Ben Bennions DFC

Ben Bennions
DFC
Battle of Britain Fighter Ace

Nick Thomas

Pen & Sword
AVIATION

First published in Great Britain in 2011 by
Pen & Sword Aviation
an imprint of
Pen & Sword Books Ltd
47 Church Street
Barnsley
South Yorkshire
S70 2AS

Copyright © Nick Thomas 2011

ISBN 978-1-84884-145-1

Typeset in 11pt Ehrhardt by
Mac Style, Beverley, E. Yorkshire

Printed and bound in the UK by CPI Group (UK) Ltd,
Croydon, CRO 4YY

Pen & Sword Books Ltd incorporates the Imprints of Pen & Sword
Aviation, Pen & Sword Family History, Pen & Sword Maritime, Pen &
Sword Military, Pen & Sword Discovery, Wharncliffe Local History,
Wharncliffe True Crime, Wharncliffe Transport, Pen & Sword Select,
Pen & Sword Military Classics, Leo Cooper, The Praetorian Press,
Remember When, Seaforth Publishing and Frontline Publishing.

For a complete list of Pen & Sword titles please contact
PEN & SWORD BOOKS LIMITED
47 Church Street, Barnsley, South Yorkshire, S70 2AS, England
E-mail: enquiries@pen-and-sword.co.uk
Website: www.pen-and-sword.co.uk

Contents

Acknowledgements

I am very much indebted to 'Ben' Bennions' relatives for their interest and support throughout the writing of this book. They supplied me not only with background information and photographs but also enthusiasm for the undertaking.

Thanks are due in particular to 'Ben's' daughter, Shirley Wilson, who very kindly supplied many of the photographs used in this book, as well as allowing me access to her late father's Log Book. Much support and anecdotal evidence also came from Philip Bennion, the youngest of George's siblings. Philip also provided family photographs and was an early driving force.

Such has been the generosity of Bennions' family that few photographs have had to be sourced elsewhere, although a small number of No. 41 Squadron photographs have come from the author's collection, one via Mr John Shipman, the son of Wing Commander Edward 'Ted' Shipman, AFC, one of Bennions' fellow pilots.

Reference has been made to an unpublished monograph by Mr Giles Browne, while operational and combat details are drawn from the Squadron Operation Record Book and Combat Reports held at Kew.

The first chapter of this book is entitled 'A Burslem Boy'. Although Bennions became an adopted Yorkshireman, he always remembered his Potteries roots, and the Potteries will always remember him.

Introduction

George 'Ben' Bennions was one of Fighter Command's most accomplished pilots and a crack shot, a fact borne out by Air Commodore Al Deere's appraisal of the Potteries ace which appeared in his book *Nine Lives*:

> He was an exceptional pilot and a wonderful shot and I firmly believe if it hadn't been for this unfortunate eye injury he would have been the top scoring fighter pilot in the War.

Bennions was born in Burslem, Stoke-on-Trent, in 1913, ten years after the Wright brothers had made the first powered heavier than air flight at Kittyhawk. From an early age Bennions idolized the First World War aviation heroes, men including 'Billy' Bishop, 'Mick' Mannock and Albert Ball, and on leaving school he and a school friend, Ralph Carnall, enlisted into the RAF in the hope of becoming pilots.

A keen sportsman, at school Bennions had played football against another Potteries hero, Sir Stanley Matthews. In the RAF he soon became 'noticed' and earned a position on a pilot training course where he quickly demonstrated his aptitude for flying. Having gained his wings, Bennions was posted overseas to No. 41 (F) Squadron, with whom he served for over seven years, flying Hawker Demons and Hawker Fury IIs, before converting onto the Vickers Supermarine Spitfire.

War declared, Bennions' first taste of action came as Deputy Sector Controller when he successfully vectored his flight commander, Norman Ryder, onto an enemy aircraft which he destroyed. The young flight lieutenant was awarded the DFC for the subsequent combat. Bennions was to serve with his squadron throughout the height of the Battle of Britain, his unit alternating between their home base at Catterick and Hornchurch and claiming over ninety enemy aircraft destroyed, making it one of the highest scoring squadrons.

Flying standing convoy patrols through much of July, the pilots were almost always at a disadvantage when they encountered the enemy, lacking both altitude and sufficient numbers. Withdrawn from No. 11 Group late in the month, they flew north to Catterick where they played a leading role in the decimation of *Luftflotte* 5's raid on the north of England on 15 August.

Flying out of Hornchurch during the last two phases of the Battle of Britain, No. 41 Squadron regularly took on mass formations of *Messerschmitt* Bf 109 fighters, and in a hectic nine week period, Bennions claimed twelve enemy aircraft with five or six more probables and a further five allowed as damaged, before he was shot down while defending a formation of Hawker Hurricanes being attacked by forty Bf 109s. Bennions had been due to go on leave but had decided to make one more sortie to raise his tally to the round dozen. His award of the Distinguished Flying Cross had been promulgated in the *London Gazette* that morning.

Burnt and badly injured by head and facial wounds, Bennions managed to bail out and was to become one of Sir Archibald McIndoe's patients at The Queen Victoria Hospital, East Grinstead. Here Bennions underwent plastic surgery and as a result became a founder member of the Guinea Pig Club.

Undaunted by his severe injuries, including the loss of an eye, Bennions fought his way back to fitness and served as a Senior Fighter Controller at Catterick. However, his real goal was to get back into the air and, at length, he persuaded the authorities to allow him to pilot an aircraft again, although he was not officially permitted to fly without a second pilot.

Unperturbed, Bennions was flying solo in early 1942 and made at least one operational flight, a convoy patrol the following February, having been posted as a liaison officer in the Mediterranean. Here Bennions served alongside members of the American 1st and 52nd Fighter Groups, who were less strict when it came to his flying restrictions.

Bennions' next posting was to Algiers where he was to command the Ground Controlled Interception (GCI) unit which was to go ashore and operate on Corsica.

It was vital that his unit be established on the island as soon as practicable and so Bennions found himself in one of the first waves of landing craft to hit the beaches at Ajaccio on 30 September 1943. As he descended the ramp, a glider bomb, launched from a Dornier Do 217, detonated, the blast throwing him onto the sands. Having received further wounds, Bennions was evacuated and returned to The Queen Victoria Hospital for treatment for splinter injuries.

Bennions' next role was as an instructor, teaching a new generation of controllers. But Bennions being Bennions, he wangled the use of an aircraft on the pretext that he needed to take his pupils up occasionally.

In 1946, with the reduction of the country's fighting forces, Bennions decided to leave the RAF. It was a difficult decision, but he was finding it more difficult to get the opportunity to fly. He took a place on an emergency teacher training course and would spend the next twenty-eight years as a schoolmaster at Catterick, teaching woodwork and metalwork, as well as mathematics and physical training. A strict disciplinarian, his pupils knew where they were with 'old man Bennions'.

A skilled craftsman, Bennions was a silversmith and had his own registered mark. Another of his post-war interests was golf, pairing up with, amongst others, Douglas Bader and Arthur Donaldson. One of his other delights was to race a Tiger Moth which he co-piloted with Bill Meynell. The pair also staged aerobatics displays at a number of prestigious air shows, helping to raise funds for charity.

Bennions later became an unofficial ambassador for the Guinea Pig Club and promoted them when ever he could. He was always full of praise for Sir Archibald McIndoe and his team, and fiercely proud of his fellow Guinea Pigs.

In his latter years, Bennions became a stalwart of the Battle of Britain Fighter Association. He was keen to help keep alive the memory of his fellow aviators, many of whom had paid the ultimate price. Bennions regularly attended Battle of Britain functions, passing on his enthusiasm for flying to a new generation.

Note

It should be noted that there are inconsistencies surrounding the spelling of the family name. Whereas for much of George's early life he was known, like his parents and siblings, by the surname Bennion, official documents also give his father's surname as 'Bennions', while Edward's marriage is indexed under both names.

During his school days and early RAF career, George was known by the surname 'Bennion'. However, according to his brother, Philip Bennion: 'When he was posted for overseas service with No. 41 Squadron, his emergency passport gave his surname as 'Bennions' and George never had it amended.'

George's RAF records and his NCO's dog tags continued to use 'Bennion', although his officer's issue, made in April 1940, adopted the alternative spelling, which was also used in the Squadron Diary and all combat reports, *London Gazette* entries and official citations.

Rather than stifle George's story by continual references to the variation in his surname, 'Bennions' is used throughout, although when referring to family members, their accepted spellings are adopted.

Chapter 1

A Burslem Boy

George Herman 'Ben' Bennions was born in Burslem, Staffordshire, on 15 March 1913, the third of five children to parents Edward and Mary Bennion (*née* Smith).

George's father was born in Burslem on 19 October 1886, where prior to the First World War, he worked as a potter's pressman for Doulton & Co. Ltd., of Burslem. Edward served as a sergeant (No. 326) with the 5th North Staffordshire Regiment. When war broke out, Bennion volunteered for overseas service and by early March 1915, was fighting in France, his territorial unit forming a part of the 46th (North Midland) Division.

Having already served in the trenches for over two years, Edward was badly wounded during the Third Battle of Ypres (31 July – 10 November 1917), when he was shot in the head while observing enemy positions through binoculars. The sniper's bullet damaged his left eye, exiting his skull above the forehead. Such a terrible head wound almost always proved fatal and his apparently lifeless body was placed with those awaiting burial. One of Edward's pals, Private Stokes, thought he saw Edward's right eye twitch and called-out to a medic who quickly realized that life was not extinct.

Evacuated to a field hospital, Sergeant Bennion was operated on, but given little hope of survival. Meanwhile, his parents received a telegram informing them that their son had been wounded in action, a second communication preparing them for the worst. His condition, however, stabilized and Edward was moved further back behind the lines where he spent several weeks before repatriation via a Hospital Ship – he was to spend the next seven years in various hospitals and rehabilitation units.

Unable to undertake hard physical labour, Edward found work after the war as caretaker at the North Road School, Burslem, Mary assisting him in his daily duties.

Due to their father's temporary incapacity, George's mother, Mary, a potter's assistant at Simpson (Potters) Ltd., Elder Works, Cobridge, was largely responsible for the early upbringing of her five children. Born in

Northwood, Stoke-on-Trent, on 6 June 1886, Mary was twenty when the couple had their first son, Jack, in 1906. Four years later came William Edwin, followed by George Herman, born in 1913, while Constance or 'Connie' was born two years later.

The couple were devoted to each other and their family, and together they pulled through the difficult times. With their children in their teens, and able to do more about the house, taking some of the strain off their mother, things were looking up and on 7 August 1926, Philip was born, completing the family unit.

Naturally, as the youngest by some years, Philip missed out on much of the family's early years, but recalled some of the stories which had been passed down via his siblings.

Bennions' parents had married in 1909 at Holy Trinity Church, Sneyd, setting up home at 9, Walley Place, Burslem. The 1911 Census reveals that Edward's niece, Martha, also a potter's assistant at Simpsons, lived for a while at the same address. With a growing family, they moved to 31, Flint Street, a small terraced house in Burslem. It was here that the Bennion children lived during their formative years. Despite the remodeling of much of the Potteries, the house still stands but as Philip explained: 'The road has since been re-named Ashburton Street, while two properties have been knocked into one and numbered No. 29.'

George attended North Road School, and later Moreland Road School, before earning a scholarship to Longton High School; while there George stayed with his uncle, Professor Andrew Bailey, whose home was close by.

Philip recalled that his brother was a keen sportsman and enjoyed a good game of football, settling into his school team in the left back position: 'He came up against another Potteries hero, Sir Stanley Matthews, who was then a pupil at the Wellington Road School, Hanley, and played for Hanley Boys.'

History does not record as to whom got the better of this competitive encounter, but Matthews, who was two years George's junior, was already on the verge of an international career, making his first England schoolboys appearance against Wales at the tender age of thirteen. A natural outside right, Matthews had clearly made a lasting impression on the young Bennions.

George trained at jujitsu as a schoolboy. While practicing throws and holds with his sister, Connie, he managed to find one of the pressure-points which sent her unconscious to the floor. Inquisitive as ever, he asked Connie to describe the feeling once she had regained her senses. Dissatisfied with her response, George asked if she would use the same grip to 'put him out', which she duly obliged. At that moment their mother entered the room and was horrified at the scene that greeted her, with George in a collapsed state and Connie unable to revive him.

His interest in science led George to save up to buy the components necessary to make a small crystal radio receiver, known colloquially as a 'cat's whisker' set. Philip later explained how their father was 'against the idea until he discovered the news programmes, after which he became an avid fan of the early radio broadcasts.'

Meanwhile, spurred on by the fact that his father had been a crack shot with the Territorials, George purchased a starter-pistol, which he modified by boring the barrel. The story nearly ended in tragedy, however, when he tested his craftsmanship; the weapon put a bullet clean through the target and nearly hit his mother!

Philip recalled that, like most teenagers, George had a thirst for speed and danger: 'He decided to save up to buy himself a motorcycle and was able to put down a deposit with Broadway Motors on a second-hand 3.49 HP motorcycle, manufactured by A J Stevens & Co. Ltd. of Wolverhampton.'

Disciplined as ever, George was able to pay-off the asking-price of £12 10s early leading to a healthy discount of £2 10s.

Naturally, owning a motorcycle added to George's independence and he was able to travel around the Potteries and further afield, enjoying the speed of the open road and the skill of negotiating the winding lanes, feeling every bump in the road on the way.

No doubt supported in his studies by his uncle, who knew full well the value of a sound education, George left school in 1929 with a good School's Certificate.

George had long fostered two ambitions; one no doubt inspired through the influence of his school masters and his uncle, the other through reading about the exploits of the First World War aces, 'Billy' Bishop, 'Mick' Mannock and Albert Ball. His dreams seemed worlds apart – he wanted to become either a teacher or a fighter pilot.

Chapter 2

Born to Fly

Bennions had his first experience of flying when Sir Alan Cobham visited Meir Aerodrome during his pre-Flying Circus days, taking novices up for a spin for five shillings: 'A school-friend, Ralph Carnall, and I had long discussed the possibility of joining the RAF with a view to training as pilots.'

The country was, however, in the depths of the Great Depression and the Services, particularly the RAF, had seen massive cutbacks. Indeed, many politicians questioned the need for an air force when the Royal Navy had dominated the seas for well over a century.

One route onto pilot training was a course at RAF Halton which took mainly grammar school boys and so the entrance exam was difficult. Despite this, both Bennions and Carnall passed and were accepted onto a three-year apprenticeship as engine fitters, straight from school. When qualified, Bennions would be in the highest trade group, earning what was then considered a good wage of three shillings a day.

The regime was very strict but Bennions received a first-class training, which he acknowledged was to stand him in good stead in later life. There was a Bristol Fighter at Halton and Bennions recalled having the opportunity to fly as a passenger on a few occasions, even being allowed to get a 'feel' of the aircraft's reaction to the controls while in straight and level flight.

While he excelled on his course, Bennions understood that he would have to get 'noticed' by the officers and senior NCOs if he was to be put forward for pilot training: 'One of the accepted routes was to become a member of Halton's sports team, which I duly did, representing them at both football and boxing.'

Among the other sportsmen at Halton at that time was the hurdler Don Finlay, who went on to win a silver medal in the 1936 Olympics. Finlay, who initially qualified as a Sergeant Pilot, rose through the ranks and in late 1940 was Bennions' CO at No. 41 Squadron, following the loss of Squadron Leaders Hood and Lister.

Philip explained that his brother's hard work began to pay dividends:

While George continued to excel in his studies and the practical aspects
of his apprenticeship, he also shone as an athlete. And it wasn't long before
George was singled-out for greater responsibilities, eventually being
promoted to the rank of sergeant apprentice, which meant that he was put
in charge of his fellow apprentices on 'A' Flight, No. 4 Wing, RAF Halton.

His CO, Wing Commander McLean, recommended Bennions for an officer
cadetship at the RAF College, Cranwell. However, although he undertook *ab
initio* flying training there, accruing six hours flying time on Avro 504Ns, a
further reduction in the annual intake, brought about by financial restrictions,
meant that he did not become a fully fledged Cranwell Cadet and undergo the
two year course. It was an understandably disappointed Bennions who was
posted to RAF Sealand at the end of 1931. Here he made the most of his
opportunities: 'George was a highly skilled technician and so he was singled
out to become the CO's engine-fitter. At the same time he continued to do well
on the sports field and represented the station in a number of disciplines.'
    In 1934 Bennions was recommended to receive pilot training and in early
April the following year he was posted to No. 3 Flying Training School
(FTS) Grantham, on an *ab initio* flying course.
    Shown to their living quarters, the trainee pilots had no sooner unpacked
their kit when they were ordered to 'B' Flight's dispersal. For many of his
fellow pupil pilots this was their first close-up view of a biplane and some
were surprised at the aircraft's flimsy appearance, built, as it was, out of a
light frame of wood and steel, covered with heavily doped fabric, the whole
held taut by wing struts and steel cables.
    Soon after they were introduced to the Avro Tutor, Flight Lieutenant
Jaques, commander of 'B' Flight, instructed them to collect their basic flying
kit: helmet and goggles, overalls, a Sidcot flying suit and gauntlet, and report
the following morning for what he referred to as 'flight familiarization'. For
Bennions this would take the form of a fifteen minute trip in the passenger
seat of Avro Tutor K3304 with his instructor, Flying Officer Broad, at the
controls.
    Standing on the wing root, Bennions leant over the front cockpit as Broad
went through the instruments and controls, including the flaps and the
rudder. Before firing the engine up, Broad hauled out his parachute pack and
demonstrated to his pupil how to put it on, before quickly going through the
drill for bailing out. Next, Bennions climbed into the cockpit and was shown
how to strap himself in. Finally, there was the firm reminder: 'Unless you are
instructed otherwise, keep your hands and feet well away from the controls.'
With all of the formalities covered, they were ready.

Taking off at 11.15 hours, Broad opened up the throttle on the 180hp seven-cylinder air-cooled Armstrong Siddeley Lynx power-plant and the Tutor bounced along the grass strip. With one final lurch it reluctantly climbed into the air as he eased back on the stick, making a gentle ascent. Broad continually talked to Bennions via the Gosport speaking-tube, making sure he was aware of what they were going to be doing and checking on his general response to being airborne. Having climbed to about 2,000ft they made a couple of circuits of the aerodrome, Broad pointing out the few navigation points on the otherwise bleak, flat Lincolnshire landscape, before making his approach and landing. Bennions rejoined the other trainees and looked on as, one by one, they too completed their circuits. With their maiden flight safely out of the way the real training would begin the following day.

At 15.50 hours on 4 April 1935, Bennions climbed into the passenger's cockpit for his first 'hands-on' training flight at Grantham. Much of that and the previous day had been spent being talked though the controls and cockpit instruments, while the first element of the flying lesson was on rudder/aileron control and taxiing. Next came a demonstration of handling the throttle, smoothly building up power. Once in the air, Bennions was given control of the aircraft in straight and level flight and was permitted to make a few gentle manoeuvres before handing back to Broad for the landing.

The flight had lasted only twenty minutes but was sufficient for Broad to be confident that his charge was potentially pilot material. During his next lesson, Bennions practised stalls, climbs, gliding and performing medium turns. By the following trip he had graduated to take-offs and landings, and, with only three hours flying time, Bennions was practising recovering from spins. Later he demonstrated his competence at other safety drills, including forced landings and 'action in the event of a fire'.

Bennions' earlier training at Cranwell stood him in good stead and throughout the programme he found himself at least one step ahead of his fellow Cadet Pilots. And so, on 15 April, with only six hours flying time, Bennions took two Flight Commander's Tests with Flight Lieutenant Jaques. On landing after the second of these assessments, a low flying test, Jaques climbed out of the cockpit and instructed Bennions to take over in the front seat and taxi around; he was judged to be ready for his first solo flight.

Bennions was given his instructions: he was to take off and fly two circuits at 1,000ft before making an approach and landing. If, for any reason, he was not happy with his approach, he was to go around again. In the event, he made a flawless flight and was on the ground again after only fifteen minutes.

By the end of April, Bennions had completed thirteen hours flying, one and a half of which had been flying solo, and was already well practised in take-offs and landings, advanced forced-landings and side-slipping. On 1 October, following more solo training, he made the progression on to the Bristol Bulldog, then one of the RAF's front-line fighters. More training followed and Bennions flew cross-country or navigational flights, often putting his aircraft into a spin first in order to ensure he had to rely on his compass for his bearings. With the basics of navigation safely mastered, Bennions was soon moving on to perform aerobatics, including loops, slow rolls and half rolls – he freely admitted that he was having the 'time of his life'.

The training schedule was hectic and there was little opportunity for home leave, while evenings were spent brushing-up on the technical aspects of the course. As the days, weeks and months raced by, Bennions and his fellow pupil-pilots celebrated passing through the various stages of their course. Their favourite watering-holes were the George or the Angel public houses in Grantham, although Bennions stuck to his usual tipple of shandy in order to maintain a clear head. He wrote home regularly to let his family know his progress, every detail being eagerly awaited by his proud parents and siblings. There were letters too for Avis Brown, with whom he had been conducting a long-distance romance and to whom he had become engaged.

In 1935, with his RAF career entering a new phase, George married Avis, whose family was from Smallthorne, Stoke-on-Trent: 'Everyone knew the Browns. Avis' father was a watchmaker from Burslem whose workshop was above Askey's fish shop.'

George's youngest brother, Philip, acted as page boy at the ceremony, which took place at St Saviour's Church, Smallthorne, on 2 March 1935. Following a reception at the Greyhound Inn, High Street, Smallthorne, the couple enjoyed a brief honeymoon before Bennions returned to complete his pilot's course.

Sergeant (745064) George Bennions was officially awarded his pilot's wings on 13 December 1935, having qualified for Certificate 'B' under King's Regulations and ACI's paragraph 811 (7): 'As a sergeant pilot, I felt I was one of the landed gentry. It was a nice feeling to be paid for flying.'

Not long afterwards and prior to his first official posting, Bennions was put on what Philip described as 'the mail run': 'George would regularly fly over Burslem on his way to Sealand near Chester. He'd perform a loop-the-loop over Cobridge Park – right opposite our house.'

Philip also recalled one of the rare times that his brother was afforded leave long enough to make the journey north:

Our father would take us to the White Swan on Elder Road, Cobridge. In order to avoid any fuss, George would wear father's rain coat over his uniform and pilot's wings. His tipple was a ginger beer shandy.

On one occasion, George was uncharacteristically agitated; this was the only time I ever heard him irate.

While sitting quietly enjoying his drink, a man came up to him and pinned a badge on father's coat. George looked at the brass badge and then at the man who announced that it was a lucky charm and that he was an Egyptian.

George looked sternly at the man and replied that, one he didn't believe in charms, two he didn't like Egyptians, and three, if he didn't remove it from his coat he would be the one in need of a lucky charm!

On 17 January 1936, Bennions' log book recorded his first assessment as a pilot. With just under twenty-one solo hours on the Bristol Bulldog, he was given an 'Average' rating but, more importantly, his instructors made no note of any flying traits which needed to be watched; his flying was good and his use of the controls measured, and above all, he wasn't prone to taking silly risks.

In February, Bennions was posted to No. 41 Squadron, then flying Hawker Demons out of Khormaksar, Aden, Yemen, where they had been stationed since the previous year, flying policing operations in response to the Abyssinian Crisis. Much as he wanted to get his first posting under his belt, Bennions was devastated at the thought of being separated from Avis, but he was in the Services and so overseas he went.

No. 41 Squadron was commanded by Squadron Leader J A Boret, who would later serve as Air Officer Commanding No. 13 Group and whose son flew with No. 41 Squadron during the Second World War. Bennions was assigned to 'A' Flight which was commanded by Flight Lieutenant G J Grindley.

Although the squadron flew a number of patrols in protection of Royal Navy vessels lying off Aden, the whole operation was little more than a demonstration of force in support of the Empire's interests in the region. But for Bennions the posting gave him the opportunity to fly an operational front-line fighter and was the fulfillment of his boyhood dreams: 'I was very much the new boy, anxious to learn and very keen to do everything the right way.'

The Hawker Demon was the fighter version of the Hawker Hart light bomber and was known within the Service as the 'Hart Fighter'. The aircraft was equipped with three 0.303 machine guns, one power-mounted in the rear cockpit and two forward firing guns controlled by the pilot. With a top speed of 180 mph, the aircraft had a service ceiling of about 28,000 ft.

Bennions' first experience in a Demon was a familiarization flight as a passenger with Sergeant Harry Steere at the controls. He then had to follow regulations and flew four hours with a ballast weight in the rear cockpit before being allowed to take off with another crewman in the second seat.

There was much excitement on the squadron when, on 22 February, No. 41 Squadron took part in a dive-bombing exercise against the Fleet. On this occasion Bennions acted as bomb-aimer, with Sergeant Kean piloting Hawker Demon K3806; this aircraft would soon become Bennions' regular 'ship', with Corporal Holdham generally acting as his gunner. While the two were able to maintain contact using the Gosport tube, communication between aircraft was via a series of hand signals made by the formation leader to indicate open throttle, throttle back, turn right or left, climb, dive, etc. The system was rudimentary and totally impractical under 'modern' air-to-air combat conditions.

The pilots and air crew needed to maintain their gunnery skills and the squadron took advantage of the vast expanse of unoccupied desert to get in valuable air-to-air firing using a towed drone. Bennions initially practised under the supervision and guidance of his flight commander, as he later recalled: 'The fighters made attack passes in pairs as one aircraft's bullets were dipped in red ochre in order to leave a mark around the bullet hole and aid with recording the results.'

Bennions received gunnery instruction from Sergeant Steere, a pilot with twelve months' more flying experience. Bennions observed that instead of firing long bursts at the drogue, as many pilots did, Steere fired several short bursts, drawing closer each time until he was nearly on top of the target. This method produced good results and Bennions adopted the same technique:

> We approached the drogue from head-on and from slightly to one side, keeping the drogue on the outer edge of the firing-ring and allowing it to fly into our bullets. This way I found I was able to get 50 per-cent of my rounds into the target.

Bennions' attitude and eagerness to learn helped him attain an 'above average' rating as a pilot while serving overseas.

Separated from his brother for over a year, Philip recalled following the exploits of 'Biggles' and imagining George's adventures abroad as a fighter pilot. His family, meanwhile, received regular mail. Philip remembered that after reading George's letters he used to carefully remove the stamps from the envelopes, sticking them into an album, which he kept along with press-cuttings and other flying ephemera:

> Of course, I was fascinated by anything related to aviation and like most schoolboys at the time, saved collector's cards which had on the one side a photograph of the RAF's latest aircraft, and on the other their armament, engine and flight statistics.

Meanwhile, by April 1936, No. 41 Squadron had moved to a new base at RAF Shaikh Othman. Bennions was generally found flying K3783, teamed up with Aircraftman Williams:

> I always flew as a part of 'A' Flight, which was composed of Red and Yellow Sections and then commanded by Flight Lieutenant Johnson. We

used red ID, while 'B' Flight used blue. They were made-up of Blue and Green Sections and were led by Flight Lieutenant R V McIntyre.

Welcome news came through of a home posting for Bennions' squadron, and his last flight in the Yemen was made on 4 August 1936, when he flew K3775 to Khormaksar. Here the aircraft were dismantled, packed and crated ready for transporting by sea back to the UK.

Most of the squadron's strength was back in the UK by the end of the month, settling into their new base at Catterick, Yorkshire, where they were to form a part of the RAF's Home Defence. Their aircraft arrived by sea and were re-assembled, many requiring new parts owing to the erosive effects of the sand, while all were given a major overhaul. By mid-November, however, the aircraft were fully serviceable and training could resume. Bennions' first flight from his new base was made on 23 November when he took off in K4540, flying a thirty-minute 'familiarization and radio transmition test'.

With the squadron now stationed in Great Britain on a permanent basis, Avis made the journey north, the couple setting up home at No. 2 Mowbray Road. It would be here that their children Connie, Shirley, Georgina and Anthony were born.

Philip recalled hearing the news of his brother's posting back to the UK:

'George had served overseas for a little over six months, but it must have seemed like a lifetime to Avis, not knowing if or when his squadron would be back in the UK. Imagine the relief when she learned that 41 and George were coming home.'

Following the enforced flightless period, Service Training continued apace and Bennions spent the next few months practicing formation flying and 'Battle Flights and Interceptions' while also honing his gunnery skills using a camera gun. It was during this period that he made his first night take-off and landing: 'The generally accepted method for helping pilots to acclimatize to night-flying was to make take-off and landings under conditions of gradually reduced light.'

The flights were both hazardous and unpopular.

Bennion's squadron reached a landmark in February 1937, when King George VI approved their badge of a double-armed cross, which was based on the arms of St Omer in France, their first overseas operational HQ during the First World War. The squadron's motto was forceful and direct: 'Seek and Destroy'.

There were important changes on the squadron with the arrival of a new CO, Squadron Leader Adams, while in June, Pilot Officer McDonald took over command of Bennions' 'A' Flight.

Training continued and in early June No. 41 Squadron's pilots practised beam, quarter and stern attacks on the firing range, Bennions taking air-gunners Collingan and Morris up, giving them the opportunity to test their aim. Meanwhile on the 16th it was Bennions' opportunity to get in gunnery practice.

Between 19th and 30th June the squadron attended the annual summer camp, which was held at Catfoss, Yorkshire. This was always a time of great excitement among the pilots and air-gunners as the week at the coastal armament practice camp gave the gunners the opportunity to fire their 0.303 Lewis guns against static targets on the sands, while dive-bombing was carried out from 800 and 5,000ft against floating targets.

Late October 1937 marked a major turning-point for the squadron, as Bennions recalled:

We converted onto the single-seater Hawker Fury Mk II, exchanging our Demons with a squadron then based at Tangmere. It was an exciting time but a sad one too, as our air-gunners suddenly became redundant and were posted away; many successful partnerships coming to an end.

The Fury II has been considered by many as the finest biplane ever built. It was the RAF's first aircraft to exceed 200mph in level flight and was designed as an interceptor. It had two 0.303 Vickers Mk IV machine guns, a ceiling of 30,000ft and an impressive rate of climb of 2,400ft per minute. Unlike the squadron's Harts and Demons, which bounced on a heavy landing, the Fury II had oleo or compression undercarriage legs which were able to cope with the impact.

Bennions made his first flight on the Fury II on 30 October, flying K7264 and gaining thirty minutes on the new type. He quickly discovered that the highly sensitive controls made it exceptionally manoeuverable and ideal as a fighter aircraft.

Having scanned the instruments, Bennions climbed into the cockpit and strapped in. Taxiing slowly he turned into the wind and opened the throttle, rapidly gathering speed until he cut the bonds with earth and became airborne: 'I returned to the airfield circuit, throttling back and brought the Fury in on a tight turn close to the boundary and, side-slipping to shed a little excess height ready to touch down.'

Bennions also recalled that:

When landing in formation; and by that I mean in a vic of three, the lead-pilot would then always open up the throttle to pull ahead of others, otherwise the side-wind effect might swing one of us into the leader. If we had swung in towards the leader, then our brakes alone might not prevent a collision and a propeller of one of the outer aircraft chewing-up the wings of the leader, or worse.

The single-seater fighter gave the pilots of No. 41 Squadron a new found freedom which they relished. 'Wally' Wallens recalled the high-jinks of one of his fellow pilots. The incident also involved Pilot Officers Douglas Gamblen and 'Tony' Lovell:

Tearing round one cloud in a vertical turn with the stick well back, I could see Douglas hard on my heels but lost sight of 'Lulu' who should have been on Douglas's tail.

Halfway round the cloud's perimeter I heard a roar behind my head and caught a flash of a silver shape that, in a moment, passed between Douglas and I, missing us by inches. The shape was a Fury with 'Lulu' at the helm travelling at the same height and at right angles to our line of flight.

We eventually rejoined Vic formation and returned, somewhat subdued, at least two of us, to the airfield. After landing Douglas and I walked over to 'Lulu's' aircraft and asked him what the hell he was playing at a while before.

'Oh', he drawled in his Irish brogue, 'I had dropped a little behind you so I thought I'd take a short-cut to catch up!'

I looked at Douglas, he looked at me, our eyebrows rising to our hairline as we both remarked, 'What can you do with a mad, bloody Irishman?' And there's no answer to that, so we walked away.

Bennions saw another side of the airman: 'One of the best pilots I flew with was Anthony "Tony" Lovell, who was not only a fellow pilot but a personal friend....'

Flying practice suddenly took on a new tone when, on 13 March 1938, Hitler's troops crossed Germany's border with Austria, which became absorbed into the new Reich. As a consequence, that year's summer camp, which was held at Loch Neagh, Aldergrove, Northern Ireland, became a more serious affair.

On 29 June, Bennions made three flights, scoring 62 to 72 per cent on the range. His score on 1 July was 200 hits out of 211 rounds, while on the 4th he hit the target with 187 out of 196 rounds during his first attack and shot the drogue away on his second! Bennions' aim was no fluke, as he proved when he shot up the drogue again on the 5th and 6th, before registering 195 out of 200 rounds during his first attack on the 7th.

Bennions had continued to make steady progress in all aspects of his flying, resulting in his being assessed as 'above average' on the Fury II on 11 August.

In September 1938, during what was to be coined the 'Munich Crisis', Europe looked to be on the brink of war. Prime Minister Neville

Chamberlain famously returned from Germany having attended a four-power conference, where he secured an agreement signed by Great Britain, France, Germany and Italy, by which Hitler was permitted to annex the German-speaking Sudetenland but guaranteed the sovereignty of the remainder of Czechoslovakia. Arriving back at Heston airport, Chamberlain was mobbed by the Press as he held aloft the signed document in triumph, proclaiming: 'I believe it is peace in our time.' Churchill, however, later attacked Chamberlain in a prophetic House of Commons speech, warning: 'You were given the choice between war and dishonour. You chose dishonour and you will have war.'

Chamberlain's hopes of peace soon evaporated with Hitler's invasion of Prague, with the remainder of the country being swallowed up as the world crisis deepened.

In response to Hitler's move, an alert went out and all squadron personnel who were on leave were immediately recalled, while the armourers were busily checking the Vickers machine guns and making up additional belts of 0.303 ammunition. In the event, Europe stepped back from war. However, few in the Air Ministry felt that it could now be avoided.

In the weeks and months that followed, the squadron spent more time on interception exercises and mock combats, flying in tight vic formation and using the RAF's standard air attacks, which were designed to take on unescorted bomber formations. These, however, would soon be proved virtually worthless against a *Luftwaffe* already blooded in the Spanish Civil War, and which had developed the technique of flying fighters in pairs or fours.

The squadron also made co-operation sorties during which experiments were being carried out with Radio Direction Finding (RDF) or radar. While No. 41 Squadron's Furys flew along a predetermined course, staff in the operations room interpreted the radar signals as the height, strength, location and direction of the 'raid' was mapped. The idea was that based on the plots, interception patrols could be flown, the pilots being given directions via radio as the progress of the plot was followed.

Later, Bennions and the officer pilots of No. 41 Squadron took turns in the Plotting Room acting as Deputy Controller; this training gave the pilots an understanding of the mechanism behind the Controller's directions.

Chain Home had twenty radar stations along the south and east coast as far north as Scotland, designed to locate high-altitude targets at up to 120 miles. A second defence system, Chain Home Low, could detect lower flying formations, but these twelve stations only became operational in July 1940.

Luftwaffe bombers could cross the Channel to Dover in six minutes and within another ten, they could be over No. 11 Group's airfields.

Chapter 3

The Road to War

In November 1938, Bennions, who had been with his squadron for over two and a half years, was promoted to the rank of flight sergeant.

Throughout late 1938 rumours circulated among the pilots that they were about to become only the third squadron to receive Vickers Supermarine Spitfires. These were further fuelled by several visits by No. 19 Squadron's CO, Squadron Leader Henry Iliffe Cozens, whose uneventful landings and take-offs confirmed the suitability of Catterick's landing-strip. Naturally the sight of the revolutionary new aircraft parked at dispersals aroused a good deal of interest, with pilots and ground crews alike gathering around to get a closer look:

> For us the introduction of 'new types' had previously meant adapting to a slightly faster aircraft with an all round improved performance of a few per cent along with a greater armament capability. The introduction of the Spitfire, however, blew away those old margins.

Little did they then know, but No. 41 Squadron had initially been selected to be the first to fly the Spitfire, until Cozens had intervened and contacted a friend at the Air Ministry suggesting that a squadron closer to London ought to be the first. With his squadron based at Duxford, near Cambridge, he had reasoned that it would be more convenient for officials to monitor the aircraft's progress, while the short landing strip at Catterick, he had argued, might pose difficulties. Consequently Nos. 19 and 66 Squadrons each received a Spitfire in August 1938, with instructions to fly them for 400 hours 'as quickly as possible' and report their findings. Understanding the need for the Spitfire to be made operational with all haste, Squadron Leaders Cozens and Fuller-Good complied and delivered their reports ahead of schedule.

Designed by Stoke-on-Trent-born Reginald Joseph Mitchell, CBE, to Vickers' specification for its Type 300, which became the Air Ministry's specification F37/34, the Spitfire Mk I had first flown at Eastleigh on the morning of 5 March 1936.

Following its maiden flight at the hands of test pilot 'Mutt' Summers, the prototype K5054 was immediately sent for official handling trials at Martlesham Heath. Early reports convinced the Air Staff of its service potential so specification F16/36 was drawn-up based on the aircraft's characteristics.

The Air Ministry immediately issued contract B527113/36 and, on 28 July 1936, placed an unprecedented initial order for 310 aircraft, ten of which were for development, the remainder to go straight into squadron service.

Sadly, Mitchell died on 11 June 1937, before any of the production aircraft became operational.

An air historian wrote shortly after Mitchell's death:

He was always ready to stand up to his seniors if he thought that their views or their decisions were wrong. And he was equally willing to listen to the suggestions of his juniors. I know of nobody who worked under Mitchell who did not love and respect him. I do not know what kind of monument can be raised to his memory, but he has the greatest monument that any man can have: he lives in the memories of those among whom and for whom he worked – that is to say, the officers and men of the Royal Air Force.

The Spitfire's first public appearance was at the Hendon Air Show on 18 June 1936. Here it astounded the audience with its speed and manoeuverability, making the RAF's other fighter aircraft appear antiquated and positively pedestrian.

Almost universally criticized for his appeasement of Adolf Hitler, Chamberlain and his 'Piece of Paper' may have given the dictator more confidence, but also allowed time for the RAF to equip its fighter squadrons with the Hawker Hurricane and, to a lesser extent, with the Spitfire. When war was declared the RAF had ten Spitfire squadrons. Of these, Nos. 19, 66 and 611 Squadrons operated out of Duxford, Nos. 54, 65 and 74 Squadrons out of Hornchurch, No. 72 Squadron from Church Fenton, Nos. 41 and 609 Squadrons at Catterick, and No. 602 Squadron out of Abbotsinch. Meanwhile, at Turnhouse, No. 603 was in the process of converting onto the new fighter.

The re-equipping of the RAF would be a painfully slow process. By the end of 1939, Spitfire and Hurricane production stood at only two of each type per day, although this had risen by three hundred per cent by the onset of the Norway campaign in April 1940. By the height of the Battle of Britain, however, production was outstripping average daily losses. The RAF were never really likely to run out of aircraft at the rates of attrition they faced during 1940, although the training of replacement pilots was another matter entirely.

It was on 13 January 1939 that No. 41 Squadron received its first Spitfire Mark Is, which arrived pre-painted in their brown and green wartime camouflage colours, with only the squadron and individual letter-codes to be added:

> Of course, everyone was as keen as mustard to climb into the cockpit and take one up. But because the 'Spit' was so different to anything anyone of us had ever flown before, we had to go through a short programme to adjust.

Following a brief read through the rudimentary flying notes, and a written examination covering familiarization with the new type and its handling characteristics, the pilots took turns to sit in the cockpit for instruction. First the controls were explained and then they were talked through the take-off procedure, during which it was necessary to turn slightly from one side to the other in order to see what was directly ahead; the nose severely restricted vision, something which resulted in accidents on every squadron, including No. 41. The undercarriage raised or lowered using hydraulics which had to be hand-pumped, an indicator light showing when each leg was locked in position.

Once a pilot was airborne, there came a difficult manoeuvre, as the lever operating the undercarriage sat to their right and it was necessary to change hands on the stick. Novice pilots could be spotted weaving up and down on take-off, because when they pumped the undercarriage up manually there was a tendency to mimic the motion with a smaller movement of the left hand; some would even stall or dive-in during take-off.

Shortly afterwards came the moment that everyone had been eagerly waiting for as the pilots took it in turns to take to the controls, the most experienced officers being given precedence.

On take-off the pilot had to be aware of the problems of torque and the side-force created by the air pushed back from the propeller into the right side of the tail. The force of the spiralling air meant that the aircraft had a tendency to want to turn around on itself – hard rudder had to be used to prevent the Spitfire from veering off a true course and putting its wingtip into the ground. At the same time the pilot kept a weather-eye on the propeller, keeping it clear of the ground as the aircraft adopted the horizontal position.

Later, engineers from Roll-Royce arrived to fit the new two-speed, metal three-bladed propellers, replacing the problematic fixed-pitch, wooden two blade airscrews. These could be set at a fine pitch on take-off and at a coarse pitch during normal flight, giving additional power when it was most needed.

Bennions' log book recorded a sixty-five minute flight in K9840 at 14.15 hours – he could not help but be astonished at the aircraft's turn of speed as familiar landmarks raced by in rapid succession rather than in the more accustomed sedate fashion.

Bennions later wrote: 'Once in the air the Spitfire was a lovely aeroplane, ladylike, smooth to handle and responding quickly.'

Remembering his instructions, Bennions came in on a curved approach so that he could see where he was going as the ground disappeared under the aircraft's nose. Keeping a close eye on the airspeed indicator as it dropped below 180 mph, Bennions pulled the canopy back (it being almost impossible to open over that speed), before checking his instruments again: airspeed, altimeter and artificial horizon.

As his speed dropped below 140 mph, Bennions selected 'wheels down' and pumped at the handle until he felt the undercarriage lock into position, looking for confirmation from the indicator lights. Turning towards the landing ground he received the 'green light' from the Watch Office Control and was cleared to land, dropping his airspeed further to 120 mph and lowering the flaps, checking his approach again as he dropped his speed to 100 and then to 90 mph. Keeping the airfield's boundary fence in sight, he made a close turn, avoiding pitching the nose too high which would reduce forward visibility and potentially result in collision with any aircraft taxiing or taking-off unsighted.

Turning to make his final approach, Bennions crossed the boundary. Still flying at 90 mph, he throttled right back, causing the nose to rise as he eased the control column gently back. The Spitfire 'floated' momentarily just off the grass, until it lost lift and dropped down, and then Bennions checked its speed with a gentle dab of the brakes in order to avoid tipping the aircraft onto its spinner. There was, however, a slight mishap which resulted in the loss of his tailwheel on the grassed strip, but he was able to bring the aircraft to a halt without it sustaining any further damage.

The next few weeks and months saw intense training on the new monoplane, the pilots practicing flying in tight squadron formation, making mock attacks and improving their gunnery skills by using gun cameras; the squadron was gearing itself towards operational combat. For all, including Bennions, the recoil of the eight rapid-firing Browning machine guns came as a surprise, compared to that of the two 0.303 Vickers Mk IV guns of the Fury.

The training included night flying exercises, something which was carried out with some difficulty in a Spitfire owing to the bright exhaust flashes:

In peacetime the night view of towns and cities was a magnificent blaze of white and orange light, while the countryside was dotted with more dimly lit cottages and farmhouses, but mostly there was a dark mass of shades of grey across which every now and then shone a neon beacon from one of the many RAF airfields flashing the station's letter code – each airfield repeated a different letter as an aid to navigation.

The squadron's pilots were 'rusty' when it came to night flying as the Fury II, like the Spitfire, had a blinding flash back from its exhaust stubs. The squadron began acclimatizing by using an old Demon, while all of the pilots completed at least ten hours on the Link Trainer, a simulator which mimicked flying conditions and which was used to practice 'instruments only' flying.

There were several aids for landing at night. These included Chance floodlights, which appeared as little more than insignificant blips of light when seen from the air. Looking down into the murk, the pilot searched for the No. 1 flare, which shone a beam of light on three segments, the top, amber, indicting that he was above the glide path, the centre, green, which indicated the correct glide path, and red below the glide path. The pilot adjusted his approach depending on the colour displayed:

> A flare-path would be laid to assist us in our final approach, which was, by the way, made on a right-hand circuit at night, as opposed to the reverse by day, something you had to remember, particularly if there were hazards in your in your flight-path that you weren't used to!

To qualify for night flying a pilot had to safely complete six landings. On one of his attempts Pilot Officer Horace 'Pookie' Overall came in on the green light but managed to hit the upper branches of a tree on the boundary of the airfield, which was aligned with the night flying flare path – one foot lower and he would almost certainly have crashed.

Night flying had other hazards, as aircraft recognition became even more difficult, particularly for the gunners several thousand feet below. The Air Ministry's answer was to use a system of daily letter and colour-codes. If fired upon, a pilot could discharge the appropriate colour Very light or flash the letter of the day using an identification lamp. In practice this method was not always successful as it relied on the pilot remembering the correct code in the heat of the moment, and it being spotted thousands of feet below – there would be many instances of night flyers giving the previous day's code a little after midnight or a faint signal remaining unnoticed amid the muzzle flashes and exploding shells.

On 19 May 1939, No. 41 Squadron took part in the annual Empire Day celebrations, flying as a part of a formation of over sixty aircraft, Spitfires and Hurricanes, on a round trip via Digby, Grantham, Nottingham, Rotherham, Sheffield, and finally back to Catterick. This was the first mass display of the RAF's new fighter aircraft and was a clear signal for Hitler to take note of the growing strength of the Junior Service. The following day saw an impressive exhibition of formation flying and air drill as No. 41 Squadron put its Spitfires through their paces in front of an appreciative crowd – this would be the squadron's last and most impressive peacetime air display.

Meanwhile, on the world stage there was another turn of the screw when on 22 May, Adolf Hitler and Benito Mussolini signed the 'Pact of Steel', a military alliance between the two Fascist nations under the terms of which, in the event of war, one would come to the aid of the other. The Treaty was particularly significant as Italy had a very strong Mediterranean fleet which rivalled that of the Royal Navy, while its air force was developing monoplanes which would certainly rival the RAF's Hawker Hurricane.

In preparation for the possibility of war in Europe, aircraft from No. 41 Squadron flew formation attacks in a co-operation exercise with No. 10 (B) Squadron on 12 June, providing the bomber air crews with practice in defending against interceptions by single-engine fighters.

Bennions was engaged in night flying on 15, 26 and 29 June. Meanwhile, daytime training continued with practice scrambles, battle-climbs and 'breaking through cloud', as well as mock attacks; these skills had to became second nature to every pilot if the squadron was to have any hope of survival as a fighting unit.

The squadron suffered its first loss on the new type on 18 July 1939, when Sergeant Kenneth Mitchell was killed during a cross-country exercise, his aircraft flying into Great Dun Fell. Mitchell had been bound for RAF Kingstown, near Carlisle, when the exercise was called-off due to the deteriorating weather conditions. Following orders, he turned back for Catterick but crashed at 2,500ft while re-crossing the Pennines in poor visibility: 'Mitchell's death was a tragic waste. There was a court of inquiry which blamed the station commander for going ahead with the exercise under such poor weather conditions.'

Such losses only served as a reminder of the ever-present dangers even in peace-time flying, when a small error in navigation due to a stronger than forecast crosswind might cost a pilot his life.

Bennions flew a seventy minute local flight on 25 July, during which he practiced formation flying; this was to be his last flight prior to the opening of hostilities, as he was temporarily posted to Deputy Controller duties, a role which gave him a greater understanding of the country's air defence system.

The system had been greatly advanced by the advent of radar. A series of masts formed what was known as Chain Home, which would eventually cover much of the south and east coasts. Information from the radar stations' plotters was relayed to Headquarters Fighter Command's Filter and Operations Room, along with details of visual sightings from shipping and Observer Corps posts. The strength, altitude, location and direction of each enemy raid were plotted on the Operations Room table, the information being updated every five minutes. To ensure the plots remained current the counters were colour-coded in synchrony with the Sector Station clock – if the plots were old, a shout would go-up 'Three colours on the table!'

HQ Fighter Command, Stanmore, forwarded details of raids to the appropriate Group Headquarters where the state of each operational squadron was displayed on a board. The Group Controller would then feed details through to their Sector Stations. The Sector Controllers contacted their Fighter Stations, changing their squadron's state of readiness accordingly, scrambling the appropriate fighter strength to identify the 'bogie' and, if necessary, to make an interception:

> If the plot was identified as a possible enemy raider, then the Sector Controller began to implement a series of responses, notifying anti-aircraft batteries and barrage balloon sites along the 'bogie's' anticipated route.
>
> Once in the air, the fighter-leader was vectored towards the enemy formation by the Sector Controller who monitored the progress of the plot of the unidentified aircraft and the position of our own fighters.

In order that HQ Fighter Command, Group HQs and the Sector Controllers had an idea of the whole picture, information was passed both ways along the chain of command.

The location of friendly aircraft was aided by the use of a transponder, which automatically replied to 'interrogation' from the ground with an identification signal. This system was known as Identification Friend or Foe (IFF) and identified RAF aircraft on the plotter's screen. The top secret IFF was codenamed 'Parrot', while the instruction for pilots to turn their system on was given as 'squawk your parrot.'

The air defence network, and radar in particular, would quickly prove its worth, successfully aiding No. 602 Squadron's destruction of a Ju 88 during the *Luftwaffe's* first raid on shipping in British coastal waters on 16 October 1939.

With political tension at an all-time height, any unidentified shipping or aircraft detected approaching the British coast attracted the attention of the RAF. One such incident occurred on 3 August and was reminiscences of the *Zeppelin* raids of the 1914–18 War.

An alert went out of a large slow-moving object approaching the east coast. The plot was believed to be the German LZ 130, *Graf Zeppelin*, monitoring transmissions and 'listening' for high frequency signals. The Germans evidently were unaware of the British use of low frequency radar and so their signals remained undetected.

The *Graf Zeppelin's* progress was monitored as it flew northwards towards the east coast and then to the Shetland Islands and back, with fighters from Dyce being scrambled to make an interception. The engines were cut as LZ 130 approached Aberdeen, feigning a mechanical failure. Meanwhile, the scientists on-board inspected and photographed the antenna masts below. As the airship drifted over the mainland it was circled by Spitfires before the engines were restarted and the airship turned for its home base, landing away from the prying eyes of British officials who were waiting to confiscate any sensitive data the scientists had managed to obtain.

A few days later No. 41 Squadron took part in a three-day air defence exercise held at nearby RAF Digby. On their return, the aircraft's radio frequencies were changed as was the squadron's call sign, while orders were given that all future patrols would be made flying fully armed aircraft as the squadron was put onto a wartime footing:

> During peace-time the squadron's aircraft were housed in their hangars or lined-up on their aerodromes in neat rows. This, of course, made them highly vulnerable to air attacks. A number of dispersal-points were created around the airfield perimeter. Each section had its own petrol bowser, starter trolleys and a bell tent with a direct telephone link to the Sector Operations room.

Located on the eastern edge of the airfield, adjacent to the River Swale, the Spitfires had sufficient grassed landing ground to take off either to the north-west or south-west depending on the prevailing wind. Initially the makeshift dispersals were fairly basic but conditions improved as the emergency continued: 'There were no 'creature comforts' and we only had hard cot beds to sleep on. We were, however, permitted to go across the airfield to use the Messes for our main meals.'

With vital ports, coal mines, heavy engineering and armament production, the north–east was clearly an important target for enemy bombing. Ack-ack positions had already been established, protecting the coast and industrial targets, while barrage balloons were soon in position around Newcastle and Middlesborough: all targets within range of Continental Europe. It was clear that in a total war, No. 41 Squadron would be called into action.

Hitler's plans for German expansionism had begun to move with frightening pace. At the centre of the growing tension in Europe lay the question of the free city of Danzig (Gdansk). Under the terms of the Treaty of Versailles, the Baltic port had been ceded to Poland although its people remained predominantly of German origin. While Poland needed the sea port to secure its independence, the corridor of land cut East Prussia off from the Motherland and thereby weakened Germany's position in the east.

Hitler favoured a co-ordinated uprising by the Germanic population, allowing Danzig to be re-absorbed. Consequently, orders had been given to permit the traffic of weapons across the border to arm pro-Nazi sympathizers. On 13 August the Polish Government issued an ultimatum demanding the reinstatement of controls. The German *Gauleiter* Forster made a statement in which he claimed there had been no such order and the crisis was temporarily averted, although Danzig was already bristling with 15,000-plus members of the *Wehrmacht*, reminding many of the situation in the Sudetenland immediately prior to its annexation.

There was a new twist on the political scene when, on 23 August, it was announced that Germany and Russia had signed the 'non-aggression' treaty known to history as the 'Molotov–Ribbentrop Pact'. This allowed both nations to pursue their own immediate goals. For Russia this was to be the invasion of Finland, while for Germany the Treaty left the way open for Hitler to continue his policy of expansionism and his next goal – the invasion of Poland.

With the German Press controlled by Nazi Party officials, the newspaper *Angriff* reported the party-line on the Treaty, perhaps unaware of the bitter irony of its words:

> The world stands before a towering fact: two peoples have placed themselves on the basis of a common foreign policy which during a long and traditional friendship produced a policy of common understanding. It is certain that the renewal of these ties has many good possibilities both in the economic and political fields.
>
> The decision of the *Führer* is so popular because the simplest man among the German peoples sees that it means the rebirth of the historical German–Russian policy, which for so long in history proved its importance.

The pact was a massive coup for Hitler. Germans believed that should war come, they would not face the potential of a long Eastern Front, their ultimate downfall during the First World War.

With Germany now free to pursue its goals, not only in the east, but also in the west, Hitler continued to apply pressure on Danzig; two days later Great Britain and Poland signed a mutual assistance treaty. Hitler was not deterred by this display of unity and the move towards the seizure of Danzig and the Corridor continued. The German people were prepared for the move by the press and by propaganda broadcasts and newsreels.

The newspaper *Deutsche Allegemeine Zeitung* ran with the headline: 'Offensive Preparations by Poland', the *Morgenpost* favouring: 'Poland has mobilized – On Eve of Polish Coup Against Danzig.' A further warning came when the Berlin newspaper *Volkischer Beobachter* suggested that war was imminent, announcing: 'Polish Army Ready to Strike Threatened Occupation of Danzig – War Preparations in the Entire German-Polish Border.'

In the main article it was alleged that a whole Polish division was stationed to the south and west of the port, while more troops were said to be massing along the border with Germany, ready to invade Reich territory.

On 26 August, in response to the deepening crisis, the station commander at Catterick ordered the hangars to be camouflaged, while all of the windows on the Station were criss-crossed with strips of brown paper to reduce the effects of splintering should the airfield be targeted by bombers. Meanwhile, all ranks were seconded to help fill sandbags for air raid shelters, machine gun posts and defensive positions.

Two days later Germany issued a statement assuring the neutrality of Belgium, The Netherlands, Luxembourg and Switzerland should war come. Hitler's promises to the Benelux nations, however, would evaporate as soon as their territory became tactically important.

Meanwhile, the British Ambassador to Berlin, Sir Nevile Henderson, met with Hitler for further talks to avert war, during which the German dictator maintained his demands on Danzig and its corridor.

With pressure continuing to mount, Poland began a general mobilization on 30 August, the news of which produced further headlines in the German press including: 'The Responsibility Is Now Established.'

Sir Nevile Henderson and Von Ribbentrop had further emergency talks. Hitler's reaction was to appoint his War Cabinet, while on the following day he issued his Directive No. 1 for the Conduct of the War. This document not only outlined Hitler's plans for the invasion of Poland but also the initial phases of the campaigns against France and Britain, stating that:

If Britain and France open hostilities against Germany, it will be the duty of the *Wehrmacht* formations operating in the west to conserve their forces as much as possible and thus maintain the conditions for a victorious conclusion of the Operations against Poland. Within these limits enemy forces and their military-economic resources are to be damaged as much as possible. The right to order offensive operations is reserved absolutely to me.

The Army will hold the West Wall and make preparations to prevent its being outflanked in the north through violation of Belgian or Dutch territory by the Western powers. Should French forces invade Luxembourg the bridges on the frontier may be blown up.

The Navy will carry on warfare against merchant shipping, directed mainly at England....

The Air Force is, in the first place, to prevent the French and British Air Forces from attacking the German Army and German territory.

In conducting the war against England, preparations are to be made for the use of the *Luftwaffe* in disrupting British supplies by sea, the armaments industry, and the transport of troops to France. A favourable opportunity is to be taken for an effective attack on massed British naval units, especially against battleships and aircraft carriers. The decision regarding attacks on London is reserved to me.

Preparations are to be made for attacks against the British mainland, bearing in mind that partial success with insufficient forces is in all circumstances to be avoided.

The die was cast and in the early hours of 1 September, Hitler's forces made their move, and under the cloak of darkness a group of *SS agent provocateurs*, dressed as Polish soldiers, launched a raid on a German radio station. This staged attack on German sovereign territory was Hitler's excuse to his own people for taking the nation to war. At dawn, *Wehrmacht* forces, including six armoured and eight motorized divisions, crossed into Poland, while the *Luftwaffe* attacked Polish infrastructure. Meanwhile, a German vessel in Danzig harbour bombarded the city with its heavy guns.

While still claiming that Poland was the aggressor, Hitler appeared in a military uniform, which he vowed he would not remove until victory was won in the 'counter-attack against Poland'.

At 5.40 am Adolf Hitler's message to his armed forces was broadcast:

Poland has refused my offer for a friendly settlement of our relation as neighbours. Instead she has taken up arms.

The Germans in Poland have been victims of bloody terror, hunted from house to house. A series of frontier violations that a Great Power cannot accept proves that Poland is not willing to respect the Reich frontiers. To put an end to this foolhardy situation, I am left with no other means than from now on opposing force to force.

The German army will lead the struggle for the honour and vital rights of resurrected Germany with hard determination.

I expect that every soldier, filled with great traditions of the eternal Germany soldiery, will fulfill his duty to the last.

In every situation know that you are the representative of National Socialist Greater Germany.

(signed) A. Hitler

The first news of the invasion did not reach the British Foreign Office until 07.28 hours, when the details were quickly verified. As the full enormity of the morning's events sank in, hurried meetings were held in Whitehall and at the Ministry of Defence. It was a sombre Neville Chamberlain who stood up in the House of Commons later that day to address Parliament and the Nation, announcing:

German troops crossed the Polish frontier this morning at dawn and are since reported to be bombing open towns. In these circumstances there is only one course open to us.

His Majesty's Ambassador in Berlin and the French Ambassador have been instructed to hand to the German Government the following document:

'Unless the German Government are prepared to give His Majesty's Government satisfactory assurances that the German Government have suspended all aggressive action against Poland and are prepared promptly to withdraw their forces from Polish territory, His Majesty's Government in the United Kingdom will without hesitation fulfil their obligations to Poland.'

Facing what by now must have been the almost inevitably of war with Nazi Germany, Chamberlain announced immediate measures to counter the future threat:

This morning we ordered a complete mobilization of the whole of the Royal Navy, Army and Royal Air Force. A Bill will be laid before you which for all practical purposes will amount to an expansion of the Military Training Act. Under its operation all fit men between the ages of 18 and 41 will be rendered liable to military service if and when called upon.

The full details of the Act would be announced by the BBC's Home Service at 4.30 pm that day, during one of its first broadcasts.

Finally, the Prime Minister in an appeal to right-thinking Germans reminded them and the world that the government's differences were not with the people of Germany but with its regime:

We have no quarrel with the German people, except that they allow themselves to be governed by a Nazi Government. As long as that Government exists and pursues the methods it has so persistently followed during the last two years, there will be no peace in Europe.

We are resolved that these methods must come to an end....

But France and Great Britain had bowed to the will of the Dictator before and Hitler felt certain the Chamberlain's words were equally as hollow as they had been in the past.

A defiant Hitler ordered his forces to continue their merciless onslaught on Poland and on 2 September the German High Command's communiqué announced:

> German troops are advancing steadily everywhere despite heavy resistance and blown-up roads. German forces captured Teschen, advanced up to Pless Nkolai, occupied Wieruszow, east of Kempen and also Klobuch Schildberg. In the Corridor the German forces reached the important railway line between Bromberg and Gdynia near Culm.

In the wake of the massacre of thousands of innocent civilians during the Spanish Civil War a few years earlier, America's President Roosevelt had made an appeal to Germany not to shell 'open' cities or civilian populations, but his words fell on deaf ears and all across Poland, towns and cities were relentlessly bombed and shelled.

In Germany the Press responded negatively to Neville Chamberlain's speech for peace, made on 1 September. The Berlin newspaper *Volkischer Beobachter* leading with, 'The *Führer* Proclaims: The Fight for Germany's Rights and Security,' while *Nachtausgabe's* headlines read: 'Our Soldiers March For Germany's Honour And Security – Chamberlain In The Chains Of The Warmongers – England Has Invited Upon Itself A Frightful Guilt – The British Prime Minister Distorted The Facts.'

In London later that day, the British Government prepared an ultimatum which would be handed to Germany at 09.00 hour on 3 September. It was intended that the document should be delivered to Hitler by the British Ambassador to Berlin. In the event, it was read to interpreter Paul Schmidt, who passed on details of its contents to Hitler and to Von Ribbentrop; the latter had assured the dictator that Great Britain would back down. Hitler turned to Von Ribbentrop and demanded: 'What now?'

Both understood the magnitude of their misjudgment.

Chapter 4

The So-called 'Phoney' War

The morning of Sunday 3 September 1939, was bright and sunny but the mood in the country was very tense. For the second time in a generation Britain stood on the verge of war with Germany.

At 11.15 am, some fifteen minutes after the ultimatum to Adolf Hitler had expired, came the unmistakable voice of Neville Chamberlain over the airwaves:

> I am speaking to you from the Cabinet Room at No.10 Downing Street. This morning the British Ambassador in Berlin handed the German Government a final note, stating that unless we heard from them by eleven o'clock that they were prepared at once to withdraw their troops from Poland, a state of war would exist between us. I have to tell you now that no such undertaking has been received, and that consequently this country is at war with Germany.

His broadcast to a numbed nation ended with the words:

> Now may God bless you all. May He defend the right. It is the evil things that we shall be fighting against, brute force, bad faith, injustice, oppression and persecution and against them I am certain that right will prevail.

Of the events that had led to war, Winston Churchill was generous to his political opponents, particularly the now broken Prime Minister, when he said:

> In this solemn hour it is a consolation to recall and to dwell upon our repeated efforts for peace. All have been ill-starred, but all have been faithful and sincere.

We must not underrate the gravity of the task which lies before us or the temerity of the ordeal, to which we shall not be found unequal. …The Prime Minister said it was a sad day, and that is indeed true, but at the present time there is another note which may be present, and that is a feeling of thankfulness that, if these great trials were to come upon our Island, there is a generation of Britons here now ready to prove itself.

Fully understanding that Hitler had designs on Europe beyond Poland, Churchill added:

This is not a question of fighting for Danzig or fighting for Poland. We are fighting to save the whole world from the pestilence of Nazi tyranny and in defence of all that is most sacred to man. This is no war of domination or imperial aggrandizement or material gain; no war to shut any country out of its sunlight and means of progress. It is a war, viewed in its inherent quality, to establish, on impregnable rocks, the rights of the individual, and it is a war to establish and revive the stature of man….

Churchill's words were statesmanlike, more like those of a prime minister than those of Neville Chamberlain – he was already demonstrating that he was the man of the hour, the man who could lead Great Britain through this war.

Meanwhile, in Berlin, the *Reich-Führer* issued further instructions:

Directive No. 2 for the Conduct of the War
SUPREME COMMANDER OF THE ARMED FORCES MOST SECRET
Berlin 3 September 1939.

1. After the declaration of war by the English Government. The English Admiralty issued orders at 11.17 hours on 3rd September 1939, to open hostilities.
   France has announced that she will be in a state of war with Germany from 17.00 hours on 3rd September 1939.
2. The immediate aim of the German High Command remains the rapid and victorious conclusion of operations against Poland.
   The transfer of any considerable forces from the eastern front to the west will not be made without my approval.
3. The basic principles for the conduct of the war in the west laid down in Directive No. 1 remain unchanged.
   The declaration of war by England and France has the following consequences:

(a) In respect of England.

Navy.
Offensive action may now begin. In carrying out the war against merchant shipping, submarines also, for the time being, will observe prize regulations. Intensified measures leading to the declaration of danger zones will be prepared. I shall decide when these measures shall become effective.

The entrance to the Baltic will be mined without infringing neutral territorial waters.

In the North Sea the blockade measures envisaged for defensive purposes and for the attack on England will be carried out.

Air Force.
Attacks upon English naval forces at naval bases or on the high seas (including the English Channel), and on definitely identified troops transports, will only be made in the event of English air attacks on similar targets and where there are particularly good prospects of success. This applies also to action by the Fleet Air Arm.

I reserve to myself the decision about attacks on the English homeland.

Meanwhile, the German forces were not to act aggressively toward the French, and the *Wehrmacht* stationed along the border with France was forbidden, for the moment, from taking the offensive, while the *Kriegesmarine* similarly could only retaliate to French attack. The *Luftwaffe* could defend against attacks on their soil: 'In general the employment of the Air Force in the west is governed by the need to preserve its fighting strength after the defeat of Poland for decisive actions against the Western Powers.'

If anyone in Great Britain ever doubted that the conflict would be an all-out war, they soon had their worst fears realized. At 14.00 hours, less than three hours after Chamberlain's speech, the German submarine U-30 torpedoed the unarmed passenger ship SS *Athenia* 200 miles off Ireland. She sank with the loss of 112 of the 1,418 onboard; many of the casualties were American. Fearing the atrocity would bring the United States into the war, Germany denied responsibility for the fatal attack, while some American Senators even suggested that the sinking might have been a deliberate act by the British to draw their nation into what they felt was a European conflict.

While the *Athenia* had been unescorted at the time of the attack, the Royal Navy was already at sea on a war footing, defending home waters, Britain's trade routes and those of the Empire; for the Senior Service there would be no 'Phoney War.'

Plans had been made for a British Expeditionary Force to cross the Channel and take up station in France, where elements of the RAF's Advanced Air Striking Force (AASF) had already been secretly deployed. With their HQ at Reims, the RAF squadrons were mainly based to the east and north-east; the fighters' role was to protect the Marginot Line, while the Fairey Battle and Bristol Blenheim bombers were to act as a strike force to attack any advancing German columns – a task for which they were to prove ill-suited.

At Catterick, No. 41 Squadron was prepared for immediate action. All aircraft, equipment and supplies were checked, while rudimentary air raid precautions were already in place and a night time black-out enforced. Bell tents sprung up at dispersals, occupied by airmen muffled in scarves and leather flying gear, warmed against the early morning and night air by the heat of makeshift braziers.

The Squadron's Operational Record Book was closed and together with the duplicate record was forwarded to the Air Ministry, while the new book was opened with the words:

First Day of Mobilization
A State of War was declared by the British Government between Great Britain and Germany. Action was taken in accordance with the Unit Mobilization Scheme.

One of the initial measures was to make the squadron's aircraft less of a target for enemy bombers. As a consequence, 'A' Flight's dispersals were moved in amongst trees on the edge of the south-east side of the aerodrome.

Acknowledging the significance of the moment, the squadron diarist recorded a nominal roll of the pilots on duty:

Squadron Leader G A G Johnson	OC
Flying Officer E N Ryder	OC 'A' Flight
Flying Officer J T Webster	OC 'B' Flight
Flying Officer H P Blatchford	
Flying Officer J G Theilmann	
Flying Officer R A Barton	
Flying Officer H F H Overall	
Pilot Officer J E Hibbert	Adjutant [ground staff]
Pilot Officer A D J Lovell	Attached to Operations B [Deputy Controller]
Pilot Officer J J H Copley	Squadron Operations Officer
Pilot Officer W J M Scott	Squadron Operations Officer
Pilot Officer B G Piddocks	

Pilot Officer R W Wallens
Pilot Officer J N Mackenzie
Pilot Officer G W Cory
Pilot Officer C Robertson
Pilot Officer O B Morrogh-Ryan
Flight Sergeant G Bennions
Flight Sergeant E Shipman
Sergeant A Harris
Sergeant I E Howitt
Sergeant R A Carr-Lewty
Sergeant Gillies

The majority of No. 41 Squadron's pilots already had between fifty and eighty flying hours on Spitfires under their belts, while they had sixteen fully operational Spitfires, with a further five available as replacements on Command Reserve. This meant that they were better prepared than most units at the outbreak of the war. Some fighter squadrons were still flying biplanes or twin-engine aircraft, including the fighter version of the Bristol Blenheim. No. 64 Squadron's pilots, for instance, only converted from Blenheims onto single-seat fighters in April 1940, but by late May they would be flying a desperate defence of the BEF at Dunkirk.

With a wealth of experienced pilots on No. 41 Squadron, Air Vice Marshal Richard Saul, Air Officer Commanding No. 13 Group, had no qualms about placing the squadron on night and day readiness. With the pressing need to bring other squadrons up to operational readiness, No. 41 Squadron would lose some of their most experienced pilots and ground crew who were posted away over the following weeks and months.

The squadron's first operational patrol under wartime conditions came at 03.15 hours the following morning, when 'B' Flight's Blue Section took off in search of an enemy reconnaissance aircraft that had crossed what was referred to as the 'action line', which lay eighty miles off the coast. The Germans appeared to be testing the RAF's defences, as the enemy aircraft, which was being closely monitored by radar, was seen to turn back for base before an interception could be made.

A detachment of ground crew was temporarily deployed to Scorton, following orders issued by AOC. The satellite aerodrome, a flattish field which had previously been used by the squadron for forced landing approach practice, was serviceable by October when it was used by No. 41 Squadron's Spitfires and the Blenheims of No. 219 Squadron.

Until ordered to the contrary, the squadron would maintain one flight at readiness at their advanced station; the second was to remain at various stages of availability. While one section was generally placed at immediate readiness, if there was the likelihood of a raid the second might be at fifteen or thirty minutes' readiness. If, however, a substantial raid was plotted approaching the squadron's sector, then they might be placed on standby, the pilots sitting in their cockpits strapped-in, with the ground crews running the engines every half-hour to keep them warm and ensure a quick take-off. When the order to scramble was given by the Sector Controller, the Spitfires would be fired up using the starter trolleys and were in the air in a little under five minutes.

Sitting at dispersals waiting for the order to take off, the pilots would try to read a book or played games; anything to take their minds off the possible combat ahead. All were following the news broadcasts and read the newspapers from cover to cover.

The news from Poland was all bad. While Polish land and air forces were putting up stiff resistance, they were hopelessly outnumbered and outgunned and suffering heavy losses. The situation was perhaps summed-up by a report in the German newspaper *Nachtausgab* which stated how Polish forces gallantly took on the *Wehrmacht* under the headline: 'Cavalry Attack Tanks!' Despite such heroics, it was only a matter of time before the whole country was overrun.

Two days after war had been declared, and with no sign of immediate action in their Sector, arrangements were made to allow some of the pilots and ground staff to rest, and while one flight was kept at readiness, the other was allowed off the Station. Meanwhile, it was decided to divide the squadron into three watches, two of which were on duty at any one time, the third being allowed off camp. The operational rota was later reorganized and with the exception of the section commanders, one pilot per flight was placed on 24 hours' duty.

On 9 September, with their campaign in Poland going according to plan, further orders were issued from Berlin:

Directive No. 3 for the Conduct of the War.
SUPREME COMMANDER OF THE ARMED FORCES MOST SECRET.
Berlin 9 September 1939.

1. Operation against the Polish Army and Air Force will continue with the necessary forces until it is safe to assume that the Poles are no longer capable of establishing a continuous front which can tie down German forces.
2. Should it be clear that some part of the eastern Army and of the Air Force are no longer necessary for the completion of this task and for the pacification of occupied territories, arrangements are to be made to transfer these forces to the west.

As the Polish Air Force becomes progressively weaker, further air defence units may be made available for use against our western enemies.

3. Even after the half-hearted opening of hostilities by England, at sea and in the air, and by France, on the land and in the air, my personal approval must be obtained.

(a) For any crossing of the German land frontier, unless they are necessary to meet heavy enemy air attack.

(b) For all flights beyond the western frontier of Germany, unless they are necessary to meet heavy enemy attacks.

(c) The air attacks against England.

The Air Force is, however, free to operate in the German Bight and in the western mined areas, and in immediate support of naval action at sea.

(d) For the Navy.... No offensive action at sea is to be undertaken against France.

(signed) Adolf Hitler.

On 13 September Air Vice Marshal Saul visited Catterick where he inspected the dispersal points and spoke to Bennions and the other pilots before being flown to Church Fenton by Flying Officer Theilmann. No doubt one of the results of the AOC's visit was the near immediate promotion of the squadron's two flight commanders, Flying Officers Ryder and Webster, to the rank of flight lieutenant, which came through within the week.

Concerns were raised that the hastily established blackout might not be one hundred per cent effective and at 22.32 hours Flying Officers Webster and Blatchford flew a sector reconnaissance during which they checked for light sources, both on the airfield and in Catterick village, but no infringements were observed.

On the following day the squadron suffered their first wartime casualty, when Pilot Officer Copley was killed while taking-off in Spitfire K 9849. His forward vision impaired by the aircraft's high nose, he ploughed into the Watch Hut. With a full fuel-tank, the Spitfire erupted in a ball of fire, killing the young pilot, whose charred remains were recovered and sent by rail to Whittles Ford on the following day. Copley's death was a ghastly reminder of the ever-present dangers of flying.

Pilot Officer (41528) James John Hawke Copley, RAF, was the son of Squadron Leader Reginald James and Josephine Myra Copley, of Newton, Cambridgeshire. He was 18 and had been with the squadron for less than three months. Copley was buried at Newton St Margaret Churchyard, Newton, Cambridgeshire.

There was another twist to the war when, at 06.00 hours Moscow time on 17 September, Russian forces invaded eastern Poland, claiming that as the Polish government no longer existed, their earlier promise to respect Polish sovereign territory was null and void. In fact, the invasion was in accordance with their pact with Germany.

With Hitler's plan for Poland on course, the German press called on the Allies to sue for peace. The *Frankfurter Zeitung* used Stalin's rationale when it claimed: 'Since the Polish state has ceased to exist, the treaties of alliance with it have no more sense.'

In Great Britain many people were dismayed that Poland, on whose behalf the country had gone to war, appeared already lost before our own forces had had the opportunity to intervene.

For his own part, Bennions did not make his first operational flight since the opening of hostilities until 18 September:

There had been little activity in our Sector and most of the flying had been non-operational. I flew several air co-operation exercises with No. 10 Squadron, flying Armstrong Whitworth Whitleys out of Dishforth.

I made mock attacks which were great fun but totally useless tactically. The bomber crews got experience of taking avoiding action against fighter attacks.

Bennions' log book records that he had been given clearance to fly in order to practise 'No. 1 Attacks'. The RAF's formation attacks would be quickly discredited once the squadron entered into combat, but it would be a costly learning-curve, with pilots spending vital time getting into formation position, time which was dangerous to waste and took their concentration away from the real objective, making them vulnerable to attack from the *Luftwaffe's* fighters which hunted in pairs.

The squadron flew further affiliation exercises on the 25th and 29th when they practised following the Controller's vector to locate a moving target and make an attacking approach. Such practice interceptions proved vital as the pilots geared themselves up for the very real possibility of intercepting enemy bombers.

Meanwhile, towards the end of the month the pilots were issued with Smith and Wesson 0.38 Service revolvers; if they were shot down over enemy-occupied territory, this would be their only method of avoiding capture, but at least there was no need for a re-issue of the 'Goolie-chits' carried in the Yemen!

On the Continent, however, the war continued to go badly for the Allies, and at 20.10 hours Berlin time on 27 September a German radio announcer read from the German High Command's official communiqué: 'Warsaw has unconditionally capitulated. The formal giving over to the German High Command will probably take place [on] September 29th.'

With the surrender of Poland, Hitler had achieved his goal, but he needed time to consolidate his gains before taking on Britain and France. In an effort to buy time, the Germans pulled back from any further escalation of hostilities, thus entering the phase known by many as the 'Phoney War', when the Allies failed to make strategic advances for fear of starting a land war in France and Belgium which would parallel the slaughter of the First World War.

The squadron was to spend many weary hours at readiness, punctuated by occasional scrambles, flying training and convoy patrols. Previously, training had always been in favourable weather, but on a war footing pilots were forced to take off regardless of the conditions if 'bogies' were reported entering their section:

> Following days of relative inactivity, we had what we thought was our first taste of action on 30th September. Red Section was put on standby at about 4 pm and scrambled a few minutes later. But once in the air the Controller quickly informed them that the 'bogie' had been identified as 'friendly' and they were ordered to land. The danger hadn't totally passed and the section remained at readiness.

This course of events became a regular occurrence, with Spitfires being scrambled to investigate radar plots which turned out to be our own aircraft returning from reconnaissance sorties and having flown off-course. On each occasion the 'friendly' aircraft were located and identified, before being escorted to an airfield.

On 3 October Bennions took part in two formation mock–attacks on radar stations and industrial targets at 12.40 hours and 14.25 hours. The 'raids' were designed to give the radar operators and members of the Observer Corps practice in recognizing plots and monitoring their progress.

There had been a sudden influx of unattached pilots and ground staff onto the Station and on the following day No. 219 (F) Squadron was reformed at Catterick on Blenheims. Their role would be to make long range shipping protection sorties, escorting vessels approaching the nearby ports of Newcastle, Sunderland and Hull. Richard 'Batchy' Atcherley, who in 1931 had flown as a part of the team that set a new world air speed record in the Supermarine S6, would arrive later to train the unit as the RAF's first dedicated night fighter squadron.

Meanwhile, during the month, No. 26 Army Co-operation Squadron, which had shared Catterick as their base, was posted to France, forming a part of the AASF. The squadron had been reformed in 1927 as an Army

Co-operation Flight and by late 1939 was flying Lysanders, which had replaced their Hectors.

Flight Sergeant Bennions made a ten minute operational patrol on 8 October, being ordered to 'pancake' almost as soon as his Spitfire had become airborne, as the sortie was cancelled.

Meanwhile, on 9 October, Adolf Hitler issued his sixth War Directive, in which he ordered that preparations should be made for: '…an attacking operation on the northern wing of the Western Front, through the areas of Luxembourg, Belgium and Holland. This attack must be carried out with as much strength and at as early a date as possible…'

In the event the Allies advance into Belgium to counter the German's invasion would prove to be a part of their downfall, stretching their supply lines and exposing themselves to attack from the rear, which came when German Panzers bypassed the French Maginot Line and instead broke through the supposedly impenetrable Ardennes forest to the north.

The squadron temporarily lost Flight Lieutenant Ryder from 10th October when he was sent to RAF Northolt on an intensive Air Fighting Instructor's Course. Here the fighter techniques already being developed by other squadrons were discussed at length. The pre-war RAF had fixated on keeping a tight formation, something which was drummed into the pilots over all else. Fighter squadrons generally flew in a vic formation, the twelve aircraft being sub-divided into four sections of three. When flying at squadron strength, the rear section acted as lookout. This was the 'weaver' section, whose job it was to constantly check the sky for the enemy, while remaining in their own tight vic. The rest of the pilots were largely concentrated on keeping together in tight formation with only the leader actively looking for targets. Fighter Command had adopted equally rigid methods of attacking formations of enemy aircraft: these were known as Nos. 1–5 Fighter Attacks. For the moment at least these remained in vogue but combat experience would soon prove their fallibility.

Friday 13 October saw one of the RN's worst losses of the Second World War, when U–47, commanded by *Kapitänleutnant* Prien, slipped through a gap in the anti-submarine nets and into the natural harbour at Scapa Flow where it torpedoed HMS *Royal Oak*, which sunk with the loss of over 840 souls. The remainder of the Fleet had already been dispersed, the guns of the *Royal Oak* being used to give the shore establishment protection from enemy shipping.

On the afternoon 16 October the air campaign stepped up and the first enemy aircraft were caught off the British coast when fifteen *Junkers* Ju 88s of I./KG 30 were engaged while attempting to attack the RN in the Firth of Forth. Nos. 602 and 603 Squadrons' Spitfires claimed two Ju 88s and damaged a third.

The following afternoon No. 41 Squadron had its first contact with the enemy when their Spitfires were scrambled to intercept a possible enemy raider.

At 15.47 hours the telephone rang at dispersals, where 'B' Flight's Green Section was at readiness. It was the Group Controller responding to reports of an aircraft flying up the coast off Whitby. Flying Officer Howard 'Cowboy' Blatchford answered the telephone and immediately barked out the order: 'Green Section scramble!'

Before the receiver was replaced, Sergeants Albert 'Bill' Harris and Edward 'Shippy' Shipman, already in full flying gear and Mae West, sprang to their feet, joining Blatchford in racing to their Spitfires.

Airborne by 15.55 hours, Green Section followed a vector which took them towards West Hartlepool at 8,000ft where they were to investigate the unidentified plot designated Raid X 18. Updated at 16.12 hours they climbed to 10,000ft, before the plot turned northwards while flying a little to the south of Whitby, and at 16.40 hours the Sector Controller ordered them to head towards Whitby. Taking the section southwards along the coast in an open vic, Blatchford ensured the sun would be behind them as they approached the 'bogie.'

Four minutes later, Green Leader reported making contact with an unidentified aircraft approaching the coast a little to the south of Saltburn; the bomber was heading north. Approaching the twin-engine aircraft from below to avoid fire from the gunner, Shipman, Green 2, positively identified his target as a *Heinkel* He 111, before pulling up and closing to fifty yards and opening fire. With tracer from the upper-gunner passing over his port wing, Green 2 expended all of his ammunition with a single fifteen-second burst, which silenced the gunner and damaged both engines. He then peeled away to allow Blatchford and Harris to make their passes. With more hits registering, the bomber limped on, but was losing altitude all of the time.

Blatchford watched the bomber trailing smoke as it descended, before it finally ditched into the sea at 16.50 hours. He reported back to the Controller that his section had shot down one enemy aircraft 20 miles out to sea, bearing 40 degrees from Whitby. It was later discovered that the He 111 of 2 (F) *Aufklarunggruppe* 122 had been searching for HMS *Hood*.

The three triumphant pilots returned to Catterick where they landed after an hour. As they came in to touch down it was clear to onlookers that their gun-port covers had been blown while the leading edges of their wings were blackened by tell-tale streaks of cordite.

At the immediate debriefing by the squadron's Intelligence Officer their accounts were gradually pieced together. To be officially credited with a 'kill', the definite destruction of an enemy aircraft had to be independently confirmed by another pilot, land forces, or by the RN. If a claim could not be verified and proven conclusively, it had to be recorded as a 'damaged', 'probable' or 'unconfirmed.' As soon as they had filed their combat reports the trio found themselves surrounded by all ranks, eager for details of the squadron's first victory, which was toasted with champagne in the Officer's Mess.

Although all three pilots were given a share in the victory, the official squadron record credited 'Ted' Shipman as the first member of the squadron to have fired his guns in anger, with the 'kill'.

Later that day a congratulatory signal was received from the AOC of No. 13 Group, based at Ouston, near Newcastle.

Of the bomber crew, *Leutnant* Joachim Kretschmer and the air gunner, Hugo Sauer, were killed, while the pilot, *Oberfeldwebel* Eugen Lange and his radio operator, *Unteroffizier* Bernard Hochstuhl, took to a dinghy and eventually came ashore near the village of Sandsend. They were escorted under armed guard to Whitby for hospital treatment and later interrogation.

On 18 October the squadron received orders to fly to Wick in Caithness, via Drem. Here their role would be to fly defensive patrols over Scapa Flow.

Two bomber raids had been made against Scapa Flow on 17 October. The first saw four *Junkers* Ju 88s bomb and sink HMS *Iron Duke*; a few hours later a formation of fifteen bombers attacked the supply liner *Voltaire*. Ackack gunners claimed one bomber during the initial raid. However, the Royal Navy Skuas of No. 803 Squadron Fleet Air Arm (FAA), based at Royal Naval Air Service (RNAS) Hatston, in the Bay of Kirkwall, arrived too late to make an interception.

While the Fleet had been largely dispersed prior to the raid, this situation could not continue due to the logistics involved in both their defence and resupply. In response to the attacks, the First Lord of the Admiralty, Winston Churchill, implemented measures to improve the defences at Scapa Flow. These included additional fighter cover based on the Orkneys and on the mainland at RAF Wick, the nearest mainland airfield to the deep-water anchorage, with No. 804 Squadron FAA being formed at Hatston, flying Gloster Gladiators. In the interim No. 803 Squadron FAA continued to alternate between the two airstrips. No. 41 Squadron's Spitfires would also provide additional air cover.

It wasn't until 15.30 hours that Bennions, flying one of the twelve Spitfires on detachment, took off on the first leg, landing at Drem some thirty-five minutes later for an overnight stop. Meanwhile, an RAF Rapide ferried five members of the ground-staff to Wick ready to service the squadron's aircraft.

At 17.30 hours, a Whitley of No. 102 Squadron, ferrying personnel, ammunition and equipment to Wick, crashed killing four members of the crew: Sergeant H J Gaut (pilot), Pilot Officer R A M Luckman, Aircraftman First Class C Paterson, Aircraftman First Class J B Clark, along with Sergeants Harris and Vincent, and Aircraftman First Class Jones of No. 41 Squadron. Two other men, Sergeant Gibbs and Corporal Jenkinson, were admitted to hospital.

The incident was witnessed by Violet Harris who was standing at her kitchen window in the married quarters. Initially reassured by the other pilots' wives that the crash had involved a bomber, it wasn't until she heard the knock at the door that the terrible truth hit home.

An investigation later blamed the accident on a starter trolley, one of several that had been incorrectly secured. Sergeant Gaut had earlier telephoned his base at Driffield, reporting that the Whitley was overloaded, but had been overruled.

Sergeant (563150) Albert H Harris, RAF, was the son of Arthur and Eva Harris and the husband of Violet Ann Harris, of Toronto, Ontario, Canada. He was 27. Harris was buried at South Hinksey (St Laurence) Churchyard, Section O, Grave 209.

Sergeant (560443) Arthur Vincent, RAF, was the son of Albert and Dorothy Jane Vincent of Sunderland and the husband of Olga Vincent, of Humbledon, Sunderland. He was 30 and was buried at Sunderland (Southwick) Cemetery, Section D, Grave 1243.

Aircraftman First Class (Wireless Operator/Mechanic under training) (533682) Horace Jones was buried at Doylsden Cemetery, Section F, Grave 482.

News of the disaster had been quick to reach Drem, where many squadron personnel, including Bennions, counted Sergeants Vincent and Harris as close personal friends. But, for the moment at least, all personal thoughts had to be put aside and the pilots continued on their mission.

Taking off from Drem at 08.30 hours on the following morning, the squadron headed north again, crossing the Firth of Forth before climbing over the Grampians and the Highlands, completing the second leg of their journey.

Despite the ban on discussing the last-minute posting and a strict radio silence, the locals in Wick had known of their impending arrival twenty-four hours before the first Spitfires landed. More disturbingly, the German daily reconnaissance sorties at 10.00 and 14.00 hours ceased abruptly.

On landing the Spitfires were immediately refuelled and placed on standby. The CO offered to mount standing patrols but the Admiralty declined, informing Squadron Leader Johnson that their vessels would fire at anything that appeared overhead!

RAF Wick was originally used by Captain E E Fresson's Highland Airways Ltd., which had handed over the grass strip to the Air Ministry in

1939, when a programme of upgrading was put into place as a matter of great urgency. This included the construction of runways, hangars and ancillary buildings, although during No. 41 Squadron's brief tenure the facilities remained rudimentary. The squadron's headquarters was in the classroom of North School, the local primary school which had been requisitioned at the beginning of the war, while the pilots were billeted in the nearby Station Hotel.

The day after the squadron's temporary detachment, No. 19 Squadron arrived at Catterick, where they assumed No. 41 Squadron's duties. However, with the Fleet moved to a safer anchorage on the west coast of Scotland, No. 41 Squadron soon returned to Catterick, having flown nothing more than a couple of air tests; the knowledge of their presence had kept the enemy at bay.

Over the following weeks, the squadron made regular flight- or section-strength convoy patrols, calling on additional aircraft when enemy aircraft were plotted approaching their vicinity. Flying out of Catterick meant wasting valuable time crossing the Cleveland Hills before reaching the coast so under wartime conditions the squadron operated out of their forward landing ground at West Hartlepool.

It was from here that the Spitfires were operating on 30 October when they had another opportunity to make contact with the enemy. At 07.39 hours Group HQ received details of Raid X 46, which was plotted heading in a north westerly direct, fifteen miles north-east of Hartlepool; the plot crossed the coast to the north of Sunderland.

Blue Section was scrambled at 08.01 hours and was vectored onto the enemy flying near Hartlepool at a height of 6,000ft. Meanwhile, members of the Durham Observer Corps reported sighting the raider '8 miles inland slightly north of South Shields'. Despite being given updated courses, the search proved fruitless and at 08.32 hours the Group Controller ordered their return. Two further operational patrols were made by Red and Blue Sections prior to 14.00 hours but frustratingly nothing was seen.

Bennions joined the remainder of 'A' Flight in taking part in another flying affiliation exercise with No. 10 Squadron on 6 November. On landing, Bennions reported to dispersal where on reading the flight log he learned that he was due to take part in 'night flying under black-out conditions' at 19.00 hours. The weather, however, closed in and the flight was apparently cancelled.

Later that evening, at 21.20 hours, three Spitfires took off, with orders to make a search for the remains of a Whitley which had crashed nearby in patchy fog. None of the pilots had made night flights recently, while the airfield itself remained partly shrouded.

Flying Officer Overall (flying K 9846) took off first, closely followed by Bennions and Norman Ryder. Overall was seen to climb to about 200ft before banking to the right in a descending turn. Bennions watched helplessly as moments later the Spitfire plunged into Catterick village, ploughing into the ground at the top of Mowbray Road, a blinding fireball appearing to engulf the heart of the village.

George's eldest daughter Connie, who had been asleep in bed at the rear of No. 2 when the plane crashed, later recalled the horrendous noise and flames. Her mother rushed up the stairs to check that she was safe, instructing her to 'stay in bed and be a good girl.' Convinced that it was her husband's Spitfire that had struck their neighbour's house, Avis wanted to shield her daughter from the carnage. High above, Bennions believed that Overall's aircraft had struck No. 2, and feared for the safety of his wife and daughter.

Disobeying orders, Bennions immediately landed and jumped into his car and raced home, arriving in time to see Avis being restrained, having already made several attempts to extricate the pilot from the burning wreckage. He recalled: 'The exact cause of the accident was never discovered but may have been due to a failure in the artificial horizon. Pookie's vision would have been almost totally obscured by the exhaust flashes.'

With the lights of Catterick concealed by a faultless blackout, fog blanking out any visible horizon and the airstrip using shielded lighting designed only to be visible on a landing approach, Overall had neither visible landmarks nor a horizon to gauge his position or altitude.

For the first time Bennions had witnessed the loss of a close friend and was forced to reflect on what might have been – had Overall's Spitfire remained in the air a fraction of second longer, or had its wing not clipped a telegraph pole, then it might well have levelled No. 2. Instead, Overall's Spitfire had crashed into the garden and frontage of No. 1, the Hughes' house, causing some structural damage. Miraculously the house next door suffered nothing more than scorch marks to the paintwork.

Mrs Hughes later wrote a letter of condolence to Overall's parents in which she mentioned her two children and her fears for their safety, living so close to an operational airfield. In their reply Mr and Mrs Overall offered to take the children in as evacuees to thank the family for their efforts to save their son, the Canadian government paying for their sea passage.

Flying Officer (39331) Horace Ernest Herbert Overall, RAF, was the son of William Joseph and Annie Sophia Overall, of Niagra Falls, Ontario, Canada. Overall, who was 26, was buried at Catterick Cemetery, Church of England Section, Row M, Grave 4.

Many Germans had opposed the rise of Hitler's Third Reich, and while thousands simply allowed themselves to be dictated to by the *Führer's* war machine, others decided to act.

During the evening of 8 November, Adolf Hitler attended the annual celebration of the Munich beer house *Putsch* of 1923, where he continued the tradition of making a keynote speech to Party members. Hitler told Goering and the nation to prepare for a 'five-year war', announcing:

> I can assure you that England will never win this second war against us. England is now up against a different Germany and will soon realize it. England doesn't want peace. We heard that from Lord Halifax yesterday. We now speak to England in terms which she understands....

Making an uncharacteristically brief address, Hitler left earlier than expected. Only fifteen minutes after his departure, a bomb exploded behind where Hitler had been standing. The dictator made great political mileage out of the attempt on his life, its victims being given a state funeral. The assassination attempt was publicly blamed not on disaffected Germans, but on agents sent by Churchill, Hitler manipulating the truth to ensure that patriotic Germans closed ranks behind him.

For the pilots of No. 41 Squadron this period saw continued training exercises. Meanwhile, there were many weary hours at readiness, only punctuated by the occasional scramble and long hours of convoy patrols, but all proved uneventful. Meanwhile, at 14.00 hours on 12 November, Bennions' 'A' Flight was released to attend the funeral of Flying Officer Overall. Naturally, it was a very solemn occasion. Overall was well liked by all of the pilots and ground staff and his loss was keenly felt:

> The accident was in my opinion wholly avoidable. But when you are in the Services and you are ordered to take off on a sortie, there is no room for discussion – no matter whether you agree with the command or not, that didn't enter into it, not at the time anyway.

On the following day, Bennions began a period of four days' leave. Meanwhile, the first bombs were dropped on British soil when a raid hit the Shetland Isles. The newspapers made light of the attack, reporting that the only casualty was a rabbit, inspiring the popular wartime song *'Run Rabbit'*.

With the rest of the squadron still engaged in almost daily local patrols, Bennions flew formation and practice attacks on the morning of 18 November, making 'interceptions' during the afternoon:

> This was my first flight after Pookie's death. I was glad to be in the air again and to be back into the routine of things. It didn't pay to dwell on the loss of a friend, not when you faced the possibility of action at any moment. If you let your concentration drift even for a second when you

were in the air – especially in tight formation – that could be the end of you and the pilots around you.

At 09.20 hours on the morning of 21 November, Bennions was airborne when 'A' Flight's Red Section was ordered to patrol Scarborough:

> We set the dial on our oxygen and climbed to operational altitude where we cruised for about forty minutes, marking the patrol-line but without sighting the enemy.
>
> The thought of possibly entering into combat for the first time filled me with a combination of excitement and trepidation. I wanted to get stuck-in and prove myself and my training. Finally the Controller's voice broke the silence and we were ordered to break-off and returned to base.
>
> Benions' first combat would have to wait.

A working party from Supermarine, Southampton, arrived at Catterick two days later, to fit head and body armour to the squadron's Spitfires, while on the 27th Browning machine guns were delivered from the BSA Works, Birmingham. Further improvements came when staff from Rolls-Royce modified the Merlin engines, giving them increased boost pressure and power. Meanwhile, every new aircraft that was flown in from a Maintenance Unit had to be modified before it could become operational: this meant fitting the correct radio, setting-up the guns and later adding reflector gun-sights, while armoured windscreens and a domed canopy gave greater protection and an all-round field of view. Some modifications required less technical support and a visit to a motor-cycle shop provided the pilots' first rear-view mirrors: essential in combat, but not originally fitted as standard.

On 24 November Bennions took part in an early morning flight-strength patrol off the Whitby area:

> Looking at my log book, it was my first 'dawn patrol' after the declaration of hostilities – the first of many. We took off in two vics of three. The sun was low in the sky, which made spotting aircraft at our own altitude and below more difficult, but as it turned out it was fairly routine and the formation landed without having been vectored onto the enemy.

Hitler already knew that victory depended on the conquest, or at least the military and political silencing of Great Britain, to which end, on 29 November, he issued Directive No. 9 for the Conduct of the War. Initially, Hitler's plan was to cripple Britain financially so she would not be able to pose an offensive threat. Prime targets included merchant shipping and their escorts and the destruction of oil, food and grain storage facilities. Troop transport was to be interrupted, while industrial plant, especially war production, was also to be targeted, as were the main ports. Meanwhile, shipping lanes were to be mined to help maintain the blockade.

The *Luftwaffe's* assault on Britain was yet to materialize and No. 13 Group's sector remained particularly quiet, with only occasional enemy reconnaissance and anti-shipping patrols being flown.

Throughout December the squadron flew almost daily local patrols in the areas of Hartlepool, Saltburn, Scarborough and Whitby, while occasional sunset patrols were also made.

The squadron had two of its Spitfires damaged on 30 November, when Sergeant (565271) Reginald Thomas Llewellyn landed heavily during his first two solo flights. Llewellyn, who had been posted from No. 263 squadron only five days earlier, didn't fly again with the squadron and was sent to No. 12 Group Pool at Aston Down at the end of the year. Llewellyn later flew with great distinction with Nos. 213 and 74 Squadrons, opening his account over Dunkirk on 29 May. He was shot down and badly wounded in the right arm while in combat with Bf 110s over Hawkhurst on 15 September 1940. Llewellyn was awarded the DFM on 22 October 1940, by which time he had thirteen and a half victories – he was commissioned and later commanded Nos. 74, 87 and 208 Squadrons.

Bennions flew on ack-ack co-operation exercises for local batteries on 1, 9, 11, 13 and 21 December, while at 14.10 hours on the afternoon of the 21st he took part in squadron formation flying.

Meanwhile, on 5 December, following their CO's recommendation for a commission, Flight Sergeants Bennions and Shipman, along with Warrant Officer J S Darrant, travelled to No. 13 Group HQ at Kenton for an interview with Air Vice Marshal Saul; in due course all three were promoted.

At 13.00 hours on 5 December 'B' Flight carried out Air Firing Training at Acklington.

At 14.45 hours on 10 December Bennions' Red Section was scrambled and ordered on an operational patrol of the Whitby area. Bennions raced to his Spitfire. Clambering onto the wing and over the pilot's side door and into the cockpit, he sat as the rigger dropped the top parachute straps over his shoulders and into his lap before he clicked them into their fast-release buckle. Seemingly in the same motion he switched the petrol on and primed the engine before grabbing his flying helmet, plugged in the ear-pieces and turned the radio on, checking the propeller pitch and trimming tabs, locking the harness, turned the engine on and signalling to the starter-trolley, where an airman pressed the started button. The engine fired up and he signalled for the chocks to be pulled away from beneath the wheels. The formation leader opened the throttle and motioned forward. Taxiing in formation,

Bennions waited for the signal to take off: all six aircraft were in the air within five minutes. Bennions patrolled for twenty minutes before being ordered to return to base.

At 15.46 hours on 17 December, two aircraft of Blue Section were scrambled and ordered to patrol Whitby, where a convoy was reportedly under attack. Vectored onto an enemy aircraft, Flight Lieutenant Webster (Blue Leader) sighted a twin-engine *Heinkel* He 115 floatplane looming indistinctly in the distance. Closing in, Webster confirmed the identity of the aircraft before engaging. Firing several bursts totalling 500 rounds, he saw pieces flying off the enemy aircraft, which emitted smoke before escaping into the clouds, hotly pursued by Pilot Officer Lovell. Despite a protracted search, the enemy could no longer be traced, so Webster, who had earlier served with Nos. 47, 17 and 80 Squadrons and had joined 41 Squadron as a Flight Commander, was only allowed to claim the *Heinkel* as a probable.

The Air Ministry's guidelines on the assessment of combat victories were necessarily strict to avoid over-claiming:

Destroyed:
a)   Aircraft must be seen on the ground or in the air destroyed by a member of the crew or formation, or confirmed from other sources, e.g. ships at sea, local authorities etc.
b)   Aircraft must be seen to descend with flames issuing. It is not sufficient if only smoke is seen.
c)   Aircraft must be seen to break up in the air.

Probables:
a)   When the pilot of a single-engined aircraft is seen to bail out.
b)   The aircraft must be seen to break off the combat in circumstance which leads our pilots to believe it will be a loss.

Damaged:
Aircraft must be seen to be considerably damaged as the result of attack, e.g. undercarriage dropped, engine dropped, aircraft parts shot away, or volumes of smoke issuing.

Quite how a single-engine aircraft was meant to get home without a pilot remains unclear.

On the following day the squadron flew an operational patrol off the Filey area with 'A' Flight's Yellow Section taking off at 13.16 hours. Bennions was to make a second operational patrol two hours later, both passing off without incident.

On the 20th 'B' Flight was ordered to intercept an enemy raid at 12.32 hours while already on a patrol. The leader followed the vector but their target somehow eluded them.

There could be no let-up in the squadron's vigilance and they remained on duty throughout the Festive Season. Squadron Leader Johnson, however, decided to help break the monotony by putting on an aerobatics show on Christmas Eve. At 10.15 hours, he led seven of the squadron's Spitfires on a 'beat-up' of Thornaby aerodrome, the aircraft peeling off after their fun and heading to Usworth where they repeated the breathtaking display.

Bennions was next in the air on 29 December when 'A' Flight flew a night training exercise, taking off at 23.30 hours.

The New Year saw only occasional local patrols, until 12 January, when the squadron flew dawn to dusk standing convoy patrols. Bennions undertook the initial two-hour long sortie; the patrols passed off without event.

The squadron once again provided standing patrols for a convoy during the morning of 21 January, with Bennions' Red Section, consisting of Flight Lieutenant Ryder, Pilot Officer Mackenzie and Flight Sergeant Bennions, carrying out the first stint, which was flown between 08.00 and 09.22 hours: 'We approached the convoy on a wide arc, showing our silhouette before making an approach to within firing range so that we were easily identifiable – no-one wanted to have to report to the CO having lost their Spit to 'friendly' fire.

All flights had to be authorized and logged in order to minimize confusion between friendly and hostile aircraft. The ack-ack gunners, however, generally proved to be trigger-happy, and in the early days of the war at least, shot at anything that appeared in their field of fire. Convoy escorts could be particularly hazardous, and from November 1939 it had become common practice for a squadron leader to be onboard the lead RN escort in order to aid aircraft recognition – even then, aircraft were not always correctly identified and were sometimes fired upon.

Red Section was scrambled at 13.18 hours and ordered to patrol Darlington and Middlesborough at 3,000ft in search of a *Dornier* Do 17. Known as the 'flying pencil', the Do 17 had a distinctive long fuselage with twin engines and a dorsal gun-turret.

The suspected aircraft was 'intercepted' but was identified as an RAF Hudson. Bennions noting that the 'Raid' landed at 13.37 hours.

Two days later the squadron carried out standing convoy patrols between 10.15 and 16.42 hours, Bennions' Red Section flew a single sortie between 12.30 and 13.35 hours. Meanwhile, a section-strength coastal patrol flown between 15.10 and 15.40 hours on the 25th was Bennions' last flight during another quiet month.

Despite the rarity of combat between the RAF and *Luftwaffe* over these shores, the pilots of Fighter Command were already growing in public popularity, which was further enhanced by a new feature film premiered at cinemas across the country on 19 January. Directed by Alexander Korda and staring Ralph Richardson, *The Lion has Wings* included flying scenes shot at RAF Hornchurch, featuring Spitfires from No. 74 Squadron's 'B' Flight, filmed the day after the so-called Battle of Barking Creek, when its pilots were mistakenly ordered to shoot down what turned out to be two Hurricanes.

Very heavy snow fell during 28 January which meant that the airfield, like many others across the country, was unserviceable:

> Around three to four hundred troops from a local army camp arrived early the following morning. We had the use of a couple of snow ploughs too and through their combined efforts they cleared us a single short and rather narrow landing strip with routes off leading to the perimeter track and to our dispersal points.

The winter of 1939/40 was particularly severe. Heavy frosts and snow regularly shrouded the landing strips, while the Spitfires' Merlin engines, which were covered overnight, had to be thawed-out by various means before they could be fired up. The mechanics ran the engines every thirty minutes to make sure they were ready for an immediate scramble.

February saw more convoy patrols, the first being flown early in the mid-afternoon of the 2nd, when Flight Lieutenant Ryder led Red Section with Flight Sergeants Bennions and Gillies. The thirty-four vessels represented a significant target and were escorted until fading light lowered the risk of attack.

Standing patrols were flown over another convoy from first light on the 9th. Bennions flew with Yellow Section during the squadron's sixth and final mission of the day, which was made between 13.20 and 14.50 hours. Three He 111s were believed to have been in the area but could not be located.

The convoy was picked-up again the following morning, Bennions flying a single sortie, while the patrols continued until late on the 11th, Bennions again flying that morning, when the last of the merchant vessels and their escort passed through the squadron's sector.

The tedium of these convoy patrols continued on and off until 17 February, although Bennions began seven days leave on the 13th.

On 21 February Bennions' Red Section, which included Pilot Officers Mackenzie and Legard, were on standby when Group HQ telephoned through: two 'Huns' were reported heading for the coast near Saltburn. Scrambled at 10.38 hours, the three Spitfires took off in section formation and were in the air within five minutes and vectored to fly over Saltburn at 5,000ft. The Section Leader followed the Controller's directions for an hour, as the pilots strained their eyes to try to pick-out the enemy on the horizon, but to no avail. Finally, having nearly expended all of their fuel, they were ordered to land back at base without having caught sight of the enemy – it had been another frustrating patrol.

Between 23 February and 2 March, Bennions' 'A' Flight operated out of RAF Thornaby. From here they carried out operational patrols on the 26th and the following day.

March saw a continuation of local, coastal and occasional convoy patrols. These were largely made at section strength. With his flight back operating out of Catterick, Bennions flew with Red Section on a convoy patrol made between 07.34 and 08.38 hours on 3 March. Standing patrols were flown over a convoy during the daylight hours on the 6th and 7th, Bennions Red Section flying one mission on both days, landing back at base a little after noon.

Bennions' next patrol didn't come until he 30th when Red Section, comprising Flight Lieutenant Ryder, Flying Officer Scott and Flight Sergeant Bennions, took off at 10.10 hours to carry out a seventy minute patrol of West Hartlepool at 2,000ft, while the squadron provided uneventful standing patrols over a convoy for much of the late afternoon.

Meanwhile, 'A' Flight's Yellow Section carried out a rapid rearm and refuel exercise, the ground crews turning the Spitfires around in fourteen minutes. During the height of the Battle of Britain the rapid turn around of aircraft would prove vital in maintaining Fighter Command's defensive screen.

On the following day the squadron was once again engaged in dawn to dusk standing patrols, with Bennions joining Flying Officer 'Butch' Barton on a single uneventful convoy patrol. This was his last flight as a sergeant pilot, as on 1 April Bennions was commissioned as a pilot officer, with his Service No. 43354: 'My promotion meant that officially I left the Service and re-enlisted as a pilot officer, having first been injected with 'blue blood'', Bennions joked. In the meantime, his first port of call was a visit to the military tailor in order to get fully kitted-out: 'I had to buy all new uniforms, each being individually fitted to ensure a smart Bennions presented himself before the CO and brother officers in the Mess.'

Along with access to the Officers' Mess, better quality meals and a bar tab, all single officers also had a batman. With Avis living just off base, however, Bennions did not require further assistance when it came to looking after his uniforms, kit and personal affairs.

It was usual for a promoted NCO to be posted away to another unit as the Service felt that it was bad for morale for NCOs and officers to socialize, either on or off the base. Squadron Leader Johnson, however, was less strict on this issue and both Bennions and Shipman, who was also promoted on the same day, had already made it clear that they wished to remain with the squadron; they had trained together and wanted to fight together. Bennions had, however, to make some concessions and was selected to become the Squadron Navigation Officer, and later on 5 May reported to RAF St Athan to attend No. 6 Navigation Instructor's Course. While the posting might enhance his promotions possibilities, it meant that he would not return to Catterick until late June, missing the whole of the squadron's first posting to Hornchurch and its role in the Dunkirk operations. In the meantime, Bennions remained at Catterick, awaiting the start of his course.

No. 41 Squadron made only occasional local patrols during April, and from the 5th they flew by sections to their advanced base at West Hartlepool early in the morning, from where they operated. Meanwhile, standing convoy patrols were made on the 2nd, 6th, and 8th and again on the 10th.

The slow-moving ships were difficult to defend and when the *Luftwaffe's* anti-shipping campaign was finally launched, casualties would be high among the defending squadrons. But for now at least, the work remained monotonous and largely uneventful.

Dowding had already warned the Air Staff and the Admiralty that he would not be able to maintain standing convoy patrols because they were proving too costly in both men and aircraft, and that this would be the only method of guaranteeing protection for shipping in the Channel. This was because even with radar there was only twenty-minutes' warning of an enemy build-up and by the time the bombers were heading in for the attack, the RAF's fighters would scarcely be off the ground.

No. 41 Squadron's hours of tireless convoy patrols and interceptions were rewarded on 3 April when Blue Leader, Flight Lieutenant Ryder (N3114), recorded a definite 'kill' when he shot down a He 111 which had attacked trawlers off Whitby.

The morning had begun quietly. A combination of low cloud and driving rain had largely grounded the enemy. A little after noon a call came through to Bennions who was acting as Deputy Controller: radar had picked-up a lone raider which was approaching fishing vessels lying off the coast at Saltburn.

Bennions immediately telephoned through to No. 41 Squadron's advanced base at West Hartlepool, where Flight Lieutenant Ryder, on standby, was scrambled. In the air by 12.20 hours, Ryder was vectored onto what Bennions calculated to be the target's projected position. Crossing the coast near Redcar, Ryder quickly located the trawlers which had only moments earlier been targeted. A trail of smoke led to a He 111 (1H+AC) flying on its starboard engine, the port engine having cut out, damaged by defensive fire from one of the armed vessels. The crippled aircraft was limping along only 200ft above the sea and veering off to port.

Throttling back so as not to overshoot the lumbering aircraft, Ryder put himself into position for a stern attack, firing long bursts at the remaining serviceable engine. Ryder's combat report takes up the commentary:

He commenced climbing towards cloud base as soon as he saw me. I then got into a stern position by a left hand-turn, (having made a circuit of the machine and turned in). On my turn I noticed very red flashes indeed from the E/A top gun. No tracer seen.

The He 111 crew had been alert to his attack and the top gunner fired at his Spitfire, recording a number of hits, which Ryder heard strike:

I commenced firing, taking starboard engine as target, for 6 or 7 seconds. I heard two bangs (may have been bullets coming in and out – a clack-clack.)

I then broke away to port and came round for another No. 1 Attack, and noticed his starboard engine was streaming both light and dark smoke (light smoke over, dark smoke under).

I did not turn in for this second attack, as he was losing height. Steadily.

I positioned myself on his starboard side, and watched him land on the water. I imagined his starboard engine completely cut out of action though prop was idling.

Having circled the crew until they were picked up by the trawler *Silver Line*, Ryder noticed there was a problem with his oil temperature, which had risen to 70°, while the cockpit was beginning to fill with oil fumes. It was clear that a bullet had damaged the oil system and that the engine was about to seize. Too far from the coast to make land, Ryder sighted a trawler, the *Alaska*, which he began to circle, using his flaps to reduce his airspeed before making an approach ready to ditch close enough to be picked up:

I then decided I would have to land, as low cloud height made it difficult to position for a parachute descent. I opened the hood and leaving flaps up, tightened my Sutton harness and closed the radiator flap. When about 400 feet off water, I reported to Control [Bennions] that I was landing.

I stalled on to the water at 65 mph with a loud crash. Aircraft immediately dug its nose in and came to vertical position, tail up, and sank immediately. I think whole touch down and sinking was simultaneous.

My next clear recollection was realizing that I was below the surface, and that everything appeared green. I undid my Sutton harness and commenced to get clear.

The a/c was sinking rapidly and when almost clear my parachute caught under the sliding roof. I then got partly back into cockpit and out again and finally got clear [and] commence to swim to the surface. The tail passed just in front of my face.

Pressure was very great and green light had changed to dull black.

Ryder gained the nick-name 'Green to Black' following his recollection of the events to his fellow pilots in the Mess.

By this time I had broke[n the] surface, my lungs had reached just about the limit. I then undid my parachute and treaded water and had great difficulty in keeping up. There appeared to be rollers at regular intervals, about 5 to 6 feet high. I passed through the centre of each of them except odd ones. I tried to remove my helmet but went under each time I tried. Then I tried to put more air into my 'Mae West', which I had failed to do in the air, but found this impossible as I was definitely winded.

I then caught sight of a trawler coming approximately in my direction.

Dragged onboard by the crew of the *Alaska*, he was landed at West Hartlepool and taken to hospital for treatment. Ryder's was the first Spitfire shot down in action; it was also the first to be ditched into the sea. On returning to Catterick, he wasted no time in filing a report in which he emphasized that it was preferable to bail out over the sea rather than to try to ditch, but if unable to do so, he made the following observations and recommendations:

If forced to land on water:
Tighten straps, and inflate 'Mae West'.
Open hood and possibly door.
Close radiator flaps and pancake, at 70 mph.
Aircraft immediately tucks its nose in (with sea running) and assumes a vertical position, tail up and sinks.
Release Sutton harness and parachute and evacuate.
Push away hard to clear tail plane.

Despite having been shot down by return fire, Ryder was later awarded the DFC for the destruction of the bomber which had led to the subsequent capture of *Gruppenkommandeur, Oberstleutnant* Hans Hafele and the remainder of the crew: *Leutnant* Rudolf Behnisch (pilot), *Leutnant* George Kempe (observer), *Unteroffizier* Albert Weber (radio operator) and *Unteroffizier* Alfred Nachle (mechanic).

The Supplement to the *London Gazette* dated 19 April 1940, carried the following announcement of his award:

The KING has been graciously pleased to approve the under-mentioned awards in recognition of gallantry displayed in flying operations against the enemy:-

Distinguished Flying Cross
Acting Flight Lieutenant Edgar Norman RYDER

During April this officer was ordered to investigate an enemy raid at sea and took off alone in bad visibility and low cloud. He sighted an enemy aircraft and observing that its port engine was out of action, he promptly attacked the starboard engine and after disabling it with one burst of fire the aircraft fell into the sea. Afterwards Flight Lieutenant Ryder found that his own aircraft was losing power and he was forced to come down on the sea, whereupon his aircraft immediately dived. When at a considerable depth he managed, with great difficulty, to extricate himself from the cockpit and was then picked up by a nearby trawler. His accurate flying made the interception a success, and his coolness and courage materially contributed to his own rescue and the collection of much valuable information. He set a splendid example of courage and discipline to his squadron.

While the citation noted Ryder's skill in locating the enemy aircraft in poor visibility, it did not acknowledge the part played by Bennions as Deputy Controller in placing Ryder in the path of the enemy aircraft[1]. No doubt, the gunners who 'winged' the He 111 and could quite rightly claim a shared 'kill' were also duly recognized.

In Britain many people were becoming dismayed at the continued inactivity of the BEF in France, while the enemy were consolidating their gains and preparing for the next phase of their campaign.

Chamberlain's position was becoming untenable and on 8 April a poll was published indicating the support for the various possible candidates as his replacement:

Sir Anthony Eden	28%
Winston Churchill	25%
Lord Halifax	7%
Clement Attlee	6%
Lloyd George	5%

In the House, however, Churchill had less support among his fellow MPs. He had a reputation as being self-serving, while many remembered the disastrous Gallipoli campaign of 1915, which he had planned as First Lord of the Admiralty.

Germany's war machine was dependant on Swedish iron ore, and during the winter months this was mainly imported via the Norwegian port of Narvik. In order to secure this supply route, Hitler invaded Norway on 9 April (Operation *Weserübung*), attacking the ports and airfields. France and Great Britain dispatched an expeditionary force, the campaign ending on 10 June with a German victory.

Meanwhile, on 20 April a new face appeared at Catterick when Squadron Leader Hilary Richard Lionel 'Robin' Hood was posted to No. 41 Squadron pending taking over command from Squadron Leader Johnson some two days later. On passing out from Cranwell, Hood had begun his career flying Gloster Gamecocks with No. 23 Squadron (1929–30), later flying the Fleet Air Arm's Fairey Flycatchers. Next came a posting as a flying instructor in 1933. Hood had previously led No. 3 General Reconnaissance Unit, flying modified Wellington DWI minesweeping aircraft, but had little or no experience on Spitfires.

Hood, like most squadron leaders, also lacked experienced as a tactical commander in the air and frequently flew a wingman to his flight commanders while on operational sorties. Similarly, it was not unusual to find more experienced sergeant pilots leading their officers while on section-strength patrols – something which was recorded on most squadrons during the Battle of Britain, when partially trained officers joined the depleted ranks of units that had already lost their more seasoned leaders to combat or exhaustion.

Bennions' log book shows that his next flight came on 26 April when Yellow Section, comprising Pilot Officers Bennions and Mackenzie, accompanied by Sergeant Gillies, was scrambled to make a thirty-minute patrol of the Saltburn area at 16.51 hours. No enemy aircraft were reported and the three aircraft were ordered to return to base.

The first few days of May saw very little activity for the squadron. While sections flew to their advanced base at West Hartlepool, where they remained at readiness, there was only a single uneventful operational patrol.

On the international scene, The House of Commons began debating the Norway campaign on 7 May. It seemed that the die was cast and following Chamberlain's speech to the Commons, Lloyd George stood to make his reply: 'I say solemnly that the Prime Minister should give an example of sacrifice because there is nothing which can contribute more to victory in this war than that he should sacrifice the seal of office.'

On the following day the House voted on the Norway issue. Chamberlain won but had his majority cut from 213 to 81. Privately he admitted to Churchill that he did not believe he could continue in office.

There was some activity for No. 41 Squadron on 9 May when three coastal patrols were flown between dawn and dusk. For many, including Bennions and the men stationed at Catterick, the war had settled into a steady pattern of hardships but little direct threat to their personal safety, but this was about to be shattered by events on the continent.

There appeared to be a new and even greater threat to Western Europe on the horizon when the Ministry of Information in London announced that two German divisions were about to invade the Netherlands. In response the German newspaper *12-Uhr Blatt* accused Chamberlain of being an 'Aggressor Seeking A New Victim.' The German words were a smoke-screen, which for the moment at least concealed the truth: British claims were accurate and an invasion was only hours away.

Note
1. Ryder, who was Bennions' flight commander for the duration of his combat time with the squadron, was finally rested from operations in January 1941, later becoming CO of No. 56 Squadron before commanding the Kenley Wing. It was while leading the Wing on a Ramrod over Gravelines that he was shot down and taken as a PoW on 31 October 1941, being one of those imprisoned at *Stalag Luft III* (PoW No. 658), the scene of the Great Escape. Group Captain Ryder, CBE, DFC and Bar, retired from the RAF in 1960.

Chapter 5

Blitzkrieg

The so-called 'Phoney War' was to end in dramatic style on 10 May when Hitler's forces were deployed in a *Blitzkrieg*, quickly overwhelming the Low Countries and denying British and French troops the possibility of containment of the enemy within Germany's pre-war borders.

The battle-plan devised by Eric von Manstein and Heinz Guderian required the element of surprise if it was to succeed with minimum cost to the *Wehrmacht*. It would involve drawing the Allies from out of their entrenched positions, across the border and into Belgium. Meanwhile a German armoured attack through the Ardennes forest and northwards to the Channel would encircle the Allies. The Germans had gambled that they could make a lightning strike and reach the bridge on the River Meuse at Sedan before the British and French could react. Sedan, they had calculated, marked the weakest point along the French front, being the hinge between the French 2nd and 9th Armies – their tacticians were to be proven right.

It was at 03.00 hours that Adolf Hitler arrived at his bunker near Aachen, Germany, from where he directed Operation *Fall Gelb* (Case Yellow). An hour later German forces began the surprise assault into Holland, Luxembourg, Belgium, and France. Thirty minutes later, in accordance with the battle-plan, *Luftwaffe* aircraft took off to attack their pre-designated strategic targets, including airfields and railway junctions in France and the Low Countries. The plan worked and half the Belgian Air Force was lost on the ground, while French airfields were also badly hit.

Glider troops landed on top of the Belgian defence system at Eben Emael, while German *Panzers* circumvented the Maginot Line and passed north through Belgium and the Ardennes forest in Operation *Sichelschnitt* (Sickle Stroke), which was designed to cut off the advancing Allied troops from their rear.

The German advance was rapid. During the afternoon, thirty-two Fairey Battle light bombers of the AASF went onto the offensive and attacked German columns in an attempt to staunch the flow of their advance through

Luxembourg. Thirteen were shot down and the remainder damaged; eleven beyond repair.

While a combined force of Hurricanes and Gloster Gladiators were already proving themselves in Norway, this was to be the first real test of the RAF's new fighters in north-western Europe.

It was the Hurricane squadrons that bore the brunt of the campaign in France rather than Spitfires as it was considered that the former's wider undercarriage would cope better with the rough airstrips, while their largely fabric-covered fuselage could be repaired on-squadron, whereas the metal-skinned Spitfire more frequently needed to be sent back to the factory for repairs. The Battle of France, therefore, was largely fought by Hurricane squadrons.

And what a test it would be, with one hundred Hurricanes of the AASF and Air Component facing over ten times their number. Amazingly, the RAF fighters accounted for fifty enemy aircraft on the first day of the *Blitzkrieg*, losing fewer than ten of their own, with three pilots wounded. For the time being at least, the RAF would hold out, but they would soon desperately need support with replacement pilots, and later, whole squadrons being rushed to France at the cost of Home Defence.

Neville Chamberlain's government was already facing a crisis. The Norwegian campaign was on the point of collapse, while the Allies' defensive lines in north-western Europe would soon be swept away. The *Blitzkrieg* that had been so successful in Poland, Denmark and Norway would lead to the loss of Luxembourg before the end of the day; the Low Countries and France would soon follow.

Leopold Amery, leading the attack on the Prime Minister in the House of Commons following the news of the new offensive, quoted the great defender of Parliament, Cromwell: 'Depart I say, and let us have done with you. In the name of God, go!' Chamberlain was shaken.

While many in Parliament favoured Lord Halifax, British Foreign Secretary, as his successor, it was Churchill who won the day. Summoned to Buckingham Palace at six o'clock, by midnight he had formed his Coalition Government: Churchill would be both Prime Minister and the Minister for War.

The War Cabinet in London had already sent four additional squadrons of Hurricanes to France by 12 May, with a further thirty-two aircraft crossing the Channel the very next day, while the equivalent of another four squadrons would soon be operating over France, flying patrols during the day before returning to their home bases across the Channel in the late afternoon. Although they inflicted heavy losses on the *Luftwaffe*, the war of attrition soon took its toll on the pilots and ground crews.

On the ground the Allies had advanced towards the River Meuse in order to counter the German offensive. However, the enemy's charge seemed unstoppable once von Rundstedt's forces discovered that the retreating Belgian Army had failed to destroy the vital bridge along the river between Givet and Sedan: the way was now open for the Germans to roll on through to the French border. Meanwhile, the Germans had already pushed the Dutch back to Rotterdam.

A secret German memorandum made Hitler's intentions clear:

> ... should the German troops encounter resistance in Belgium or Holland, it will be crushed with every means. The Belgian and Dutch governments alone would bear the responsibility, for the consequences and for the bloodshed which would then become unavoidable.'

On 13 May Churchill made his maiden speech in the House of Commons as Prime Minister, this in the wake of the losses in the Norway campaign and the grievous blows already suffered by the Allies in the Low Countries:

> ... we are in the preliminary phase of one of the greatest battles in history.
> I would say to the House as I said to ministers who have joined this government, I have nothing to offer but blood, toil, tears, and sweat. We have before us an ordeal of the most grievous kind. We have before us many, many months of struggle and suffering.
> You ask, what is our policy? I say it is to wage war by land, sea, and air. War with all our might and with all the strength God has given us, and to wage war against a monstrous tyranny never surpassed in the dark and lamentable catalogue of human crime. That is our policy.
> You ask, what is our aim? I can answer in one word. It is victory. Victory at all costs – Victory in spite of all terrors – Victory, however long and hard the road may be, for without victory there is no survival.
> Let that be realized. No survival for the British Empire, no survival for all that the British Empire has stood for, no survival for the urge, the impulse of the ages, that mankind shall move forward toward his goal.
> I take up my task in buoyancy and hope. I feel sure that our cause will not be suffered to fail among men. I feel entitled at this juncture, at this time, to claim the aid of all and to say, come then, let us go forward together with our united strength.

The news from the front was, however, uniformly bad. By the following day the Germans had broken through the French defences at Sedan, and everywhere the French were reeling under a devastating barrage from land and air.

Amid the bulletins detailing enemy gains and the plucky defence put up by the members of the BEF, the BBC Home Services made a number of public information announcements including an apparently insignificant item, the response to which would help change the course of history:

> The Admiralty have made an Order requesting all owners of self-propelled pleasure craft between 30 foot and 100 foot in length to send all particulars to the Admiralty within fourteen days from today if they have not already been offered or requisitioned.

The requested was made because the Royal Navy's Small Vessels Pool had been depleted due to the shipyards turning to the manufacture of wooden hull minesweepers. Many of the vessels that were identified as a result of the broadcast would form a part of the convoy of 'little ships' that saved an army from the beaches at Dunkirk.

With the situation in France continuing to deteriorate, the French premier, Reynaud, telephoned Winston Churchill on 15 May. During a difficult conversation the despondent Reynaud announced: 'We are beaten: We have lost the battle.'

By that evening the French and British had retired to the River Senne, reaching the Dendre the following day and the Escaut and the area around the Sedan by 17 May.

Churchill, aware of the seriousness of the situation, wrote to Roosevelt: 'We expect to be attacked here ourselves, both from the air and parachute and airborne troops in the near future, and are getting ready for them....'

On 16 May Air Chief Marshal Hugh Dowding, who had already reported growing losses to the Cabinet on the previous day, wrote a letter in which he expressed his views on sending more fighters across the Channel at the expense of fatally damaging Home Defence. The latter had already been depleted from the fifty-two squadrons accepted as the minimum requirement, to the equivalent of thirty-six. Churchill had, however, already agreed to the French Prime Minister Paul Reynaud's request for more fighters.

Hugh Dowding was summoned to the War Cabinet Room at No. 10 Downing Street. Also present were the Air Minister, Sir Archibald Sinclair, Minister for Aircraft Production, Lord Beaverbrook, and Chief of Air Staff, Sir Cyril Newhall.

Churchill explained the predicament and his earlier promise to provide more fighters to support the French and the BEF. Dowding, however, remained adamant: 'I am well aware of the situation Prime Minister, but my task at hand is for the air defence of this country and it is my belief that I cannot achieve this if half my aircraft are in France.'

Dowding produced figures to demonstrate that Hurricane losses could not be sustained at the same rate otherwise he would be in short supply of both fighter aircraft and pilots: 'We are losing aircraft at far quicker rate than we can produce them,' he explained, further emphasizing that his thirty-six remaining squadrons were nowhere near enough for a successful defence of Britain, adding, 'We need more aircraft, and more pilots to fly them.'

Churchill flew to Paris for further talks with the French Prime Minister, during which Paul Reynaud, only appointed on 21 March, stated that unless he got support, France would fall far sooner than he would have anticipated. Churchill immediately telephoned the War Cabinet asking for six squadrons of Hurricanes to be dispatched at once, claiming that Dowding had informed him that only twenty-five squadrons would be needed to defend Britain.

Sir Cyril Newhall informed the War Cabinet of Churchill's resolve to win the Battle of France, and Dowding's fears should the air strength of Britain be further reduced. A compromising solution was reached. Six Hurricane squadrons would be sent to France, operating from French bases close to the Channel, from where they could be rapidly withdrawn should the French campaign collapse.

On 19 May, Churchill broadcast to the nation setting the tone of the war years and making it clear from the outset that Hitler would be fighting a united nation under a strong leader; it was his rallying call:

> I speak to you for the first time as Prime Minister in a solemn hour for the life of our country, of our empire, of our allies, and, above all, of the cause of Freedom.
>
> A tremendous battle is raging in France and Flanders. The Germans, by a remarkable combination of air bombing and heavily armoured tanks, have broken through the French defences north of the Maginot Line, and strong columns of their armoured vehicles are ravaging the open country....
>
> It would be foolish to disguise the gravity of the hour. It would be still more foolish to lose heart and courage or to suppose that well-trained, well-equipped armies numbering three or four millions of men can be overcome in the space of a few weeks, or even months, by a scoop, or raid of mechanized vehicles, however formidable....

Despite the supreme gallantry of the infantry and their immediate commanding officers, the BEF would ultimately be forced to withdraw from Belgium and France in the face of the German onslaught. The RAF had fared better, although many on the ground accused them of leaving the Army to their fate. Aware of the criticism wrongly levelled at the pilots of Fighter Command, Churchill extolled their successes:

> In the air – often at serious odds, often at odds hitherto thought overwhelming – we have been clawing down three or four to one of our enemies; and the relative balance of the British and German Air Forces is now considerably more favourable to us than at the beginning of the battle. In cutting down the German bombers, we are fighting our own battle as well as that of France. My confidence in our ability to fight it out to the finish with the German Air Force has been strengthened by the fierce encounters which have taken place and are taking place.

For the time being at least, Churchill and the High Command believed that the BEF could still turn what appeared to be an overwhelming tide:

> We must expect that as soon as stability is reached on the Western Front, the bulk of that hideous apparatus of aggression which gashed Holland into ruin and slavery in a few days will be turned upon us. I am sure I speak for all when I say we are ready to face it; to endure it; and to retaliate against it....

And facing the possibility that France too would fall and Britain and her Empire might stand alone, Churchill said:

> Our task is not only to win the battle – but to win the war. After this battle in France abates its force, there will come the battle for our Island – for all that Britain is, and all that Britain means. That will be the struggle.

Then, looking to the great Bard for inspiration, Churchill added:

> Today is Trinity Sunday. Centuries ago words were written to be a call and a spur to the faithful servants of Truth and Justice: 'Arm yourselves, and be ye men of valour, and be in readiness for the conflict; for it is better for us to perish in battle than to look upon the outrage of our nation and our altar. As the Will of God is in Heaven, even so let it be.'

Churchill had already intimated that, despite the BEF's efforts, France might well fall and at a meeting of the War Office a number of subjects were under discussion, including the 'possible but unlikely evacuation of a very large force in hazardous circumstances, via Boulogne, Calais and Dunkirk'. At the time the plan for the evacuation of the BEF was simply a contingency in the unlikely event of the need to withdraw; in fact the collapse of the front would be so rapid that the plan, codenamed Operation Dynamo, would be put into almost immediate effect.

Vice-Admiral Bertram Ramsey, Flag Officer Commanding Dover, who had been given the task of putting together plans for the withdrawal of non-essential staff, recognized that the Dunkirk beaches shelved gently out to sea and that he needed to be able to ferry men out from the shore to the deep draft vessels; the Navy's own small boats were buffeted by the breaking waves and would be virtually impossible to use in the shallows: 'It would be necessary to have a very large number of small boats to carry troops from the beaches to the off-shore ships.'

Meanwhile, the BEF continued to withdraw towards Dunkirk and other open ports, including Boulogne. On 23 May the RAF lost two fighters with two more damaged by RN gunfire while flying over the port, this was at the same time Dowding received a series of messages from the Admiralty complaining at the lack of air cover, adding that: 'Our destroyers fire at any aircraft that comes within range whether they make our recognition signals or not.'

This stance showed how twitchy the Admiralty had become since their early losses, but flew in the face of the extensive inter-service co-operation flights made by RAF's fighter and bomber squadrons since 1938. These had been designed to give RN gunners experience at correctly identifying the RAF's front-line aircraft and to establish a system of warning the naval vessels of the approaching 'friendly' aircraft.

With the war going very much to Hitler's plans, he issued his Directive No. 13 from Supreme Headquarters, Berlin, on 24 May 1940, ordering the destruction of the Belgian, English and French forces in what would become the Dunkirk 'pocket'. Meanwhile, the *Luftwaffe* was tasked with preventing the remnants of the BEF from being evacuated across the English Channel.

During the day the War Cabinet met in London where it was learned that President Roosevelt had expressed the view that: 'It would be nice for him to pick up the pieces of the British Empire should Britain be overrun.' Churchill was understandably furious.

On the Continent, Calais fell to the advancing Germany army on 25 May, while Boulogne too would fall on the following day. Now Dunkirk was the main route of escape for nearly 400,000 allied troops.

Having already lost a quarter of its fighter strength during the Battle of France, the RAF was now called upon to cover the BEF's retreat and evacuation from the beaches.

Vice-Admiral Ramsay received orders to put Operation Dynamo into action, 'with a view to lifting up to 45,000 of the BEF within two days, at the end of which it was probable that evacuation would be terminated by enemy action.' While Ramsay would co-ordinate the evacuation from Dover, Air

Vice Marshal Keith Park, AOC No. 11 Group, had tactical control of the air defence of the English Channel, Dunkirk and its hinterland.

The situation was dire and the day had already been designated a 'Day of National Prayer' for the Army. Viscount Gort spoke candidly to the Secretary of State for War when he said: 'I must not conceal from you that a great part of the BEF and its equipment will inevitably be lost even in the best circumstances.'

With Hitler concentrating his efforts on the French and Norway campaigns, No. 41 Squadron's sector remained extremely quiet, and while sections had regularly flown to their forward base at West Hartlepool over the previous few days, they were seldom called upon and only made the occasional patrol.

Monday 27 May was the first full day of the Dunkirk evacuation. The naval operations were covered by the RAF including Nos. 17, 19, 54, 65 and 74 Squadrons, flying out of Hornchurch: between them they destroyed nineteen enemy aircraft.

Towards the late afternoon No. 74 Squadron's pilots, led by their CO, Squadron Leader White, flew north to Leconfield, their place being taken by No. 616 Squadron, who landed on the grassed strip at Rochford, Hornchurch's satellite airfield. Here they had use of the pre-war flying club buildings for their Operations Room and Mess, while bell-tents served as dispersals. No. 74 Squadron had scored fifteen confirmed 'kills' with another eleven probables and four damaged during their tour of operations. Meanwhile, No. 65 Squadron's place at dispersals had been taken by No. 222 Squadron, which included among its pilots the then unblooded Flight Lieutenant Douglas Bader.

The pilots of No. 41 Squadron were in the Mess that morning when Squadron Leader Hood informed them that they would be flying down to Hornchurch the following day. Pilot Officer W Stapleton later recalled: 'We loaded up what little things we could take, into bundles wrapped in newspapers, then stuffed them into the flare-tubes and flew down.'

Flying over Dunkirk the RAF was forced to make standing patrols. While fighters were able to fly in small numbers over the Channel and the beaches, they could not defend the town itself, which was heavily bombed.

Meanwhile propaganda leaflets were dropped on British and French troops. Written in both languages, they carried a map outlining the gravity of Allies' position: 'British soldiers! Look at the map: it gives your true situation! Your troops are entirely surrounded – stop fighting! Put down your arms!

While it was obvious to the troops that it was pretty-much a free-for-all to get to the coast and Dunkirk, the call to surrender found few who would comply.

As the momentum of the evacuation grew, employees of the Ministry of Shipping's Small Craft section were busy telephoning boat owners and shipping agents, giving them instructions to deliver shallow-draught vessels, suitable for the transportation of troops, to collection-points on the Thames estuary and elsewhere.

Hundreds of vessels off the Upper Thames were gathered together and towed to Sheerness. Here they were fuelled-up and taken to Ramsgate where they were crewed by Royal Naval Officers, Ratings and volunteers, before crossing the Channel to Dunkirk. Over the following few days many of the flotilla of over 850 'little ships' would be lost to the waves or enemy action, but they would be instrumental in saving one third of the troops who made it out of Dunkirk. Some ferried troops from the shallows out to the Royal Navy vessels, others made the voyage across the Channel with their precious cargo.

During the first day of the operation only 7,669 men were safely evacuated, while there were a number of tragedies including the loss of the *Queen of the Channel* in mid-Channel, although many of the 1,000 troops on-board were picked-up by the *Dorien Rose*. Meanwhile, the destroyer HMS *Wakefield* went down with 650 onboard and the *Grafton* was torpedoed while rescuing survivors. Another dark note occurred when the trawler *Comfort* stopped to save men off the *Wakefield* but was rammed by the drifter *Lydd* whose captain believed she was a German vessel, while there were reports that survivors were shot as they tried to board the *Lydd*.

The situation worsened when at midnight on 27 May the Belgium government surrendered, Leopold III, King of the Belgians issuing the following communiqué to his army: 'We have been forced to capitulate. History will give the verdict that the Army did its duty. Our honour is unimpaired.'

This was a devastating blow, which opened a gap to the north-east of the BEF's defensive perimeter and threatened to lead to an immediate collapse. Disaster was, however, averted and the gap plugged.

Chapter 6

Hornchurch Operations

Sir Cyril Newall informed Dowding that 28 May was 'likely to be the most critical ever experienced by the British Army.' As a consequence Dowding was ordered to ensure strong formations of RAF fighters were over Dunkirk and the beaches from dawn until dusk to give the waiting troops the best protection.

Keith Park, only recently appointed to command No. 11 Group, studied intelligence reports and made a Hurricane sortie over the beaches to assess the situation on the ground. Speaking to his squadron commanders, it quickly become apparent that his fighters were often heavily out-numbered and as a consequence suffered casualties without necessarily breaking-up the enemy attacks. Park issued orders that squadrons should fly over Dunkirk in pairs or at wing strength. Although this left the beaches unprotected for long periods of time, when the fighters were able to give protection it was in sufficient numbers to make a difference. There were other drawbacks to the wing concept, one of which was that the squadrons all operated on different radio frequencies and could not communicate with each other in the air.

The Spitfires had had their more powerful VHF radio set removed and replaced by the older HF sets, in case they might fall into enemy hands. This meant that if they flew inland over France, they lost contact with the Dover Controller. The Germans, however, were monitoring the airwaves and on one occasion the squadron was 'recalled' by an enemy radio operator.

Dowding penned a letter to 'My Fighter Boys' in which he wrote:

I don't send out many complimentary letters and signals but I felt that I must take this occasion, when the intense fighting in northern France is for the time being over, to tell you how proud I am of you and the way in which you have fought since the *Blitzkrieg* started. I wish I could have spent my time visiting you and hearing your account of the fighting but I have occupied myself working for you in other ways. I want you to know that my thoughts are always with you and that it is you and your fighting spirit which will crush the morale of the German Air Force and preserve our country through the trials which yet lie ahead.

A wing patrol was flown over Dunkirk by the Spitfires of Nos. 19, 54 and 65 Squadrons. However, poor visibility meant that they were unable to operate as a wing. This was the last mission by No. 54 Squadron, commanded by Squadron Leader James 'Prof' Leathart, which by the 26th had already been reduced to eight aircraft and a dozen effective pilots. Ordered to stand down it was sent north to Catterick to rest and regroup. Having been heavily engaged since the eve of the Dunkirk evacuation, their pilots, whose numbers included the likes of Colin Gray and Johnny Allen, were in desperate need of a rest. Their place was taken by No. 41 Squadron, while No. 222 Squadron, led by Squadron Leader H W 'Tubby' Mermagen', had already flown down from Kirton-in-Lindsey, Lincolnshire. Throughout the spring and summer Nos. 41 and 54 Squadrons would relieve each other, alternating between Catterick and Hornchurch.

Nos. 19, 65 and 616 Squadrons made a second patrol at 09.00 hours, led by No. 65 Squadron's Desmond Cooper. They heavily engaged enemy fighters and bombers, claiming four Bf 109s and two bombers destroyed, with two Bf 109s as probables.

No. 41 Squadron's composition on its posting to No. 11 Group 'D' Sector's HQ at RAF Hornchurch was:

'A' Flight (Red and Yellow Sections):
Flight Lieutenant Ryder, Pilot Officer Legard, Flying Officer Scott, Pilot Officer Mackenzie, Pilot Officer Cory, Pilot Officer Boret, Flight Sergeant Sayers, Sergeant Carr-Lewty, Sergeant Ford.

'B' Flight (Blue and Green Sections):
Flight Lieutenant Webster, Flying Officer Gamblen, Pilot Officer Shipman, Pilot Officer Morrogh-Ryan, Pilot Officer Wallens, Pilot Officer Stapleton, Pilot Officer Boyle, Pilot Officer Lovell, Sergeant Howitt, Sergeant Darling.

At 07.00 hours eighteen of No. 41 Squadron's Spitfires took off from Catterick and headed south. Squadron Leader Hood was at the head of the formation, which included Flight Lieutenants Webster and Ryder, Flying Officers Legard, Scott, Gamblen and Lovell, Pilot Officers Wallens, Morrogh-Ryan, Mackenzie, Cory, Stapleton and Shipman, along with Flight Sergeant Sayers and Sergeants Carr-Lewty, Howitt, Ford and Darling. In the meantime two NCOs and thirty-six airmen travelled down by RAF Air Transport.

On arrival the pilots were briefed by the Station Commander, Wing Commander 'Boy' Bouchier, who explained to the senior officers the gravity of the BEF's position and the urgent need for the squadrons to fly operations in support of the withdrawing troops of the BEF.

Meanwhile, at lunch in the Officers' Mess, Ryder, Lovell, Mackenzie and many of the other officer pilots met up with Al Deere, who had only just made it back from Dunkirk, less than a day after being shot down on one of No. 54 Squadron's last sorties over the beaches.

The newly arrived airmen were shocked at the appearance of many of the pilots who were already on-station. They looked tired and dishevelled and had several days' stubble. Some carried their Service revolvers tucked into the top of their flying boots, which was initially taken as a 'line-shoot'.

There would be no time to settle-in and make sector familiarization flights, as at 14.10 hours the squadron took off in four sections to make their first offensive patrol over the French and Belgium coast – they would have no difficulty locating their patrol-line, as the thick black smoke which billowed up from the burning oil storage tanks near the harbour at Dunkirk could be seen for miles. On this operation Squadron Leader Hood led twelve Spitfires. Their orders were to remain out to sea and not to follow the enemy inland. The squadron remained on patrol until about 16.00 hours, landing back at base without having engaged the enemy.

Pilot Officers Wallens recalled:

The thousands of troops on the beaches were a fantastic sight. It seemed a colossally unco-ordinated operation which I suppose it was at first. The blokes were hiding in the sand dunes from the German bombs. A lot were lying dead on the beaches or floating in the water.

On 29 May the Hornchurch Squadrons made a dawn wing patrol over Dunkirk, Nos. 19, 41, 222 and 616 Squadrons forming-up after taking off at 04.25 hours.

Squadron Leader Hood led six Spitfires of 'B' Flight's in tight squadron formation through low cloud; they maintained a strict radio silence as they headed for the beaches, arriving less than half-an-hour later at around first light. Below could be seen the detritus of war, burnt-out shells of buildings and the damaged hulks of shipping still smouldering following the attention of the *Luftwaffe*.

By reducing their speed the Spitfires were able to conserve sufficient fuel to allow them to patrol for over an hour, still making some allowance for the rapid fuel consumption of a dogfight before recrossing the Channel.

During their patrol one enemy aircraft was pursued but escaped by diving into cloud. The weather had closed-in by the time No. 41 Squadron returned and they had to be redirected to Biggin Hill, landing at 06.45 hours.

Wallens later explained that during the Squadron's first combats the enemy escaped due to the inexperience of the pilots:

> In the early days, we were always firing out of range. You thought you were opening fire at the right distance but you weren't. You were miles out. That's what our gun cameras showed. A fellow would say, 'Oh yes, I was in range.' Then his camera gun would be developed and he'd see that instead of a German bomber up close, all he had in front of him was a little spot in the sky. It got us to move in closer.

'A' Flight left Biggin Hill at 09.10 hours, making the short hop to Manston where the fighters were refuelled, ensuring the Spitfires would be able to spend as long as possible over Dunkirk. Manston's role would soon be appreciated by the enemy and the Station became a regular target for enemy bombers and land-based heavy artillery.

It was at 10.15 hours that one section of 'B' Flight and two sections of 'A' Flight carried out an offensive patrol between Dunkirk and Calais, landing back at Manston at 12.05 hours. Refuelled, the Spitfires returned to base.

At Dunkirk itself the troops were being lifted-off via the Mole. During the evacuation, enemy dive-bombers damaged the *Calvi*, the *Crested Eagle*, the *Grenade*, the *Fenella* and holed the *Polly Johnson*, which later sank, while the *Canterbury* and the *Jaguar* limped back to England for lengthy repairs. Three destroyers and twenty-one smaller vessels were lost, causing the Admiralty to temporary withdraw all modern vessels, leaving Ramsey with only fifteen destroyers, greatly reducing the lifting capacity. Some 13,752 men were rescued off the beaches, while a further 33,558 were rescued via the harbour, bringing the daily total of men saved to 47,310.

A communiqué issued by German High Command illustrated the continued pace of the Allied collapse and the successes of the German bombing campaign:

> The resistance of the last part of the encircled French army in northern France has been broken. At Lille alone, 26,000 prisoners have been taken.
>
> The attack on the remainder of the British Expeditionary Force on both sides of Dunkirk has made good progress despite stubborn resistance and the difficulties of the terrain.
>
> Despite difficult weather, the German air force attacked successfully around Dunkirk. Five transports were sunk and three cruisers or destroyers as well as ten transports damaged by bombs.

During the day three out of five raids were successfully intercepted. The enemy raids that did get though, however, wreaked havoc and caused substantial damage and casualties.

Meanwhile, the Germans claimed that the air-battle taking place over Dunkirk had resulted in the destruction of sixty-eight RAF aircraft.

The squadron was at readiness before dawn on 30 May, then at 08.30 hours No. 41 Squadron carried out an uneventful offensive patrol over Dunkirk. The second mission of the day began at 11.30 hours when Squadron Leader Hood led four sections off. They returned to base without having made any combat claims.

The weather remained poor and no further patrols were flown by any of the Hornchurch squadrons.

That evening the German High Command issued its daily communiqué:

The great battle in Flanders and the Artois approaches its end, with the destruction of the English and French armies still fighting there. Since yesterday the British Expeditionary Force has been in a complete state of dissolution. Leaving behind its entire mass of war material, it is fleeing to the sea. By swimming, or on small boats, the enemy is attempting to reach the English ships lying off the shore on which our air force is falling with devastating effect. Over sixty ships have been hit by our bombs, sixteen transports and three warships sunk, and twenty-one merchant ships and ten warships damaged or set on fire.

Despite the losses some 53,823 men were evacuated, almost 30,000 being ferried to destroyers from the beaches by ship's lifeboats, cockle-boats, motorized yachts and pleasure boats.

By 31 May the Germans had advanced close enough to the Dunkirk perimeter that their artillery had the beaches well within their range and they began pounding the shoreline, causing carnage amongst the troops.

While it appeared to those on the ground that the *Luftwaffe* bombed at will from dawn until dusk, the RAF continued the fight high above Dunkirk, often engaging the enemy before they reached the beaches.

Air operations began early, with Squadron Leader Hood and four sections taking off from Hornchurch at 04.30 hours to make a joint patrol over Dunkirk with No. 222 Squadron, before landing at Manston at 06.40 hours.

During the patrol No. 222 Squadron lost Pilot Officer GGA Davies who was shot down by French gunners and made a forced landing on the beach.

Nos. 41 and 222 Squadron flew a second offensive patrol over Dunkirk between 10.45 and 13.05 hours, when Squadron Leader Hood took four sections over the beaches.

Flight Lieutenant Webster shot down a Bf 109 and shared a He 111 with Flying Officer Lovell, while Pilot Officer Tim Vigors of No. 222 Squadron claimed a probable He 111.

Webster's combat was recorded by the squadron's Intelligence Officer and was timed at 11.49 hours:

2 aircraft of 'B' Flight's Blue Section flying 15 miles N of Ostend at approximately 2,900ft sighted a formation of one He 111 escorted by 3 Me 109s. Claimed 1 He 111 and 1 Me 109 firing bursts of 5 and 6 seconds from 200 yards, closing to 50 yards and expending 2100 and 1274 rounds. Two a/c fired.

Wallens recalled the 'cat and mouse' tactics over Dunkirk:

When we went back, before a relief squadron could take over from us, that's when the German bombers would move in. The Jerries were listening to our radio talk. We finally realized what was going on. So we pre-arranged a simulated return to base with the Controller at Dover. We said over the radio that we were returning early for various reasons and he said he'd try to get a relief squadron in as soon as possible. It was a set-up. We'd been running our planes on a very lean mixture, conserving petrol. We swept inland instead of back out to sea. Thinking we'd gone, the Jerries came roaring in. They believed another squadron wasn't likely to arrive for fifteen minutes or so. But we came right back and gave them a hell of a clattering. That was a good day's work.'

A communiqué issued by German High Command read:

The rest of the defeated British Expeditionary Force tried today to escape on small craft of all kind to the transports and warships lying offshore near Dunkirk. The German Air Force frustrated this attempt through continuous attacks, especially with *Junkers* dive-bombers, on the British ships. According to the reports received so far, three warships and eight transporters [were] set on fire or damaged. Forty English fighter-planes protecting the ships were shot down. The attack is still going on, so that further successes may be reckoned.

While the British suffered heavy losses, some 68,014 troops were safely evacuated, bringing the total rescued to 194,600 men.

A wing-strength offensive patrol was flown by Nos. 19, 41, 222 and 616 Squadrons between 04.25 and 06.35 hours on 1 June. Squadron Leader Hood commanded four sections, arriving over the beaches at 05.00 hours.

Thirty minutes into the patrol and the pilots of No. 19 Squadron saw about a dozen Bf 110s flying at 4,000 to 4,500ft some 2–3 miles east of Dunkirk. Flight Lieutenant Brian 'Sandy' Lane took the squadron into the attack and forced the enemy into a defensive circle. Meanwhile, Bf 109s flying above the battle dived down onto the Spitfires which were also joined in combat by No. 222 Squadron. During the ensuing dogfight No. 19 Squadron's pilots claimed a total of seven Bf 110s destroyed and one damaged, with three Bf 109s also destroyed. Sergeant Jack Potter's Spitfire was hit while he engaged a Bf 110 and he was forced to ditch but was picked up safe.

The pilots of No. 222 Squadron also added to their tally, claiming four Bf 110s and one Bf 109 destroyed, a further Bf 109 being reduced to a probable. One of these Bf 109's was awarded to Douglas Bader as his first 'kill'. The victories came at a cost with three pilots shot down: Pilot Officer Roy Morant force-landed on the beach but later escaped, while Pilot Officer H Falkust was made a PoW. Sergeant L J White, of May Bank, Newcastle, Staffordshire, was killed in action. He was twenty-three.

Refuelled and rearmed. No. 41 Squadron was on patrol again at 08.30 hours when Squadron Leader Hood led four sections on an offensive patrol over Dunkirk in the company of Nos. 19, 222 and 616 Squadrons. Some thirty-seven Spitfires patrolled from Nieuport down to Dunkirk at 1,000–3,000ft. Arriving over the beaches, No. 41 Squadron found the beleaguered troops under attack from Ju 87s, Ju 88s and He 111s and quickly joined in combat. The action came thick and fast, as with most aerial duels, the combat taking place in short, sharp bursts.

During the patrol, Flight Lieutenant Webster shot down two Do 215s, one of which was unconfirmed. Flying Officer Lovell and Pilot Officer 'Buck' Morrogh-Ryan attacked the same He 111 which they hit in the starboard engine, with thick volumes of black smoke seen pouring out as it descended; they were awarded one 'shared destroyed'.

No. 41 Squadron's Intelligence Officer filed the following report:

One unidentified aircraft appeared underneath the cloud layer and Red Section swung into a right hand turn and identified it as a Ju 88; they followed it in pursuit. Immediately black smoke appeared from the enemy aircraft (on opening his throttle wide) and a salvo of about 8 bombs was dropped harmlessly into the sea. Red Leader attacked and the enemy aircraft dived to the sea doing gentle evasive turns to right and left; it then used full throttle. Red Leader's attack – quarter developing to almost astern – resulted in no apparent damage to the enemy aircraft.

Red leader opened [fire] at 500 yards closing to 350 yards and fired 2,720 rounds. Red 2 and 3 followed; the former estimated enemy aircraft speed at 340 mph at sea level. Red 3 encountered enemy aircraft diving to sea by means of gentle evasive turns to left and right. He was only able to get in a short burst at 400 yards and then broke off the engagement as he had difficulty in holding his level – his left wing being very low – he arrived back at Hornchurch safely.

Yellow Section was following and Yellow Leader and Yellow 3 (missing) had short bursts at the Ju 88. Yellow 2 was astern of his section and flying at 280 mph (by pressing boost cut-out) slowly overhauled the enemy aircraft. One astern attack (6 seconds burst at 400 yards closing to 300 yards) was followed by a quarter-attack; the enemy aircraft turned towards Yellow 2. A second quarter attack (6 seconds burst) resulted in the enemy aircraft doing a slow turn straight into the water.

The general enemy aircraft tactics were steep turns about 20 feet above the water. Cannon was fired from the top rear gunner. The camouflage was standard.

Two aircraft of Blue Section sighted 1 He 111 at 3,000 feet going into clouds. Blue Section did a No. 1 Attack on the He 111 which kept a level course in and out of cloud (which was not all at one height.) Blue 2 opened at 450 yards firing 3 short bursts. Blue 3 followed opening at 200 yards closing to 50 yards. The starboard engine of the He 111 (which was the old type) was set on fire. No evasive tactics were employed. No enemy aircraft fire was experienced in this engagement.

Blue Leader sighted 3 aircraft NE of Dunkirk which on investigation proved to be Do 215s – two in tight formation and one straggler, which was attacked by another Squadron. Blue Leader attacked the other two Dos from dead astern above and at an angle of 30 degrees. Giving full deflection, he opened at 200 yards closing to 50 yards. One enemy aircraft was seen to catch fire and Blue Leader last saw it ablaze upside down. Blue Leader then attacked the second giving it a 5 second burst. The enemy aircraft glided down from 3,000 feet under control with the port engine smoking and the airscrew idling.

Blue Leader had one bullet hole in starboard mainplane.

These Do 215s employed no evasive tactics.

The remainder of the squadron, with the exception of Pilot Officer Stapleton and Flying Officer Legard (Flying N3107), returned to base safely.

The result of the engagement was one Do 215 (unclaimed) which was seen on fire in mid-air and one Ju 88 in difficulties at sea level, which dived into the sea when S/L Hood, who had no ammunition left, dived as if to attack it.

[No. 41 Squadron landing at 10.40 hours]

The following are the casualties. Certain, 2 Do 215, 2 Ju 88, 1 He 111, and probably 1 Do 215.

The other squadrons engaged recorded the following successes during the same patrol:

No. 19 Squadron:
1 He 111   destroyed
3 He 111s   probable
2 Do 215s   probable

No. 222 Squadron:
1 He 111   probable

No. 616 Squadron:
I Ju 88   destroyed
3 He 111s   probable
4 Ju 88s   probable

That evening Sir Archibald Sinclair visited Hornchurch where he spoke to the pilots, congratulating them on their recent combat victories. The celebrations on No. 41 Squadron were, however, severely muted, as the fates of Stapleton and Legard were as of yet unknown.

It was later learned that Pilot Officer Stapleton, who had not fired his guns before, had ditched into the sea after being hit by ack–ack while attempting to strafe a German airfield. He was rescued by some of the gunners who swam out to him. Badly wounded in the legs, the nineteen-year-old Stapleton was taken as a PoW and was later held at *Stalag Luft III* (PoW No. 50):

We were told to stay seaward of the coast so that if the Germans turned inland, as they always did, we were not to follow them. The day I was shot down I had actually followed an '88, which was my mistake! The minute they saw us they would drop their bombs and make off straight for home.

Legard, flying Spitfire N3108, was on his sixth operational patrol over Dunkirk when he was shot-down and killed while engaging He 111s and Do 215s.

Flying Officer (34045) William Ernest 'Billy' Legard, RAF, was the son of Digby and Elaine Legard; husband of Alice Legard, of York. He was 29. Legard's body was never recovered and he is remembered on the Runnymede Memorial, Panel 6. Legard had joined the squadron from No. 2 FTS Brize Norton on 26 November 1939.

RAF fighter pilots had little chance of survival if shot down over the Channel. While they had a sea-green Mae West, there was no dinghy, flare or dye-marker to aid their chances of survival. Even strong swimmers, hampered by their Mae West, would make little progress, while hypothermia would soon take its toll.

A German High Command communiqué summed-up the day's events from the enemy's perspective:

> In hard fighting, the strip of coast on both sides of Dunkirk, which yesterday also was stubbornly defended by the British, was further narrowed. Nieuport and the coast to the north-east are in German hands. Adinkerk, west of Furnes, and Ghyvelde, six and a quarter miles east of Dunkirk, have been taken....
>
> Altogether, four warships and eleven transports with a total tonnage of 54,000 tons were sunk by our bombers. Fourteen warships, including two cruisers, two light cruisers, an anti-aircraft cruiser, six destroyers and two torpedo boats, as well as thirty-eight transports with a total tonnage of 160,000 were damaged by bombs. Numberless small boats, tugs, rafts were capsized and troop concentrations along the beach successfully attacked with bombs.

Meanwhile, German radio broadcasts labeled the retreat as a 'cowardly flight', although a war correspondent in the *Völkischer Beobachter* begrudgingly acknowledged: 'We must admit that our enemy has been fighting with unusual stubbornness against our hard-hitting infantry,' adding: 'The activity of the enemy in the air has been very lively. One minute it's enemy planes; the next minute, our own. British fighters attack our observer posts, but miss. We keep experiencing a fluctuating fight in the air.'

Despite the gallant efforts of Fighter Command the *Luftwaffe* continuing to take a terrible toll on the beaches and on RN vessels and the 'little ships' caught in mid-Channel. New orders were issued on 2 June restricting the evacuation to around dawn and dusk.

At 04.35 hours Squadron Leader Hood led four sections on an offensive patrol over Dunkirk.

The voice of one pilot (possibly Sergeant Ford), who was having his first taste of operational flying over enemy-held territory, was heard over the R/T asking what the black puffs of smoke in the near distance were. The explanation was short and sharp:

> That's *Flak*, you bloody fool. If you can see it and hear it you're reasonably safe, but if you see it about two feet from your aircraft you won't hear it – you'll be dead. If it gets really thick and your engine stops, you can get out

and walk on it. Now stop asking silly bloody questions and get back into formation!

The air and sea operations continued on the following day. No. 41 Squadron made its only offensive sweep between 04.30 and 06.50 hours, when Flight Lieutenant Webster led four sections on a patrol over Dunkirk. The squadron made no combat claims.

The squadron received a telegram from Winston Churchill, acknowledging the desperate situation facing the troops on the beaches as Operation Dynamo was coming to a close on the morning of the 4th, asking that 'if humanly possible' they were to give one last effort to give air cover as the RN made a desperate effort to lift the rearguard off the beaches, their positions along the perimeter defences having been taken by French troops. The last vessel was planned to leave Dunkirk at 03.40 hours, beginning the perilous journey across the Channel.

Squadron Leader Hood led four sections of No. 41 Squadron on an offensive patrol, escorting the final convoy's withdrawal. The patrol took off at 04.00 hours. Several enemy aircraft were encountered and driven away during inconclusive dogfights. Flying Officer Lovell was, however, able to record one success. Having already exhausted all of his ammunition, he gave chase to one Ju 88 at very low level. The *Luftwaffe* pilot was so preoccupied with trying to shake Lovell off that he touched a wingtip on the sands and the bomber cartwheeled and blew up.

Having stayed over Dunkirk until the last possible minute, several aircraft landed at Manston owing to a shortage of fuel, one landing with wheels up due to combat damage. Poor weather conditions over Hornchurch meant that the remainder touched-down at Tangmere.

The pilots who fought over Dunkirk had initially expected that the fighting would take place at under 1,000ft, but quickly they found themselves in combat at 10–25,000ft. Although their efforts were largely unseen by the troops below, had they not fought so doggedly, the beaches would have been remembered as the graveyard of the BEF and there would have been no 'Miracle of Dunkirk.'

The following message was received at RAF Hornchurch:

Signal from Headquarters, No. 11 Group
To Hornchurch, A291.

Air Officer Commanding sends following message to pilots and all personnel of the Fighter Stations, Sector Stations and Forward Airfields:

The Admiralty reports that the Dunkirk operations were completed this morning.

During the last two weeks our Fighter Squadrons operating over France have shot down a total of 527 German bombers and fighters, 371 of which have been confirmed as destroyed, for the loss of 80 of our pilots. By their successes in air combat our squadrons have protected the Army during retreat, have enabled the Navy to embark the Army from Dunkirk and the beaches, and also protected our bombers and reconnaissance aircraft and established moral ascendancy over the German bombers and fighters. The Air Officer Commanding congratulates the pilots on their magnificent fighting and highly commends the technical and administrative personnel whose work made it possible for the pilots to succeed.

It is hoped that we shall be given a short respite in which to organize refit and train new pilots in order to inflict yet heavier casualties on the German fighters and bombers when they attack this country and coastwise shipping.

Bennions, still on his Navigation course, would later learn something of the reality of the Dunkirk air operations, but for the moment followed events via the press, BBC Home Services and the Newsreels.

The newspapers were still filled with images of smiling Tommies onboard ship, disembarking back at home or leaning out of railway carriages giving the thumbs-up and saluting the cameraman with a sandwich and a mug of warm tea. The nation was yet to get a grasp of how defenceless Britain really was – while they had the men, they had left their weapons in France and Belgium, something not lost on the Premier.

At the close of the evacuation, King George VI sent a message to Winston Churchill:

I wish to express my admiration of the outstanding skill and bravery shown by the three Services and the Merchant Navy in the evacuation of the British Expeditionary Force from Northern France.

So difficult an operation was only made possible by brilliant leadership and an indomitable spirit among all ranks of the Force. The measure of its success – greater than we had dared to hope – was due to the unfailing support of the Royal Air Force, and, in the final stages, the tireless efforts of naval units of every kind.

While we acclaim this great feat, in which our French allies, too, have played so noble a part, we think with heartfelt sympathy of the losses and suffering of those brave men, whose self-sacrifice has turned disaster into triumph.

George R.I.

In private, Churchill acknowledged that Dunkirk, despite the rescuing of 338,000 Allied troops, still represented 'the greatest military defeat for many centuries.' Over 68,000 soldiers had been lost, killed or taken as PoWs, while virtually all of the BEF's equipment was destroyed or captured, including 2,500 guns and 77,000 tons of ammunition, 84,000 vehicles, 416,000 tons of supplies and 165,000 tons of petrol.

At sea and off the beaches, 235 vessels of all types were lost, along with 106 fighters and 80 pilots. During the air operations the RAF had claimed 130 enemy aircraft as destroyed during over 2,700 sorties; Hornchurch alone had lost 23 pilots killed or made PoWs. Meanwhile, as the German forces advanced, they released 400 *Luftwaffe* pilots and aircrew, many of whom rejoined their units and the air war. Among their number was the fighter ace Mölders.

Winston Churchill remained bullish when he spoke before Parliament later that day:

We must be very careful not to assign to his deliverance the attributes of a victory. Wars are not won by evacuations.

I have, myself, full confidence that if all do their duty, if nothing is neglected, and if the best arrangements are made, as they are being made, we shall prove ourselves once again able to defend our Island home, to ride out the storm of war, and to outlive the menace of tyranny, if necessary for years, if necessary alone.

At any rate, that is what we are going to try to do. That is the resolve of His Majesty's Government – every man of them. That is the will of Parliament and the nation.

Even though large tracts of Europe and many old and famous States have fallen or may fall into the grip of the Gestapo and all the odious apparatus of Nazi rule, we shall not flag or fail.

We shall go on to the end. We shall fight in France, we shall fight in the seas and oceans, we shall fight with growing confidence and growing strength in the air; we shall defend our Island, whatever the cost may be. We shall fight in the fields and in the streets, we shall fight in the hills; we shall never surrender; and even if, which I do not for a moment believe, this Island or a large part of it were subjugated and starving, then our Empire beyond the seas, armed and guarded by the British Fleet, would carry on the struggle, until, in God's good time, the New World, with all its power and might, steps forth to the rescue and the liberation of the Old.

Meanwhile, a German High Command communiqué announced the fall of Dunkirk and the capture of British troops and the munitions and weapons of the greater part of the Army:

The Fortress of Dunkirk has been taken after a hard fight. 40,000 prisoners and booty that cannot yet be estimated is in our hands. The entire Belgian and French Channel coast extending to the mouth of the Somme has thereby been completely occupied by German troops.

The British newspapers had referred to the evacuation as: 'A withdrawal according to plan.'

It wasn't until later that many, including Bennions, would understand how serious things had become, but by then the disaster had been averted and the bulk of the BEF were safe.

However, Ramsay, who was not fully aware of the part played by the RAF's fighters, later wrote on 18 June:

Rightly or wrongly full air protection was expected, but instead for hours on end the ships off shore were subjected to a murderous hail of bombs and machine-gun bullets.... In their reports the COs of many ships, while giving credit to the RAF personnel for gallantry in such combats as were observed from the ships, at the same time express their sense of disappointment and surprise at the seemingly puny efforts made to provide air protection during the height of this operation.

On the 5th, with the air operations over Dunkirk drawn to a conclusion, No. 19 Squadron returned to Duxford, while No. 616 Squadron flew north to Leconfield on the following day.

No. 41 Squadron's Red Section was scrambled at 17.15 hours and ordered to patrol base. The unidentified aircraft was quickly taken off the plotter's table and the squadron recalled, landing at 17.30 hours.

In a speech in Berlin, Adolf Hitler warned of 'A war of total annihilation against the enemy,' while a German High Command's daily communiqué claimed:

Early this morning, new offensive operations began on the defensive front in France....

Our army this morning began an attack against the enemy the army of France on a wide front. The crossing of the Somme between its mouth and Ham and over the Oise-Aisne Canal was forced and the so-called Weygand Line, which was in process of construction on the other side, fell at many points.

At 13.35 hours on 6 June, Red and Yellow Sections were ordered to scramble as a flight. Once in the air, the Controller ordered them to the forward patrol line at 20,000ft as the first of the raids against the UK threatened. However, the raid didn't develop and the Spitfires were recalled and landed after only twenty minutes in the air.

The Germans meanwhile began a new offensive, crossing the Somme on 6 June when they broke through the Weygand Line, while on the following day they began operations south of the Somme and the Oise–Aisne canal and continued their seemingly relentless advance.

Chapter 7

Return to No. 13 Group

On 8 June Squadron Leader Hood led the sixteen Spitfires of No. 41 Squadron on their return to Catterick, having been relieved by No. 54 Squadron. Meanwhile, No. 74 Squadron returned to Leconfield and No. 222 Squadron flew back to Kirton-in-Lindsey. All were in much need of a rest.

Back serving within No. 13 Group's area, the squadron found things much quieter, making only occasional local and convoy patrols from their forward base at West Hartlepool. Meanwhile there were also regular patrols flown against 'Weather Willie' a regular *Luftwaffe* weather reconnaissance made along the east coast.

While one section or flight was at their advanced landing ground at various states of readiness, there was time to concentrate on restoring the squadron's serviceability. The daily routine, however, reverted to that of the early months of the war. The day began at about half past four with a wake-up call and a cup of tea. After washing, dressing, and eating a quick breakfast, usually in silence, the pilots reported for duty in what was still the half-light of the dawn.

Those pilots who were at 'dawn readiness', had to be at dispersals fully kitted-up and ready to take-off within three-minutes of being given the order to scramble.

One section might be detailed to fly a dawn patrol, looking for German reconnaissance planes while a second remained at readiness. Sitting in Lloyd Loom chairs, reading, sleeping or playing cards, they listened-out for the sound of the telephone as an old gramophone ground out a familiar tune. Boredom was tempered with high tension and when the telephone rang everyone stopped what they were doing and looked up anxiously. Nine times out of ten it would be a weather update or someone taking a sandwich order.

When the Controller's voice was heard, however, all hell was let loose as the order to 'scramble' was given.

The long hours at dispersal while at readiness or on standby helped to break down any barrier between the ranks. Off station the pilots mingled freely in the George at Piercebridge, while the fact that the Regulars' married quarters were close at hand meant that there was a strong sense of 'community' on the base and off. Visits to the theatre at Darlington, and boating, and even swimming in the Tees were not uncommon during quieter times; all very different from their time at Hornchurch.

On 10 June Mussolini finally declared his hand and took Italy to war as one of the Axis Powers. The King of Italy sent the following message to Hitler:

> The almighty has willed that against our own intentions we have been forced to defend the freedom and future of our people in battle against England and France.

Two days later the Germans were closing in on Paris, which had been declared an open city and which would fall on the 14th. The French government established a temporary HQ at Bordeaux, the First World War hero, Marshal Petain assuming the premiership from Reynaud.

Meanwhile, on the 13th the squadron flew sections to West Hartlepool, making their first patrol of the day between 10.33 and 11.17 hours when 'A' Flight's Yellow Section was ordered to investigate an unidentified aircraft, thought to be a lone German intruder searching for a target out to sea.

While a single sortie was flown in the afternoon of the following day, elsewhere Keith Park held a meeting with combat-experienced squadron commanders from No. 11 Group at Northolt where he discussed tactics for the campaign ahead. Among the many points under discussion was the best use of aircraft, whether this was in sections, by flight, squadron, or multiple squadrons. The merits of the so-called 'Big Wing', which had already been used over Dunkirk, were also discussed.

During the air campaign, the fighters' targets were to be the enemy bombers; the destruction of their fighters was simply a means to an end.

Park advocated head-on attacks on the bombers to break up their formation: 'Attack the ones in front. If you shoot them down, the formation will break up in confusion. Then you can take your pick.'

This, however, didn't give the fighter pilots much of a chance to shoot down the enemy due to the high closing speed. The tactic had high risks attached, as head-on collisions were common, with enemy aircraft breaking in the same direction as the fighter, or neither breaking. Meanwhile the rear-gunners got a clear shot as the fighters wheeled by. The enemy's fighter cover might also be above and to the rear ready to catch the fighters in a cross-fire or to dive down onto them.

Keith Park sent out a warning to all of his fighter stations that they would be subject to air attack. They would be pushed to their limits in the air while facing the ever-present threat of bombing and strafing between ops.

At readiness from dawn on 15 June, the squadron flew to West Hartlepool by sections; the only operational sortie was a patrol over base made by Flight Lieutenant Webster flown between 06.15 and 07.58 hours.

By 17 June only Nos. 501 and 17 Squadrons were still operating from French soil, providing air cover for the remaining British contingent in their retreat towards evacuation from the remaining open ports. The situation had become critical during the previous twenty-four hours and at 13.00 hours, Marshal Petain spoke to the French nation: 'People of France, it is with grief in my heart that I have to tell you to stop fighting....'

In England, a little known French tank general, General de Gaulle, who had escaped the German advance later made a broadcast promising his people liberation would come one day: 'Rien n'est perdu parce que cette guerre est une guerre mondiale. Les mêmes moyens qui nous ont vaincus peuvent faire venir un joir la victoire.'

The fall of France meant that Great Britain, her Commonwealth and Dominions now stood alone, and on 18 June Churchill stood before the House of Commons and made a speech in which he reflected on the events surrounding the extrication of the larger part of the BEF from the beaches of Dunkirk and the realities of the struggle that lay ahead:

> During the last few days we have successfully brought off the great majority of the troops ...that is to say, about 350,000 out of 400,000 men... are safely back in this country.... We have, therefore, in this Island today a very large and powerful military force.
>
> Thus, the invasion of Great Britain would at this time require the transportation across the sea of hostile armies on a very large scale, and after they had been so transported they would have to be continually maintained with all the masses of munitions and supplies which are required for continuous battle – as continuous battle it will surely be.

During the day No. 41 Squadron saw a new intake of pilots, when Pilot Officers Eric S Lock, Gerry A Langley, and Sergeants Frank Usmar and Johnny McAdam were posted straight from No. 6 FTS, Little Rissington. All were RAFVR but none had flown Spitfires before, only Harvards. It was considered too risky for the new pilots to make their first flights on the shorter runways at Catterick and a Spitfire was ferried to a nearby bomber station, from where each made three or four familiarization flights on the 21st before being permitted to join operational patrols flown from their new home base.

After gaining a few hours on type, the newly posted pilot would need to develop the art of formation flying, which relied not only on an ability to handle the aircraft with the minimum use of the controls and throttle, but also anticipation. The new pilots were fortunate to join the squadron while it was 'resting' back in No. 13 Group. The old hands who had been blooded over Dunkirk were able to pass on their hard-earned combat knowledge:

> Keep your eyes on the sun – there's probably a Hun up there... If you hear machine gun then break fast... Never follow the Hun who dives past you at 45 degrees but just out of range, he's drawing you in... remember the enemy hunt in pairs... learn when to use your radio and when to remain silent... if you come across a lone pilot and have cover, attack from 95 degrees starboard and not from astern as its more natural for a pilot to turn to his left to look behind him... remember, under attack a pilot always breaks to the left... always leave an aircraft above you.

The new boys would be put through an intensive programme of squadron training to ensure they had a fighting chance once the squadron was back in the thick of the combat, fighting as a part of No. 11 Group. This included battle climbs, mock combats and formation practice. Keeping tight formation was crucial when going into action, as Bennions recalled:

> One young pilot was shot down simply because he could not keep formation at 25,000ft. He lost the protection of his leader and was picked off by a 109 coming down on him from behind. He probably didn't even know what had hit him and had no time to take avoiding action or to bail out. Air combat could be a cruel business and you rarely got a second chance.

All of the recently posted pilots got time to make their mark on the Battle, in particular, Eric Stanley 'Sawn Off' Lock who was born at Bayston Hill, near Shrewsbury. He would go on to win the DSO, DFC and Bar while with the squadron, remarkably earning all three gallantry awards in 1940, before being killed on 3 August 1941. Lock has no known grave and is remembered on the Runnymede Memorial, Panel 26.

Meanwhile, there was time for Flight Lieutenant Webster to travel down to Farnborough where he carried out performance trials against a captured Bf 109, the flights adding to the RAF's and the squadron's data on the leading German fighter aircraft.

Bennions would become well versed in the tactics gleaned from these and other trials and in combat he demonstrated that the Spitfire was effective against the Bf 109 in a turn combined with a steep climb (combat report 5 September 1940).

Of the Spitfire versus *Messerschmitt* Bf 109 duel, the squadron's most experienced flight commanders Norman Ryder later wrote:

Firstly the Spitfire was a very rugged and reliable aircraft. No matter how bad the damage, I always got them down in one piece and never had any engine trouble.

Secondly, it was very sensitive and responsive. One really needed to fly it all the time, but it had no vices and one really felt 'man and machine' being one unit.

Penetrating over England German air force fighters were not inclined to mix it, because of their fuel limitation for combat, but their main advantage was height advantage obtained on the climb out from their bases in France. We were then invariably climbing underneath them to gain height to attack; often at low speed and frequently into the sun, as they [Hurricane squadrons] were detailed to attack bomber formations, whereas the faster Spitfire supplied cover against attack by the escorting fighters. I seldom remember being able to attack a nice juicy bomber.

...the 109 was a good fast aircraft: good acceleration in the early part of the dive, not so good as far as manoeuvrability was concerned. Their first tactic, if taken by surprise, was to flip over and go hell-for-leather diving for the coast and home. If caught at the lower level on their way out, say 7,000 feet, there was nothing they could do. If they tried any manoeuvre the Spit cut the corner and got there quicker. This was not to say it was easy – far from it – and even on good days there was often the coastal cloud. However, with surprise on their side, they were dangerous and had good weaponry. Who saw who first was the name of the game. It wasn't for some time that we realized that the Spit could catch them in a dive – after the initial advantage had gone. A heavy, flush-riveted Rolls after a stud-riveted Ford.

Churchill, aware of the role that Fighter Command would play in the next phase of the war emphasized the RAF's part in the previous week's fighting and the struggle ahead:

...we have a very powerful Air Force which has proved itself far superior in quality, both in men and in many types of machine.... Anyone who looks at the photographs which were published a week or so ago of the re-embarkation, showing the masses of troops assembled on the beach and forming an ideal target for hours at a time, must realize that this re-embarkation would not have been possible unless the enemy had resigned all hope of recovering air superiority at that time and at that place....

I am happy to inform the House that our fighter strength is stronger at the present time relatively to the Germans, who have suffered terrible losses, than it has ever been; and consequently we believe ourselves possessed of the capacity to continue the war in the air under better conditions than we have ever experienced before. I look forward confidently to the exploits of our fighter pilots – these splendid men, this brilliant youth – who will have the glory of saving their native land, their island home, and all they love, from the most deadly of all attacks.

While the might of the *Luftwaffe* would soon be directed at Great Britain, there would be a brief period while they established themselves in their new bases in Northern France before launching the main offensive.

Churchill then spoke of the dangers to be faced on the Home Front where the ordinary man, woman and child in the street would be on the front line. Since the Spanish Civil War many had feared the indiscriminate bombing of civilian targets in a so-called 'Total War':

> There remains, of course, the danger of bombing attacks... I do not at all underrate the severity of the ordeal which lies before us; but I believe our countrymen will show themselves capable of standing up to it.

To this end the Civil Defence (CD) and Air Raid Precautions (ARP) had already been formed. Although Churchill did not mention the use of poison gas, this was a real threat, and by late 1938 gas masks had been issued to every family in the country.

And of the weeks, months and years Churchill said:

> What General Weygand called the Battle of France is over. I expect that the Battle of Britain is about to begin. Upon this battle depends the survival of Christian civilization. Upon it depends our own British life, and the long continuity of our institutions and our Empire. The whole fury and might of the enemy must very soon be turned on us.
>
> Hitler knows that he will have to break us in this Island or lose the war. If we can stand up to him, all Europe may be free and the life of the world may move forward into broad, sunlit uplands. But if we fail, then the whole world, including the United States, including all that we have known and cared for, will sink into the abyss of a new Dark Age made more sinister, and perhaps more protracted, by the lights of perverted science.

And then, borrowing from Shakespeare's *Henry V*, Churchill finished with words which spoke of sacrifice but promised ultimate victory:

> Let us therefore brace ourselves to our duties, and so bear ourselves that if the British Empire and its Commonwealth last for a thousand years, men will still say, 'This was their finest hour.'

The Ministry of Information, meanwhile, issued a pamphlet entitled *If the Invasion Comes*. Amongst other things, the document told civilians to stay where they were in the event of landings – thousands of refugees had congested the roads in Flanders, hampering the movement of the military. The document continued: 'When you receive an order make sure that it is a true order and not fake… if you keep your heads you can also tell whether a military officer is really British or pretending to be so.'

The British press inadvertently added to the tension with repeated warning of spies, parachutists and fifth columnists, the fear of which became almost an obsession for many.

As the enemy stepped-up their offensive, the night of 19/20 June saw heavy raids, which were later described in the newspapers as 'The Greatest Air Attack Of The War.' While most of the bombers' targets were in the south of England, the north west was not spared.

Enemy bombers were plotted entering Catterick's air space and at 22.59 hours, 'B' Flight's Flight Lieutenant Webster was ordered to patrol at 10,000ft. Vectored onto the enemy he spotted the distant glow of the bomber's engine exhausts. Closing in undetected Webster fired several accurate bursts, seeing his target catch fire. He claimed the He 111 of KG 4 as destroyed, but was only allowed a probable, although post war research has since confirmed the 'kill'.

Squadron activity continued, and solo standing patrols were maintained until 02.55 hours, but no further raiders were encountered.

At readiness before dawn on the 22nd, one Spitfire from 'A' Flight was ordered to patrol the coast at 04.45 hours but no enemy aircraft were seen.

On 22 June, in an act of humiliation, the French were forced to sign an Armistice, which came into effect three days later. Hitler chose the location for the ceremony, a rail carriage at Rethondes in the middle of the Compiegne Forrest. A generation earlier this had been the scene of Germany's capitulation at the end of the First World War. Following the surrender, Hitler gave orders that the carriage should be destroyed.

Two days later, Squadron Leader Hamish West was posted to No. 41 Squadron from No. 5 OTU, Aston Down, as supernumerary squadron leader. West had previously served with No. 32 Squadron before joining Nos. 801 (Fleet Fighter), and 803 (Fleet Fighter) Squadrons. Later he went to CFS Upavon for an instructor's course. West would later take command of No. 151 Squadron at Digby on 8 September 1940.

Over the previous few nights, No. 41 Squadron had flown patrols into the early hours of the morning. On 27 June Pilot Officer Shipman was on the squadron's last night patrol when a lone raider attacked Middlesborough, while four more bombers attack Hutton Hall. Although in the air at the time,

Shipman was not vectored onto the enemy aircraft which escaped unmolested.

No. 41 Squadron began July with twenty-six pilots of all ranks, including Bennions, who by then had completed his navigation course at St Athan. The routine for sections to operate from their forward base at West Hartlepool continued, and over the next few days, they were ordered to fly local patrols over Saltburn, Seaham Harbour, Hartlepool, Scarborough and Whitby.

The losses of both trained fighter pilots and their aircraft was discussed at a War Cabinet meeting held on 1 July, following which Sir Archibald Sinclair announced that pilot training courses were to be shortened, while the numbers of schools of instruction were increased. Meanwhile, a number of RN pilots were to be seconded to RAF to supplement Fighter Command's understrength squadrons and requests by fully trained pilots for a transfer into Fighter Command would be looked upon favourably.

The *ab initio* course was usually followed by a forty-four week instruction. This was later cut to twenty-one weeks followed by a six week period at an Operational Training Unit (OTU). Under the new conditions those who 'showed promise' were posted straight to operational squadrons being rested and brought back up to strength in a quieter sector. They would learn combat techniques on-squadron.

Throughout 1940, many young, inexperienced pilots filtered through from the much shortened training programme to replace casualties and the tour expired – their fates were mixed.

On 2 July, Goering issued the first *Luftwaffe* operational orders for the campaign against England and the RAF. Bad weather, however, meant they could not be properly implemented until 10 July, the date later established by the Air Ministry as the beginning of the Battle of Britain.

Two days later came the first concentrated raids on Britain, with an attack on a small convoy in the Dover Straits. No. 74 Squadron was scrambled from Hawkinge to intercept the bombers but was attacked by their Bf 109 escort, losing one fighter without making a claim. Then at 19.00 hours No. 32 Squadron engaged a formation of Bf 109s, losing three aircraft but with the pilots safe. They claimed one Bf 109 destroyed and another as damaged. The battle began inauspiciously for the RAF who were vastly outnumbered and would need to destroy the enemy's aircraft at a ratio of 4:1 if they were to defeat the *Luftwaffe*.

On the following day a concerned Winston Churchill sent a memo to the Vice Chief of the Naval Staff marked 'Action this day' in which he stated:

Could you let me know on one sheet of paper what arrangements you are making about the Channel convoys now that the Germans are all along the

French coast? The attacks on the convoys yesterday, both from the air and by E-boats, were very serious, and I should like to be assured this morning that the situation is in hand and that the Air is contributing effectively.

Meanwhile, Lord Beaverbrook, who had been appointed to step up the manufacture of munitions and armament, made a public appeal:

Women of Britain, give us your aluminium. We want it and we want it now… We will turn your pots and pans into Spitfires and Hurricanes, Blenheims and Wellingtons. I ask therefore that everyone who has pots and pans, kettles, vacuum-cleaners, hat-pegs, coat-hangers, shoe-trees, bathroom fittings and household ornaments, cigarette boxes or any other articles made wholly or in part of aluminium, should hand then in at once to the local headquarters of the Women's Voluntary Services.

The call was answered and tens of thousands of tons of aluminium, which would otherwise have needed to be imported, were recycled in aid of the war effort.

At 22.12 hours on 6 July. Red Section, which included Pilot Officers Bennions, Mackenzie and Flight Sergeant Sayers, was ordered to patrol forward base at 2,000ft: 'The sortie lasted a little over thirty minutes, with the suspect plot having been removed from the table and, as the Controller had no further business for us, we were ordered to conserve our fuel and to pancake.'

No. 41 Squadron was able to claim a part-share in the destruction of a Ju 88 off Scarborough on the morning of 8 July. The squadron flew section patrols throughout the day, but at 10.50 hours Blue Section was scrambled and ordered to patrol Seaham Harbour at 20,000ft. The patrol, which was led by Flight Lieutenant Webster, was vectored onto the lone Ju 88 which was attacked and damaged south-east of Scarborough at about 11.00 hours. Three Hurricanes of No. 249 Squadron from Church Fenton later finished off the bomber, which they claimed as destroyed, hotly disputing the earlier part played by No. 41 Squadron's Spitfires.

Sergeant Jack Allison's combat report read:

F/O Lovell attacked & I saw a large piece of what appeared to be a portion of the tail fall off. I then proceeded with my attack when the enemy went amongst the clouds. I then saw F/O Lovell following him again & got into position, but lost him in the clouds. Three Hurricanes [No. 249 Squadron] were circling round at the time. I saw no enemy fire. I gave two bursts & fired 221 rounds.

There was little activity in the squadron's sector on 10 July. Elsewhere, after mid-day there were heavy raids on a convoy in the Straits of Dover, while harassing attacks were made along the west, south and east coasts; these were particularly fierce in the west.

Downing was disturbed to learn that while there had been a small number of combat victories, Fighter Command flew over six hundred sorties; as many as during the height of the Dunkirk operations, and this at a time when the enemy offensive against Great Britain had only just begun in earnest – such levels of activity could not be maintained indefinitely.

That night twelve small raids were plotted between the Firth of Tay and Beachy Head, with bombs being dropped on Guisborough, Canewdon, Hertford, the Isle of Grain, Tobermory, Colchester, Welwyn and Ely.

Early the following morning four sections from No. 41 Squadron made the short hop to West Hartlepool from where they operated for much of the day. While the *Luftwaffe* flew a number of solo raids between Yarmouth and Flamborough Head, the squadron only patrolled between 06.00 and 09.00 hours. Bombs were dropped at Bridlington. Here an ammunition-laden truck was hit and blew up.

Flight Lieutenant Webster was scrambled at 11.00 hours and ordered to patrol Whitby at cloud base, but was unable to locate the enemy.

There were a number of minor raids in the south and a little after 11.00 hours, enemy bombers attacked Portland, while a convoy off the coast was attacked by fifty-plus bombers, with five fighter squadrons intercepting the enemy and claiming eight Bf 110s with the same number probably destroyed. Ack-ack at Portland destroyed a further three enemy aircraft.

Convoys off the Suffolk coast were attacked during the afternoon, with standing patrols successfully defending the shipping against enemy bombers.

At 17.45 hours, a raid of fifty-plus enemy aircraft bombed Portsmouth, setting fire to the gas works and causing a number of casualties. Nos. 145 and 601 Squadrons successfully intercepted the enemy, claiming seven He 111s and two Bf 110s destroyed and a further four He 111s probably destroyed. One Hurricane was shot down but the pilot was reported as safe.

That night there were raids in the south-west of England, East Anglia, and Portsmouth. The *Luftwaffe* also hit targets along the Yorkshire coast; there were no reports of No. 41 Squadron's aircraft having been scrambled to deal with the threat.

On 12 July it was the turn of Blue and Green Sections to operate out of West Hartlepool, but no enemy aircraft were reported and they returned to Catterick without incident.

There were a number of raids across the country and between 06.00 and 09.00 hours a number of minor raids occurred in the Portsmouth area, while later that morning the *Luftwaffe* made two attacks on a convoy sailing off the Norfolk–Suffolk coast, losing six aircraft destroyed and two more which were allowed as probables. The RAF lost one Hurricane. Another anti-shipping raid resulted in the loss of eleven more enemy aircraft, with six damaged.

In the afternoon bombers attacked targets between the Isle of Wight and Portsmouth, one He 111 being shot down by No. 43 Squadron. Meanwhile, five raids were reported in the south-west, with bombs dropping on Cornwall, Devon, Weymouth, Falmouth and St Eval. During the night the *Luftwaffe* targeted north Wales and the Bristol area.

At 18.00 hours on 13 July, Red Section, comprising of Flying Officer Scott, Pilot Officers Bennions and Morrogh-Ryan, was scrambled and ordered to investigate Raid Y 1, but no enemy aircraft could be located and after an hour in the air, and following Controller's orders, the three headed for base.

During the day eight unsuccessful raids were made on shipping off the east coast, while Warmwell was hit.

At 14.20 hours shipping off Portland was attacked by twenty enemy aircraft. Nos. 238 and 609 Squadrons were scrambled to intercept, claiming three Bf 110s destroyed and one unconfirmed, along with one Do 17 destroyed and another unconfirmed. Throughout the afternoon the *Luftwaffe* attacked Channel shipping, other raids concentrating on Dover. No. 64 Squadron claimed two enemy aircraft and No. 56 Squadron claimed three Ju 87s and two Bf 109s destroyed and one Ju 87 probably destroyed, but at a cost, with two Hurricanes lost during the engagement.

Two raids crossed the south coast during the morning and No. 501 Squadron destroyed a Do 17 west of Southampton, while in a separate raid at 11.15 hours No. 43 Squadron claimed a He 111 near Spithead.

Night raids were made with mines being laid along the Thames estuary.

Three sections operated out of West Hartlepool on 14th, with the squadron flying a section-strength patrol over their home base and later making a patrol.

Standing patrols were made over convoys off Norfolk and Dover, while elsewhere, five raids were plotted over the Channel from Start Point to Dungeness between 09.00 and 11.00 hours, while two raids approached Swanage at 11.00 hours, a naval unit being bombed.

A formation of forty-plus Ju 87s and their Bf 109 escort made an attack against Channel convoy *Bread* at 15.30 hours. The Ju 87s screamed down onto their targets, using their airbrakes to reduce speed, hitting two merchantmen in the convoy along with one of their escorts. Three Ju 87s and three Bf 109s were destroyed with a further Ju 87 and Bf 109 probably destroyed; all for the loss of one Hurricane. Meanwhile, a convoy off Harwich was located and fighters sent to ward off the enemy.

One Norwegian vessel was damaged along with HMS *Vanessa* and the SS *Balder of Bergen;* both had to be towed, while the *Gronland* and the *Island Queen* were slightly damaged.

Three fighter squadrons were engaged and during the general dogfight the RAF destroyed seven enemy aircraft. However, a fighter of II./JG51 shot-down Pilot Officer Mudie who was KIA.

The events was captured for posterity by BBC reporter Charles Gardner who gave a running commentary of the attack which was broadcast on the news three hours later.

The convoy attacks were reported in the German Press: 'Air victory over the Channel – superior enemy forces beaten – bombs on British convoy.'

While, German radio also described a fictitious raid on London when the Royal Family was allegedly forced to take cover, claiming that: 'The King threw himself quickly to the ground. Among those with him there was a general panic.'

Speaking to the House of Commons, Churchill gave a stark warning, saying that: 'Should the invader come to Britain, there will be no placid lying down of the people in submission before him, as we have seen, alas, in other countries. We shall defend every village, every town, and every city.'

While only four days into the Battle of Britain and with Fighter Command committed to the draining tactic of mounting standing patrols over Channel convoys, the Prime Minister could boast:

This has been a great week for the Royal Air Force, and for Fighter Command. They have shot down more than five to one of the German aircraft which have tried to molest our convoys in the Channel, or have ventured to cross the British coast line. These are, of course, only the preliminary encounters to the great air battles which lie ahead. But I know of no reason why we should be discontented with the results so far achieved; although, of course, we hope to improve upon them as the fighting becomes more widespread and comes more inland.

That night enemy bombers raided Bristol, the Isle of Wight, Kent and Suffolk.

Operating out of West Hartlepool during the afternoon of the 15th, No. 41 Squadron flew a number of patrols, including two convoy escorts, the first of which was made between 14.39 and 16.29 hours by Black Section, handing over to Red and Yellow Sections, with Squadron Leader West leading six Spitfires, including that flown by Bennions. The work was unglamorous and tiring, the pilots having to remain on their guard against the enemy at all times in case they approached under the radar, but in the event there was no threat from enemy aircraft and the Spitfires landed before 18.30 hours.

Poor weather meant that there was little enemy activity across the whole country with a few raids over the Cardiff, Swansea, Portsmouth and Southampton areas, as well as over the Thames estuary, the Norfolk coast and on convoys on the south and east coasts.

Once again severe weather conditions reduced enemy activity on all fronts on the following day and No. 41 Squadron saw no operational flying, the enemy only making general and convoy reconnaissance sorties; an evening raid was made on the Isle of Wight.

This was, nevertheless a momentous day in the campaign: Adolf Hitler issued his Directive for the Conduct of the War No. 16, for the invasion of England. The preliminary phases were to be completed by the middle of August, by which time the dictator specifically decreed that 'the English Air Force must be so reduced morally and physically that it is unable to deliver any significant attack against the German crossing.' The assault was codenamed Operation *Seelöwe* (Sealion).

The document was intended only for his Commanders in Chief, but was forwarded by *Reichsmarschall* Goering to his Air Fleet Commanders via the Enigma coding machines. Thanks to Polish resistance workers, the British had secured an Enigma machine and the Germans' plans, once intercepted, were quickly deciphered at Bletchley Park.

Directive for the Conduct of the War No. 16
Berlin, 16 July 1940.

As England, in spite of her hopeless military position, has so far shown herself unwilling to come to any compromise, I have decided to begin preparations for, and if necessary, to carry out the invasion of England.

This operation is dictated by the necessity to eliminate Great Britain as a base from which the war against Germany can be fought. If necessary the island will be occupied. I therefore issue the following orders:

The landing operation must be a surprise crossing on a broad front extending approximately from Ramsgate to a point west of the Isle of Wight. The preparations must be concluded by the middle of August.

The following preparations must be undertaken to make a landing in England possible:

The English Air Force must be eliminated to such an extent that it will be incapable of putting up any substantial opposition to the invasion troops....

The task of the Air Force will be:

To prevent interference by the enemy Air Force.

To destroy coastal fortresses which might operate against our disembarkation points, to break the first resistance of enemy land forces, and to disperse reserves on their way to the front. In carrying out this task the closest liaison is necessary between individual Air Force units and the Army invasion forces.

Also, to destroy important transport highways by which enemy reserves might be brought up, and to attack approaching enemy naval forces as far as possible from our disembarkation points. I request that suggestions be made to me regarding the employment of parachute and airborne troops. In this connection it should be considered, in conjunction with the Army, whether it would be useful at the beginning to hold parachute and airborne troops in readiness as a reserve, to be thrown in quickly in case of need.

The Germans were meanwhile preparing 20 divisions across the Channel ready for the possible invasion of Britain.

No. 41 Squadron sent 'A' Flight to their forward base a little after first light on the 17th. Waiting at dispersals, Red Section was scrambled and made a patrol of Saltburn between 08.08 and 08.31 hours.

There were no further indications of enemy activity and in the mid-afternoon Squadron Leader Hood organized a station defence practice, which included members of the 33rd 'Rough Riders' who manned four Bofors guns. In the late evening 'A' Flight practiced formation flying and mock interceptions.

Elsewhere, bombs were dropped on Glasgow, while attacks were also made on shipping off Dundee and Beachy Head. In the south, there were raids in Surrey, Kent and Portland, while in the mid-afternoon a small formation of dive-bombers attacked trawlers sailing along the east coast in the area of Bawdsey.

There were minor engagements off Dover, the *Luftwaffe* targeting vessels off Clacton and south of the Isle of Wight.

On the afternoon of 18 July, a raid on Dover harbour resulted in several hits on the 11,500 tons tanker *War Sepoy* which sank in the harbour, while No. 141 Squadron's Boulton Paul Defiants were badly mauled. But the enemy didn't have everything all their own way, and eleven of the 120 raiders were destroyed.

A month after the surrender of French forces, the victorious German Army marched through Paris.

On the following day, Adolf Hitler made a speech before the *Reichstag* in which he laid the blame for the war on England and France and their insistence on German's adherence to the rigid terms of the Treaty of Versailles, which he claimed were:

Intolerable, not only because of their humiliating discrimination and because the disarmament which they ensured deprived the German nation of all its rights, but far more so because of the consequent destruction of the material existence of one of the great civilized nations in the world, and the proposed annihilation of its future.

The dictator continued:

All attempts made by democratic Germany to obtain equality for the German people by a revision of the Treaty proved unavailing.

It is always in the interests of a conqueror to represent stipulations that are to his advantage as sacrosanct, while the instinct of self-preservation in the vanquished leads him to reacquire the common human rights that he has lost.

The programme of the National Socialist Movement, besides freeing the Reich from the innermost fetters of a small substratum of Jewish-capitalist and pluto-democratic profiteers, proclaimed to the world our resolution to shake off the shackles of the Versailles Dictate.

Hitler played to German Pacifists when he reasoned for peace:

In this hour I feel it to be my duty before my own conscience to appeal once more to reason and common sense – in Great Britain as much as elsewhere…. I can see no more reason why this war must go on.

I am grieved to think of the sacrifices which it will claim. I should like to avert them, also for my own people….

Possibly Mr Churchill will again brush aside this statement of mine by saying that it is merely born of fear, and of doubt in our final victory. In that case, I shall have relieved my conscience in regard to the things to come.

Herr Churchill ought perhaps for once to believe me when I prophesy that a great empire will be destroyed – an empire which it was never my intention to destroy or even to harm.

It almost causes me pain to feel that I should have been selected by fate to deal the final blow to the structure which these men [Churchill and the House of Commons] have already set tottering.

Great Britain's reply would come from Lord Halifax in a broadcast made on 22 July when he responded to what he called a 'summons to capitulate', declaring that: 'We shall not stop fighting until freedom is secure.'

At readiness since before dawn on the 20th, Yellow Section was scrambled and vectored to Whitby where they patrolled between 06.47 and 07.25 hours, landing after the enemy turned away.

A second patrol was flown between 09.50 and 10.40 hours when Green Section was ordered to Saltburn to patrol at cloud base. The squadron then flew to Thornaby, which they were to use as their forward base until 26 July.

They would fly several operational patrols from here but without engaging the enemy – it would be the calm before the storm. While No. 41 Squadron's sector would remain quiet for weeks to come, this was not true of the rest of the country as the pace of the battle increased.

Further south, a raid approached Peterhead, but was turned back by RAF fighters, while two reconnaissance sorties were flown, with one Do 17 being shot down off Kinnaird's Head. Meanwhile, as a result of enemy reconnaissance missions, raids were made on convoys and shipping in Dover Harbour.

During the night the *Luftwaffe* laid mines from the Needles, Isle of Wight, to Land's End, the Bristol Channel and off the east coast.

On 21 July the *Luftwaffe* attacked convoys in the English Channel and the Dover Straits. The 1,360 ton destroyer HMS *Brazen* was sunk by concerted attack by twenty-plus enemy aircraft.

Night raids were focused on Merseyside.

During the following day the enemy flew a number of reconnaissance missions searching for convoys and other shipping activity, mainly off the east and south coasts. The RAF's standing patrols, however, were successful in preventing any attacks from developing.

A few raids were made over land, and during an attack on Tangmere one enemy aircraft was destroyed.

Night raids included minelaying along the east coast.

Following a reconnaissance mission along the east coast on 23 July, a convoy off Yarmouth was bombed, while trawlers in the vicinity of North Foreland were also targeted. Later a raid was made on Kenley and others near Kinnaird's Head and on naval vessels off Harwich and Yarmouth.

At night the *Luftwaffe* laid mines in various operations from Dover to the Tyne and Forth estuary.

On 24 July the *Luftwaffe's* raids focused on minesweepers operating outside Dover and also attacked the Channel convoys. At mid-day a large enemy formation was engaged off Deal and North Foreland. At its height the dogfight involved ninety fighters. A few raids attacked further inland but without inflicting serious damage.

The next day the enemy concentrated their efforts against a Channel convoy. The first attack saw the destroyers HMS *Boreas* and *Brilliant,* which were acting as escort to twenty-one merchant vessels, bombed off Lydden Spout. Four of the merchantmen were lost as a result of the attack. A second wave of bombers struck when the convoy was off Folkestone, the Spitfires of Nos. 54 and 64 Squadrons attempting to drive them off. A third attack came off Shoreham, by which time all but three of the convoy had sustained damage.

A few raids bombed the mainland, dropping their payloads but without causing any serious damage, while that night the Germans laid mines in the Firth of Forth and Thames estuary.

Chapter 8

Into Battle

On 26 July orders were received for the squadron to transfer back into No. 11 Group and to fly south to relieve No. 54 Squadron. Squadron Leader West, however, was posted on attachment to No. 219 Squadron, Catterick, for Flying Duties.

On the same day the enemy made a number of raids, varying in strength to up to fifty aircraft, many of which turned back when RAF fighters closed on them as they approached the coast.

Night operations were limited to minelaying in the Thames estuary and off the Norfolk coast and around Bristol.

Later that day No. 41 Squadron flew south to Hornchurch to relieve No. 54 Squadron who flew to Catterick for a much needed rest having been heavily engaged: only twelve pilots remained out of the seventeen who had begun the campaign a little over a month earlier. The move was probably prompted by the deaths of two of their most experienced pilots, Flight Lieutenant Basil 'Wonky' Way and Pilot Officer Finnie, both killed during the previous day's air operations.

Landing at Debden to refuel, No. 41 Squadron flew on at first light the following morning to begin what was to be an intensive two week tour of operations.

The *Luftwaffe* raided Dover twice during the day, damaging naval barracks and the destroyer HMS *Codrington*, which later sank, also setting fire to the repair ship the *Sandhurst* which was then alongside. Meanwhile, a great pall of smoke hung over the port, created by burning oil from ruptured storage tanks on the cliffs above, which spewed flaming liquid into the harbour. The ease at which raids could hit the port meant that the RAF had effectively lost the first phase of the battle so the Admiralty gave orders to abandon Dover as a forward base for its destroyers.

There was little activity in the Hornchurch sector during the morning and it wasn't until 12.50 hours that thirteen aircraft took off for formation flying before landing at Manston, the RAF's closest base to continental Europe, which it was to use as a forward base. The squadron was immediately refuelled and placed at readiness. They were to fly seven patrols before the day was out, protecting a convoy running the gauntlet in the English Channel.

Taking off from Manston in response to enemy raiders, the squadron's Spitfires had little time to gain altitude, which made them particularly vulnerable to being 'bounced' by enemy fighters. Even with the use of long-range radar, the RAF only had twenty minutes' advanced warning, while it took three minutes to scramble and a further twelve to climb to an operational altitude.

At 14.30 hours, ten bomb-carrying Bf 109s crossed the Straits on a hit-and-run raid. Ten minutes later, No. 41 Squadron scrambled and Squadron Leader Hood led thirteen Spitfires, one flown by Pilot Officer Bennions, into the air. The Controller ordered the squadron to intercept the enemy reported between Dover and Manston but they were unable to prevent the fighter-bombers from hitting the docks:

> We were vectored onto the enemy and spotted a formation of 109s some distance off and making for France. We pursued them for about six minutes but were unable to overhaul them to engage. Eventually our CO gave the order to turn back.

At 15.52 hours a raid of six-plus enemy aircraft was reported heading towards Dungeness, turning west to damage a steamer off Sandgate before fighter cover came to its aid.

Another raid was plotted approaching the Hornchurch Sector and at 17.20 hours No. 41 Squadron was scrambled, joining Nos. 501 and 615 Squadrons in an interception in the Dover area. During the engagement, No. 615 Squadron shot down one *Heinkel* He 59 but No. 501 Squadron lost one Hurricane.

Squadron Leader Hood led 'B' Flight into the air at 17.30 hours, when they were immediately vectored onto the enemy who were by this time heading for home.

Half an hour into their sortie Flight Lieutenant Webster, flying as Green 1, spotted way below them the tale-tale shell-bursts as a formation of Bf 109s came under fire from the Dover Barrage, and led the flight into action. They dived onto the Bf 109s and a low-level combat ensued. Webster latched onto one Bf 109 which he chased at fifty feet. Closing to 200 yards he fired a long burst and hit the Bf 109, which was seen to plunge into the Channel eight miles off the French coast, where it sank without a trace. The Squadron's Intelligence Officer, however, downgraded the claim to a probable as it could not be independently verified.

Turning back for base, Webster was engaged by two Bf 109s. He managed to get three short bursts at the fighters as they twisted and turned at low altitude, trying to evade his bullets and get onto his tail. With his fuel and ammunition now running low, Webster broke off and made a dash for home.

Meanwhile, at 18.05 hours 'A' Flight's Flight Lieutenant Ryder led five Spitfires, including Bennions', on a scramble with orders to carry out a patrol over Dover and the Channel. For thirty-five minutes they cruised up and down their patrol line without sighting the enemy. The thought of possibly entering into combat at any moment filled Bennions with excitement but at the same time a certain amount of anxiety. The longer the patrol continued, the more this feeling heightened. Finally, the Controller gave Ryder the recall and the Spitfires turned for home: 'On landing our Spits were quickly checked-over and refuelled, while we had a quick cuppa but didn't stray far because as soon as the "erks" had turned our aircraft around we were placed at immediate readiness.'

Red Section was the first back into the air when at 19.20 hours they were scrambled to carry out a patrol, but were soon recalled.

Bennions joined Yellow Section's Flying Officer Scott and Pilot Officer Cory on an uneventful patrol over the Channel between 19.50 and 21.20 hours, landing back at Hornchurch. Meanwhile, Red Section was ordered to carry out a routine Channel patrol before landing back at base.

A little before 20.10 hours an enemy raid was plotted approaching the coast and Squadron Leader Hood led 'B' Flight on a scramble with orders to carry out an interception patrol. No claims were made, and after an hour the Spitfires landed at Hornchurch. It had been a busy but ultimately fruitless first day at Hornchurch, but the pilots' fortunes would soon change.

On the 28th 'A' Flight, including Bennions, were at readiness from before dawn, and at 05.30 hours they took off from their advanced base at Manston with orders to carry out a routine fighter patrol over the Straits of Dover and the English Channel. The patrol landed at Hornchurch at 07.40 hours, the ground staff quickly getting to work to turn the aircraft around, ready for the next scramble.

Meanwhile, 'B' Flight had already taken off from Hornchurch for Manston at 08.10 hours. Here they were joined by the remainder of the squadron some thirty minutes later.

Blue Section was scrambled at 10.10 hours and ordered to carry out an interception patrol, landing at 11.35 hours.

Flight Lieutenant Ryder led 'A' Flight on a scramble to carry out an interception over Manston but the recall was given at 11.10 hours, after only ten minutes in the air.

At 12.04 hours, a large number of aircraft were plotted circling around the Calais–Boulogne district before setting a course for Dover. In response 'A'

Flight was scrambled but the enemy turned back towards the French coast and gradually dispersed. Bennions patrolled for an hour before landing back at base at 13.10 hours, where 'B' Flight had landed some fifty minutes earlier.

Meanwhile the *Luftwaffe* bombed trawlers off Dungeness at 13.00 hours, the Spitfires of No. 610 Squadron engaging the enemy and probably accounting for one Do 215.

Several enemy reconnaissance aircraft were plotted off the east coast and one of these, a He 111, was reconnoitring a convoy off Harwich when it was shot down by No. 17 Squadron. A Do 17 was also claimed as a probable by No. 85 Squadron.

A formation of 100-plus 'hostiles', including Ju 87s escorted by Bf 109s of III./JG 26 and I and II./ JG 51, was plotted heading for a convoy sailing off Dover at 14.00 hours.

'Sailor' Malan led the Spitfires of No. 74 'Tiger' Squadron to intercept the fighter escort, thirty-six of which were engaged at 18,000ft, while the Hurricanes of No. 257 Squadron, based at Hawkinge, were joined by a second Hurricane squadron to take on the bombers.

At 14.30 hours, as the raid was developing, No. 41 Squadron was scrambled and ordered to carry out an interception patrol over the convoy at 20,000ft. Within minutes eleven Spitfires were in the air, led by Squadron Leader Hood.

Minutes into their patrol and the squadron was still making a circling climb up to 20,000ft, while several thousand feet above them and lying in wait, was a formation of Bf 109s. Two Bf 109s, flown by *Major* Mölders and *Gefreiter* Gebhart, broke away and dived down into the attack. Bennions flying N3264 EB-J as Yellow 1, was acting as rear-cover for the squadron when he saw the Bf 109s chasing Lovell, Blue 2, and his CO, as they broke to port ahead of him. George pulled the booster switch and latched onto the enemy fighter which was attacking Hood's Spitfire. Adjusting the reflector sight for the wingspan of a Bf 109, Bennions turned the safety-catch on the gun-button to the 'off' position and pressed. There was a rattle of machine-guns as he opened fire with a quick burst, a cascade of spent cartridge cases and clips pouring out of the starboard wing (his port guns had failed to fire). As he followed the Bf 109, possibly that flown by Gebhart, diving away vertically, Bennions gave it two more bursts before it disappeared from his vision at about 5,000ft, still plunging towards the sea. The combat took place between Dover and Calais. Aware the enemy flew in pairs, Bennions was wary of being caught in the sights of his victim's wingman, and broke away.

Bennions fired off 2,464 rounds in three 4-second bursts from 200, closing to 75 yards, although the details of his combat report say 100 yards. His combat report read:

Yellow Section of No. 41 Squadron were detailed to act as rearguard for the squadron, which was climbing to engage the enemy at 20,000 feet, when I sighted two enemy aircraft diving onto leading section from above. At that moment Red 3 sighted Me enemy and called a warning to the leading section over the R/T. The leading Section then took avoiding action by turning to port. One of the enemy aircraft turned to port and closed with Mitor Leader. While this was happening, I ordered Yellow Section to carry out a Number One attack on this aircraft. Using the emergency boost I closed right in using full deflection and firing from 200 Yards to 100 Yards. The enemy turned over on its side and went almost vertically downwards, I followed using full boost and gave two more bursts of about 4 Seconds each from a position slightly left of astern, and after the second burst the whole of the enemy fuselage was enveloped in black smoke. I pulled out at 3,000 feet, to see what was happening, and looking in the mirror found two aircraft on my tail. I called to ascertain if they were Yellow Section and received no reply.

Since practically all my ammunition was exhausted, I evaded these aircraft and returned to base at Sea Level from a position about 3 miles South of Dover.

(signed) G Bennions. P/O

(annotated) 'confirmed by P/O Wallens' statement attached.'

Pilot Officer Wallens, flying with 'B' Flight, engaged five Bf 109s at 22,000ft, one of which he destroyed. In his combat report, Wallens also confirmed the details of Bennions' engagement:

I was No. 2 a/c in Green Section 41 Squadron, ordered to orbit Dover at 20,000 feet. I saw two e/a 2,000 feet above as Green Leader warned Blue Leader.

I was left behind by Green Leader and Green 3 and was unable to catch up. Whilst still 1,000 feet below I saw one e/a attack Blue Leader. One aircraft of Yellow Section then attacked this e/a (PO Bennions). The e/a then turned over and dived vertically for several thousand feet giving off a trail of thick blue smoke. I did not see this e/a crash, but saw it last at approximately 5,000 feet diving steeply.

(Signed) R W Wallens P/O

During the battle Bennions' Spitfire ('J'), was damaged by enemy fire and he 'returned to Manston in a hurry aircraft u/s through bullet holes,' landing without flaps. This was the first time that he had ever seen the Bf 109, let alone engaged in a dogfight with one. It had been his baptism of fire and he had not only survived it but was awarded one Bf 109 as confirmed.

Meanwhile, Flight Lieutenant Webster, flying as Green 1, had called out a warning to his CO, at the same time latching onto the Bf 109 diving for Lovell's Spitfire, but not before Flying Officer Lovell, Blue 2, had been wounded in the thigh, possibly by German ace, *Major* Werner Mölders, *Geschwader Kommodore* of *Jagdeschwader 51* who was on his first operation with his new unit.

During the brief combat that followed, Webster got in a short burst at the Bf 109, while Shipman followed close behind his leader and made a quarter-attack. The enemy fighter broke off the engagement, pulling up suddenly before diving away in a spin. Mölders had received a leg wound during the engagement and crash-landed back at base. Webster was credited with a Bf 109 damaged.

Mölders' account of the combat read:

I flew together with my wingman *Oberleutnant* Kirchheiss, north of Dover.

Suddenly I saw three British fighters, far behind them a lot of Spitfires in the mist. The three Spitfires were somewhat below us. I attacked this section. When I approached, both the outer Spitfires turned, but the Spit in the middle flew straight on. I got behind it and opened fire from 60m. At once the right wing caught fire, thick smoke and flame, and the Spit went down. I pulled up and saw 8–10 Spitfires behind me. I was frightened for a moment. There was only one chance – to go straight through the formation. I swept through the crowd. The first Spitfires were surprised, but one of the rearmost was watchful. He fired with all guns and hit me! It rattled in my aircraft; I had hits in the cooling system, wing and fuel tank. I broke away, and dived with everything I had, 700 kph towards the Channel. The engine was working well thank god! The Spitfire chased me and my flag of smoke, but then *Oberleutnant* Leppla, who had seen the incident, rushed to my assistance. He snapped the Spitfire sitting directly behind me [Pilot Officer P C F Stevenson of No. 74 Squadron, who returned to Manston with a seized engine], and after a few seconds it went down wrapped in a large cloud of smoke. When I reached the coast the engine began to stutter and, during the landing, the undercarriage collapsed and I made a perfect belly-landing. When I tried to get out of the cockpit my legs were strangely weak, and I saw bloodstains. In hospital I discovered the reason: three splinters in the thigh, one in the knee and one in the left foot. I had felt nothing in the heat of combat.

Lovell's aircraft (P9429) had been hit and suffered a ruptured fuel-line with fuel entering the cockpit. Despite the fact that it could have ignited at any moment, he limped back to Manston where he made a crash-landing. Lovell, who roomed with Bennions, was taken to Margate Hospital suffering from a slight thigh wound.

Meanwhile, Webster selected a second enemy fighter, firing short bursts from astern as he closed from 150 to 50 yards and seeing thick black smoke pouring from its engine, claimed one Bf 109 as a probable. He spotted two Bf 109s diving down towards him and was forced to break off the attack before firing the *coup-de-grâce*, flying back towards the coast at wave-top height.

During the same engagement, No. 74 Squadron claimed three Bf 109s destroyed with the loss of one pilot, Pilot Officer J H R Young, whose Spitfire fell into the Channel near Goodwin Sands. Meanwhile, Sergeant E A Mould was shot down while flying over Dover and was hospitalized. Hurricanes from No. 111 Squadron were also engaged, claiming two He 59s as destroyed.

At about 17.20 hours, thirty-two-plus aircraft were plotted approaching a convoy off North Foreland. Seven squadrons were despatched to intercept the raid. Only No. 151 Squadron's Hurricanes made contact, accounting for two Bf 110s with a third only allowed as a probable. One Hurricane crashed on landing; the convoy made a safe passage.

At 04.55 hours on the following day, twelve of the squadron's Spitfires took off from Hornchurch for Manston where they refuelled in preparation for active operations.

At 07.18 hours four raids assembled in the Calais–Boulogne–St Omer area and by 07.34 hours they had formed into a single medium-sized raid of eighty-plus aircraft which headed for Dover.

No. 41 Squadron was scrambled at 07.25 hours, Squadron Leader Hood taking off at the head of eleven Spitfires. The aircraft were quickly airborne with orders to patrol Manston from where they were vectored to engage a strong force of Ju 87 dive-bombers and their eighty Bf 109 escorts, which were reported as closing on their target.

Bennions later recalled arriving over Dover at 15,000ft some fifteen minutes later, seeing the harbour and shipping already under attack by about forty Ju 87 flying in two waves of twenty, each escorted by around forty Bf 109s which were flying with the sun behind them. At about 09.45 hours, Squadron Leader Hood ordered 'B' Flight to attack the Stukas while 'A' Flight went in line astern as the Bf 109s headed down to make their own pass.

Hood selected a Bf 109 and closed in before firing a three-second burst, the 109 catching fire and plunging into the sea, witnessed by Pilot Officer

Morrogh-Ryan flying as Red 2. Hood dived after a second Bf 109 but pulled out to avoid a collision. He finished off his ammunition on a Ju 87 which was trying to escape at low level. The Stuka was seen to crash into the sea about seven miles off Dover.

Leading Yellow Section (the third section in the squadron's formation) into the attack, Bennions (flying N3264) ignored the 109s and latched onto a Ju 87 just as it was beginning its deadly dive onto a destroyer. He was just about to fire when the Stuka's rear gunner spotted him and the aircraft veered under his nose and he overshot it. Quickly adjusting his position, Bennions fired at another Ju 87 but suddenly saw the tracer of a Bf 109 pass his port wing and felt an impact. Turning sharply to port Bennions saw the Bf 109 dive past so gave chase.

Bennions' account of the combat at his de-briefing read:

On receiving the order Line Astern from Mitor Leader, Yellow section moved into Line Astern and commenced a No. 3 attack on 6 87s diving towards Dover. On opening fire on the Ju 87 I noticed tracer passing over my Main Port Plane and felt a hit on the Port Side. I broke off the attack immediately and turned about to Port and saw a Me 109 diving past. I followed him down and he commenced circling at about 8,000 feet climbing at low speed. I closed to 200 yards and opened fire. Only my starboard guns firing. The first two bursts [3 seconds] had no effect but the third [a burst of 3 seconds, closing to a range of 50 yards] appeared to strike the engine from which smoke began to pour. The aircraft then began to climb almost vertically and the aircraft['s propeller] stopped turning.

At that moment I was again attacked from the rear. I felt bullets penetrating and half-rolled in almost a stalled condition. On pulling out I found that oil was streaming over my Port Main Plane, the oil pressure had fallen to Zero [and I could smell burning metal and the stench of cordite], and the temperature had risen to 85°C so I decided to return to base.

Arriving at forward Base [Manston] and switched off before crash-landing I found that only one flap (Port) would come down, so I landed without flaps, but found that the port tyre has been punctured. The aircraft arrived without fire or damage occurring but on inspection appeared to be completely u/s.

(signed) GH Bennions PO

Bennions later explained what happened when his port undercarriage collapsed and his aircraft span to a halt, the Station's fire engine racing to the scene to render assistance: 'I hit the deck and gyrated across the airfield. It was most peculiar to see hedges and hangars going round and round. When I came to rest I was completely bewildered but unhurt.'

Flying Officer Scott, Yellow 2, had attacked the Ju 87s alongside Bennions, when they were bounced by the 109s at 07.50 hours. His Spitfire was damaged and he limped back to Manston, where his undercarriage also collapsed on landing and his aircraft (N3100) was declared unserviceable.

Bennions recalled how:

Scotty and I managed to hitch a flight back to Hornchurch off one of the Blenheim crews from No. 600 Squadron a little before noon.

I wasn't used to the pedestrian speed and lack of manoeuvrability of the Blenheim compared to the Spit.

As far as I was concerned it took a very brave man to fly the Blenheim Fighter and I was mighty thankful to have my Spit.

After a quick visit to the MO to check they were not suffering any injuries after their heavy landings, Bennions and Scot were ready for action again the following day.

During the engagement Sergeant Carr-Lewty, Yellow 3, had seen a Bf 109 on the tail of a Hurricane from No. 56 Squadron and latched onto it, shooting the German down, spinning out of control. Breaking off the attack he engaged a Ju 87 but without results.

Green 1, Flight Lieutenant Webster (flying N3113), who was acting as rear-cover, had given a warning before attacking the Bf 109s, setting one on fire, which was seen going down in flames and spinning out of control. Next he latched onto the rearmost Ju 87 of a formation which was lining up to dive-bomb the harbour, but Webster was forced to peel away as another Bf 109 fired on him. Getting onto the tail of the Bf 109, Webster pressed the gun-button but nothing happened – he was out of ammunition and so he made mock attacks before diving to sea-level and heading for Manston where he crash-landed owing to combat damage.

Pilot Officer Mackenzie's Spitfire (N3112) was also hit during the melee. Unable to open the hood and bail out, Mackenzie remained composed and managed to shake off his attackers before selecting a patch of obstacle-free ground in a field at Ringwould, near Deal, where he coaxed his Spitfire down, making a heavy landing.

Flying Officer Gamblen (flying N3038) was hit in the course of the action and posted as 'missing presumed killed in action'. Ted Shipman saw his Spitfire dive vertically into the sea just outside Dover harbour at about 07.45 hours. Wally Wallens was flying alongside Gamblen and witnessed his friend's demise:

We were diving down and closing on an Me 109. Douglas was within range and just about to fire when I spotted two 109s above and behind him. I called out a warning but he didn't hear, or had no time to react. I peeled off moments before one of the *Messerschmitts* opened-up. His concentrated fire ripped into the Spitfire, which dived vertically, streaming thick black smoke behind it. He went in and disappeared.

Wallens had been powerless to act and could only look on in horror. It was a somber Wallens who returned to base; Douglas and he had been very close: 'He was one of the "old" boys on the squadron. I missed him. He was a good man and an outstanding pilot. He just got unlucky, I guess – but it could so easily have been me.'

Wallens would later recall with amusement an incident which occurred on the day before his friend was killed. While at readiness at Manston, the pilots often played cards. There was a poker school and in the tension that existed while waiting their next sortie, bets could occasionally get a little heavy: 'There was a rule that if we were scrambled, your hand would be folded if you arrived more than ten minutes after the reminder of the school.'

On this occasion the normally reserved Gamblen had put heavily into the pot when the pilots were scrambled. Everyone laid their cards flat on the table and ran to their Spitfire, strapped in and were airborne within three minutes.

During the patrol the Spitfires engaged the enemy, Gamblen's aircraft receiving several hits, but he was able to use all of his skills to shake off the Bf 109s and made it back to forward base, although his excursions meant that he landed later than the remainder of the formation:

As we were about to declare Douglas 'out' of the hand, his Spitfire came into view as he made a rapid landing and taxied at speed towards us at dispersals. Almost before the wheels stopped turning the side door was lowered and he sprang down from the wing root and raced over, announcing: 'I make that nine minutes and fifty seconds,' adding that 'if you ratters have pinched my money I'll do the bloody lot of you.'

Looking past Douglas, we noted the holes in his Spitfire. He'd been hit, but hadn't been fazed at all. He was as calm as anything, more concerned about his 'winnings' that the enemy's cannon shells!

Flying Officer (39657) Douglas Robert Gamblen was 25. His body was never recovered and the Channel remains his grave. Gamblen is remembered on the Runnymede Memorial, Panel 5.

The squadron's Intelligence Officer filed a report based on the day's combats:

07.17 hours No. 41 Squadron ordered to patrol Manston later Dover to engage enemy fighters.

07.22 hours Airborne. Climbed towards Dover. Bandits reported 5,000 feet and 10,000 feet and almost immediately seen approaching Dover from the sea 1,000 feet below No. 41 Squadron from starboard. No. 41 Squadron was flying at 10,000 feet. 41 Leader ordered line astern and attacked but simultaneously another squadron of 109s was sighted 1,000 feet up to port wheeling across the sun in line astern to attack our squadron from astern. Still more 109s were seen above them.

A general engagement ensued at about 07.36 hours which turned into a dogfight.

P/O Shipman reports evasive stall by Ju 87, and F/O Scott was attacked from too close by Me 109, both wings hit by 8 cannon shells, little damage to fuselage.

Enemy Casualties:

S/Ldr Hood	1 Me 109 confirmed
	1 Ju 87 unconfirmed
F/Lt Webster	1 Me 109 unconfirmed
	1 Ju 87 damaged
P/O Bennions	1 Me 109 unconfirmed
Sergeant Carr-Lewty	1 Me 109 confirmed

Three other squadrons had been involved in the combat, including No. 56 Squadron, and between them they shot down eight Ju 87s, seven Bf 109s, with five Ju 87s and two Bf 109s unconfirmed. The ack-ack gunners, so often forgotten when it comes to recording the battle, accounted for two further Ju 87s.

Despite the squadron's efforts, some of the dive-bombers had got through and one merchantman, which had already suffered extensive damage in an earlier attack, and one small yacht were both sunk, while one naval vessel was also hit.

At 10.10 hours, six of the squadron's Spitfires lifted off from Manston and flew back to base from where convoy patrols were flown by Blue and then Green sections between 13.40 and 15.25 hours.

Poor weather conditions on both sides of the Channel meant that the squadron could be rested on the morning of the 30th. At 12.40 hours three sections left Hornchurch for Manston, where they remained at readiness.

At 14.20 to 14.25 hours Squadron Leader Hood led three sections on a scramble from Manston, ordered to intercept an enemy formation approaching the Manston area at 2,000ft. However, the Controller recalled them almost immediately and they flew little more than a wide circuit of the airfield before making their approach and landing. Such false alarms were very bad for the nerves as the pilots landed on an adrenalin high and remained on edge as they sat at dispersals awaiting their next scramble.

Back on the ground the Spitfires were topped-up with fuel, while the pilots remained at readiness. Flight Lieutenant Ryder, Pilot Officers Bennions and Morrogh-Ryan of Red Section flew a routine patrol over Manston at 16.30 hours but with no sign of raiders they were ordered to land fifteen minutes later.

With no further business from the Controller, No. 41 Squadron took off for Hornchurch at 20.00 hours and was stood down.

Early the next morning the radar plotters followed the progress of an enemy formation which crossed the Channel at 06.35 hours. The raid appeared off Berck, making for Dungeness, where No. 111 Squadron's Hurricanes made a successful interception.

At 08.00 hours, No. 41 Squadron's Spitfires took off for Manston, landing fifteen minutes later. There were two aborted section-strength interceptions flown during the late morning and early afternoon, on each occasion the enemy raiders turning back before they came into range.

There were two further actions in the squadron's sector at around 16.00 hours when Bf 109s entered their airspace. No. 74 Squadron was scrambled and engaged the enemy, losing Sergeant Fred Eley and Pilot Officer Harold Raymond Gunn killed in action. The enemy came again, when an hour later the Dover Balloon Barrage was attacked by Bf 109s.

Enemy activity continued on a reduced scale on 1 August and mostly consisted of reconnaissance sorties and raids on shipping by lone aircraft or small formations.

No. 41 Squadron flew four flight or section-strength convoy protection patrols between 08.10 and 12.30 hours: 'I flew on the last patrol, leading POs Morrogh-Ryan and Mackenzie and taking off from Manston at 10.40 hours.'

Basing their tactics on faulty intelligence, the Germans believed they were winning the Battle of Britain and that Fighter Command would soon cease to exist as a fighting force. As a part of the *Nazi* propaganda machine the newspaper *Börsen Zeitung* led with the headline: 'England's position is hopeless.'

The air campaign took a further turn when, from his headquarters in Berlin, Hitler issued his Directive No. 17 for the Conduct of Air and Sea Warfare Against England:

In order to establish the necessary conditions for the final conquest of England I intend to intensify air and sea warfare against the English homeland. I therefore order as follows:

1. The German Air Force is to overpower the English Air Force with all the forces at its command, in the shortest time possible. The attacks are to be directed primarily against flying units, their ground installations, and their supply organizations, but also against the aircraft industry, including that manufacturing anti-aircraft equipment.
2. After achieving temporary or local air superiority the air war is to be continued against ports, in particular against stores of food, and also against stores of provisions in the interior of the country.

   Attacks on the south coast ports will be made on the smallest possible scale, in view of our own forthcoming operations.
3. On the other hand, air attacks on enemy warships and merchant ships may be reduced except where some particularly favourable target happens to present itself, where such attacks would lend additional effectiveness to those mentioned in Paragraph 2, or where such attacks are necessary for the training of air crews for further operations.
4. The intensified air warfare will be carried out in such a way that the Air Force can at any time be called upon to give adequate support to naval operations against suitable targets. It must also be ready to take part in full force in Operation *Seelöwe*.
5. I reserve to myself the right to decide on terror attacks as measures of reprisal.
6. The intensification of the air war may begin on or after 5 August. The exact time is to be decided by the Air Force after completion of preparations and in the light of the weather.

   The Navy is authorized to begin the proposed intensified naval war at the same time.

(signed) Adolf Hitler

The early hours of 2 August saw only minor enemy air activity. At 12.50 hours No. 41 Squadron took off for Manston where they were placed at readiness. Meanwhile, three plots were followed by radar, but, following the pattern of the previous days, the most threatening raid turning back when only five miles from Dover.

Bennions flew on a squadron-strength patrol of the Manston area in the mid-afternoon and was still in the air when two enemy formations were plotted crossing the Channel a little after 16.00 hours, bombing a convoy ten miles north of Herne Bay thirty minutes later.

On landing the Spitfires taxied to dispersal where the ground crews quickly began the process of refuelling the aircraft and checking with the pilots for any faults that needed attending to. After the briefest of rests Bennions and the other pilots were back in the air again, scrambling at 17.00

hours, with orders to patrol forward base; they were, however, recalled sixty minutes later.

Less than half an hour had passed before radar picked up several large enemy concentrations. The plotters monitored the situation as the build-up continued, concentrating in the Calais–Bolougne area before the bombers and their escort began flying on different courses over the Straits of Dover. No. 41 Squadron was scrambled at 18.30 hours. This was Bennions' third patrol of the Manston area in rapid succession. The squadron landed back at base at 19.30 hours. Returning to Hornchurch at 21.05 hours, the squadron was stood down for the day.

On the following day the *Luftwaffe* made a number of shipping reconnaissance missions off the south and south east coasts. Operating out of Manston, No. 41 Squadron flew a section-strength patrol in the late morning and chased off one enemy sortie. In the afternoon four raids numbering fifteen or more enemy aircraft approached Dover but these turned back before crossing the coast and so the squadron was ordered to return to Hornchurch at 13.30 hours.

A little before dusk, Bennions' section took off to patrol, but no enemy aircraft were reported and the Spitfires returned to Hornchurch where they were stood down.

At readiness since before dawn, on 4th August No. 41 Squadron flew a single uneventful operational patrol at 11.20 hours.

Elsewhere the day's activities began at 06.00 hours when one aircraft was engaged at 17,000ft over a convoy off North Foreland, but without results.

At 09.15 hours enemy activity developed into an attack by about 150 aircraft. One group of eighty flew into the Thames estuary and on towards Eastchurch, Hornchurch, North Weald and Debden, while the remainder headed for Biggin Hill. With several fighter squadrons in the air and ready to engage, most of the *Luftwaffe* aircraft turned back and by 09.45 hours were re-crossing the coast.

A second raid was spotted over Dover at 12.58 hours and within ten minutes 200 aircraft crossed the coast between Dover and Littlehampton flying at 20,000ft, some heading over the Thames estuary. Meanwhile, a formation of about fifty aircraft flew along the coast to the west of Shoreham, making for Kenley, but turned back. Eighty Bf 109s remained on patrol in the Straits to escort returning aircraft but failed to prevent the RAF taking a heavy toll over land.

During the day Fighter Command claimed fifty-two enemy aircraft destroyed and a further nineteen were allowed as probables with twenty-two damaged, while their own losses were seventeen aircraft destroyed with six pilots killed or posted as missing.

That night the *Luftwaffe* returned to attack Liverpool.

At about 08.30 hours on the 5th, four raids, estimated at fifty-plus aircraft, crossed the French coast and headed for Dover. Four RAF squadrons and one section were scrambled to make an interception but the enemy turned for home and were pursued by two squadrons of Spitfires which claimed three Bf 109s destroyed and four as probably destroyed. One Spitfire failed to return.

The *Luftwaffe* had been shadowing a convoy sailing down the east coast and launched an attack between Hastings and North Foreland. Seven of No. 41 Squadron's Spitfires had only minutes earlier landed at Manston at 12.55 hours and were in the process of being refuelled when they were scrambled and ordered to patrol. The enemy turned away before being engaged, but the threat to the convoy remained high, with No. 41 Squadron maintaining a flight-strength presence until 20.00 hours.

'B' Flight was on-station over the convoy when Flight Lieutenant Webster received a message from the Controller: an enemy formation was approaching. Minutes later a lone He 111 was sighted. While ordering the remainder of the Spitfires to maintain altitude over the convoy to providing top-cover, Webster dived down and made several attacks through heavy cloud, stopping one engine before Bf 109s intervened. The bomber was only allowed as a probable.

Webster was later to discover that Green Section, which was acting as the 'weaver' section, had split from the formation to close with the enemy without permission, leaving the rest of the squadron vulnerable to attack.

A large formation of enemy aircraft were approaching, climbing towards the three Spitfires of Green Section, but suddenly they turned *en-masse* and headed back to France.

That night the *Luftwaffe* dropped tens of thousands of propaganda leaflets across the country – they were English translations of Hitler's previously rejected *Last Appeal to Reason*. The fliers were gathered-up for waste paper or turned into impromptu bonfires.

At readiness since before dawn on 6 August, the pilots of No. 41 Squadron took off by sections before forming-up to fly to their forward base. Flying Officer Scott was ordered to take off at 08.00 hours and vectored onto a Barrage Balloon which had broken free. Dragging its heavy mooring cable the balloon, which could leave a path of destruction in its wake, severing power cables and telephone lines, had drifted some distance from its first reported position and it was nearly half an hour before the hazard was removed.

With no further sign of air activity, the squadron was stood down at 13.55 hours, some of the pilots heading off for the London clubs, pubs and theatres for some much needed letting-off of steam.

The squadron flew a single patrol between 06.40 and 07.40 hours the following morning, when four Spitfires were scrambled to combat an anti-shipping reconnaissance. Despite a wide search they were unable to locate the lone enemy aircraft.

Over the previous few months the enemy had been probing Fighter Command's defence network. German analysis of the RAF's early warning and Sector Controller systems would give Goering further reasons for over optimism for his air campaign:

> As the British are controlled from the ground by radio telephones, their forces are tied to their respective ground stations and are thereby restricted in mobility, even taking into consideration the probability that the ground stations are partially mobile. Consequently the assembly of strong fighter forces at determined points at short notice is not to be expected.

Enemy reconnaissance missions had been monitoring the steady progress of Convoy *Peewitt*, which comprised twenty-nine merchant vessels and their RN escort. By 8 August the convoy was off the south coast. The *Luftwaffe* launched three major raids against the convoy during the day, engaging 300 aircraft from JG 3, 26, 51, 53 and 54.

Radar had been monitoring a raid developing in the Le Touquet area and Nos. 41, 64 and 65 Spitfire Squadrons were scrambled to intercept. Twenty-plus enemy aircraft crossed the Channel at 11.45 hours, approaching Dover before turning west along the coast towards Beachy Head on a south easterly heading.

Squadron Leader Hood took-off at the head of thirteen Spitfires, which were airborne a little after 11.25 hours and ordered to patrol.

While patrolling, three Spitfires of Green Section were ordered to leave the main formation and investigate six or seven unidentified aircraft plotted as approaching Manston. Webster, flying as Green 1, dived from their patrol height of 25,000ft to about 12,000ft, identifying the aircraft as Bf 109s. Webster and Wallens, Green 3, attacked the rear Bf 109 in the formation, which plunged into the sea.

Webster went on to claim a further three Bf 109s shot down into the Channel. Wallens claimed another, which he managed to get close behind, firing a short burst and sending it diving straight into the Channel; suddenly the sky appeared empty of aircraft and he returned to Manston. Wallen's Spitfire was refuelled and re-armed and, realizing his was the only aircraft to have left the battle, he was back in the air within fifteen minutes, climbing to 12,000ft where he intercepted a lone Bf 109 which was heading for home. He attacked with a short burst from 50 yards, seeing it dive into the sea and sink almost immediately.

The remaining *Messerschmitts* escaped as Lovell, flying as Green 2, experienced oxygen trouble just at the crucial moment and was unable to make any claims. However, despite this lost opportunity the squadron returned to base in good spirits. Landing, they taxied to dispersals, handing their aircraft over to the ground crews who got to work while the pilots went over their part in the battle with the Intelligence Officer, Flying Officer, Lord Gisborough, who only allowed two 109s as destroyed and one damaged.

Meanwhile, convoy *Peewitt*, which was still off Dover, was targeted by two more raids between 15.00 and 16.00 hours. No. 41 Squadron took no part in these later patrols, however, as they had already been ordered to stand down, ready to fly north to Catterick, No. 54 Squadron taking their place, having been rested.

A German High Command's Communiqué claimed that during the day the RAF had lost thirty-four aircraft shot down, against only three *Luftwaffe* aircraft. These figures had been revised by the following day to forty-nine for the loss of twelve.

The RAF claims of fifty-three *Luftwaffe* aircraft destroyed were rebuffed by the German newspaper *Deutsche Allgemeine Zeitung*, which claimed: 'THEY LIE WE WIN.'

Chapter 9

The Decimation of *Luftflotte* 5

The squadron was back at Catterick by the late afternoon of 8 August. Over the next few days there would be time for pilots to reflect on the events of the previous weeks. During their time at Hornchurch they had flown 234 operational sorties and made contact with the enemy on five occasions, claiming eight Bf 109s and a Ju 87 as destroyed, damaging three Bf 109s, and one He 111, with three further 109s allowed as probables.

Of these Bennions had claimed one Bf 109 and a second damaged, with his own aircraft suffering combat damage which resulted in it being written-off during a difficult landing.

Meanwhile, the squadron had lost six more Spitfires damaged and one destroyed; that of Flying Officer Douglas Gamblen who was killed on 29 July. Gamblen had been with the squadron since November 1937 and was a greatly admired and respected figure within the Service. Since the outbreak of hostilities he had regularly led his section and flight, taking a leading role on operational patrols, particularly during Operation Dynamo. His loss was a major early blow to the squadron.

The squadron continued its previous practice of operating with one section taking off at dawn for West Hartlepool where they were refuelled and placed at immediate readiness. Another section was at readiness at Catterick, while the remaining sections were at fifteen and thirty minutes' readiness. The pilots worked on rotation, when the three Spitfires at West Hartlepool were on patrol, their place was taken by one section from Catterick.

The day after their return was generally quiet, with only isolated raids along the east coast, with several approaching the Yorkshire coast, leading to scrambles for the squadrons based at Catterick and Church Fenton.

At readiness since before first light, the squadron's carried out their first operational activity at 09.00 hours when three Spitfires were ordered to patrol Whitby at 10,000ft. They landed after only fifteen minutes, the danger having passed.

Further south, a He 111 was located and shot down over the North Sea by No. 79 Squadron's Hurricanes a little before noon, but not before it had dropped its payload on targets in the Sunderland area.

At 13.30 hours Pilot Officers Bennions and Lock, along with Sergeant Carr-Lewty, were scrambled and ordered to patrol, a possible raider having been plotted approaching the coast. This may have been in response to a hostile reconnaissance which was reported off Spurn Head, but the raider didn't stray into the squadron's sector and the Spitfires landed without making contact.

That evening there was party in the Officers' Mess, the champagne flowing in celebration of Anthony Lovell's 21st birthday. Both Lovell and Bennions steered away from the alcohol, however, as both preferred a clear head. No doubt the remainder of the station's pilots took up any 'slack'.

Further raids were directed at shipping off the Yorkshire coast on 10th, the squadron flying a section-strength convoy escort at 07.15 hours, while a section patrol of Whitby was made between 13.25 and 14.05 hours.

Bennions took off at 18.00 hours as part of a flight-strength patrol led by Flight Lieutenant Ryder:

> Ordered to patrol we climbed to an operational altitude and made for our patrol-line. The Controller gave us a vector with further updates but we were unable to make contact with the enemy. After about an hour in the air we were ordered to land. The danger had passed and the squadron was stood down.

The squadron's sector remained quiet until early the following evening when, at 18.25 hours, Green Section was scrambled. Once in the air they were vectored towards Teesmouth.

While flying at 18,000ft in the vicinity of Thirsk, Flying Officer Boyle, Green 2, sighted a Ju 88 of I./*Aufklarungsgruppe* 121 based at Stavanger, Norway. The enemy aircraft, which was flying some 2,000ft above the Spitfires, was on a long-range reconnaissance of the area between Dishforth and Linton-on-Ouse. Spotting his would-be assailants, the Ju 88's pilot dived for cloud cover at 10,000ft, closely flowed by Boyle who got onto its tail and fired a burst at 500 yards, experiencing return fire from the dorsal gunner. Pilot Officer Wallens was also in hot pursuit and, closing from forty to twenty-five yards, saw his de Wilde rounds striking the Ju 88's port engine which he put out of action. Wallens lost his target in the cloud and throttled back to avoid a collision; at the same time the Ju 88 fell away. Meanwhile, Sergeant Darling, who was flying at a lower altitude, saw the bomber emerge from cloud cover and made a beam attack before getting dead astern and launching a second strike. The Ju 88 went into a shallow dive and crash-landed on Newton Moor: three crewmen were taken as PoWs.

Flying Officer R W Wallens, Pilot Officer J G Boyle, and Sergeant E V Darling were each credited with a half share.

It was at about this time that Flying Officer Scott went on leave. Meanwhile, Sergeant Roy Ford was given permission to perform low flying, taking off in Scott's usual Spitfire EB-J. A few minutes into his flight Ford sighted the *Flying Scotsman* heading north on the line between Thirst and Northallerton. Ford decided to 'buzz' the passenger train and dive down to tree-top height in pursuit. Disaster struck when Ford failed to spot a high tension power line, which he sliced through. Miraculously, the young sergeant-pilot managed to maintain height and limped back to Catterick where he landed without causing further damage. Brought before his CO, Sergeant Ford was torn off a strip and grounded for two days. A member of the RAFVR, Ford had joined the squadron on 15 December 1939 and was to serve throughout the battle, before a brief role as a ferry pilot. He volunteered to join the newly formed Merchant Ship Fighter Unit in May 1941, providing air cover for both Atlantic and Malta convoys.

Elsewhere during the day there were heavy raids on Portland and on convoys in the Thames estuary and off East Anglia, the BBC News carrying a graphic commentary of one convoy battle which took place in the Dover Straits.

A feint attack on Dover was launched by Bf 109s which drew fighter cover away from the bombers' intended targets, which included the airfields defending the port, with 200 aircraft attacking in eleven waves. There were also attacks directed at the radar stations along the coast. The Ventnor Station on the Isle of Wight was hit, resulting in a loss of cover which was not resumed until the Bembridge Station came on-line eleven days later.

An official communiqué issued by German High Command announced: 'The battle over the Channel continues', claiming seventy-nine aircraft destroyed, while the *Luftwaffe's* losses, or: 'The planes which have not yet returned', were given as fourteen. These figures were later updated to eighty-nine RAF aircraft destroyed for the loss of seventeen.

On 12 August there were heavy raids on Portsmouth and on a convoy in Thames estuary, while radar stations and coastal airfields were again singled out for attack. The first raid put the Dover radar temporarily out of action. This success was quickly followed by attacks against the airfields at Hawkinge and nearby Lympne. These missions were timed to coincide with the bombing of radar stations at Rye, Romney and Dunkirk in Kent. A few hours later and it was RAF Manston's turn and the landing ground was heavily cratered, although the Spitfires at dispersals escaped unscathed.

Further north and the scene was very different. During the early afternoon, with no sign of enemy action, No. 41 Squadron took part in mock attacks on No. 51 Squadron's Whitleys.

The *Luftwaffe* launched their temporarily postponed new offensive, christened '*Adler Tag*' or 'Eagle Day', on 13 August. Bad weather led to the cancellation of the early morning's raids. The signal failed to reach all of the units involved, however, and a part of the force was dispatched. The first of these raids arrived over the coast, on a line between Dungeness to North Foreland, at about 05.30 hours. Some aircraft from the same formation peeled off and headed for a convoy in the Thames estuary. Forty-five minutes later, four raids totaling 250 aircraft approached the coast between the Isle of Wight and Selsey Bill, heading for Portsmouth. Fighter squadrons from Nos. 10 and 11 Groups were already in the air to meet the bombers, which suffered heavy casualties with only small losses to Fighter Command.

A little after noon a smaller raid consisting of ten enemy aircraft crossed the coast to the east of Portland. These merged with a second formation, numbering some twelve aircraft. The enemy was intercepted and several of the intruders were destroyed.

The raids continued with a large formation crossing the coast between Portland and the Thames estuary at 15.25 hours. Half-an-hour later six formations totalling 150 aircraft closed-in on their targets at Poole, Portland, Portsmouth, Southampton and Andover airfield, with another raid hitting Bristol. Fighters were scrambled to counter the enemy threat, resulting in a number of enemy aircraft claimed as damaged or destroyed.

Meanwhile, a mixed formation numbering some 150 aircraft headed for Ramsgate, Deal and Dover, while Eastchurch Aerodrome was also hit. Other targets in East Kent included Detling airfield, which was attacked by Ju 88s.

Further north and a convoy was attacked off East Anglia at 19.36 hours, with fighters successfully fending off the bombers.

There was little enemy activity in No. 13 Group's airspace. No. 41 Squadron flew two section-strength patrols between 10.25 and 11.10 hours, but without being vectored onto the enemy. At 17.25 hours, fighters from the Church Fenton Sector were scrambled to deal with aircraft shadowing a convoy sailing off Flamborough Head. The enemy headed for cloud and made for home on sighting the fighters.

The RAF's tally for the day was forty-five *Luftwaffe* aircraft claimed as destroyed for the loss of fourteen fighters, with seven pilots reported as safe.

Following the previous day's peak of activity in Nos. 10 and 11 Group's sectors, the morning of the 14th was relatively quiet with only fairly isolated reconnaissance sorties off the coast. At about midday, however, a number of large raids flew over Kent, attacking the Manston, Dover,

Folkestone and Deal areas. No. 11 Group's fighters engaged the enemy with some successes.

More raids followed at 16.00 hours, when the *Luftwaffe* employed a different tactic, sending a large number of smaller raids. These crossed the coast near Weymouth and Lyme Bay, heading for targets in south Wales, Gloucester and the area around Middle Wallop.

Two raids were plotted in the north-east, the second crossing the coast near Whitby. In response No. 41 Squadron scrambled six aircraft, with Pilot Officer Lovell leading. Airborne by 16.20 hours they were ordered to patrol. The enemy was reported to have turned back when still out to sea. Aware that the bombers might return, the Spitfires handed over to a second patrol, with Bennions being joined by Pilot Officers Lock and Mackenzie, but no enemy aircraft were seen and the section landed at 17.30 hours.

There were five major raids on 15 August, the day labelled 'Black Thursday' by the *Luftwaffe*. These were made in the north-east and the south of England, with *Luftflotte 2* flying from Holland, Belgium and northern France, Goering also employing *Luftflotte 3* from north and west France. The main targets were No. 10 and 11 Group's airfields and No. 11 Group's Sector Station at Tangmere, along with a number of coastal locations.

The first raid, which was estimated at 100-plus enemy aircraft, arrived over the coast between Dover and Hawkinge at 11.00 hours, the enemy's targets including the Thames and Eastchurch Docks as well as Biggin Hill.

At 14.30 hours a raid composed of 200 aircraft flew over Martlesham, Dover, Deal and Lympne, their targets including Detling, Hawkinge, Lympne and Hornchurch. During the raid the Sector Room at Biggin Hill was badly damaged.

Several large raids were reported in the areas of Portsmouth, Weymouth and Middle Wallop between 17.20 and 18.10 hours. These involved a total of nearly 400 enemy aircraft.

Thus far No. 13 Group's sector had generally only experienced sporadic raids. Generally the enemy made solo reconnaissance sorties, occasionally dispatching larger forces on anti-shipping raid. However, believing that No. 13 Group's defences had been depleted in order to support No. 11 Group in the south, Goering dispatched *Luftflotte 5* from its airbases in Norway; the bombers would fly largely without fighter escort. Group HQ had been informed by intelligence of the possibility of a heavy raid – German communications had been intercepted and, with the help of a captured Enigma machine and the code-breakers at Bletchley Park, the *Luftwaffe's* plans were known. Consequently, Dowding had received a message marked 'Most Secret', detailing information which he was told came from a 'reliable source'.

The morning had begun quietly for No. 41 Squadron, with an uneventful section patrol flown between 08.00 and 08.45 hours. A telephone call came through from Group HQ during the mid-morning, warning No. 41 Squadron that a Hull convoy would pass through their sector. Meanwhile, a little before noon radar picked up a raid which was heading towards the east coast of Scotland. The enemy aircraft closed to within a few miles of land, making a few jinks to further throw the Controller off the scent, before turning back for their bases. The flight had been a feint to draw the RAF's fighters further north, as another raid, estimated at thirty-plus enemy aircraft, was plotted approaching the Yorkshire coast.

Ten Spitfires from No. 41 Squadron were scrambled at 11.40 hours, with orders to make an interception, but were jumped by the higher flying escort of Bf 109s. Tony Lovell opened-fire at the rear aircraft of the formation at a range of 250 yards, firing one burst of five seconds and two of six seconds. The *Messerschmitt* fell in flames by the railway line between Adisham and Bekesbourne, the pilot, *Feldwebel* Herbert Tschoppe, bailing out to become a PoW.

Flying Officer Lovell's combat report read:

...flying as Blue 2, we broke up to attack Me 109s who were attacking us. I sighted my Me 109 turning east and diving. I dived after him and chased him for some 15 miles in and out of cloud. After my first burst white fumes came from his port wing rout, (sic) but he carried on. I gave him two more bursts and he caught fire and I saw him bail out and was being attended to on the ground.

The remainder of the squadron was able to avoid the Bf 109s' fire but was unable to break-up the enemy raid.

With a further raid, estimated at thirty aircraft, detected by radar, No. 41 Squadron was brought to immediate readiness and scrambled at 12.40 hours, with Flight Lieutenant Ryder leading a formation of thirteen Spitfires. Taking off by sections, they received orders to patrol West Hartlepool at 15,000ft.

Making the initial contact over the Farne Islands, No. 72 Squadron, based at Acklington, reported the formation's position and true extent, which was nearer 100 aircraft. The Controller had already scrambled Nos. 79 (Acklington), 605 (Drem) and 607 (Usworth) Squadrons which followed-up the initial attack. Meanwhile, No. 72 Squadron's attack had succeeded in shooting down three of the unescorted bombers, breaking up the enemy into two smaller formations which continued towards the coast to the south of Durham, where No. 41 Squadron was patrolling.

RAF Halton's Tug of War Team in 1931 (Bennions top left).

Winners of the King's Cup 1931, RAF Halton Athletic Team with trophies (Bennions back row, fourth from right).

L/AC's MAURICE. EMANUEL. SALTER. BERTRAM. ROSS. FLYNN. MITCHELL. MARPOLE. PRIESTLEY. BENNIONS.
A/P/O's WALKER. FRYER. WILLIAMS. FULTON. RICHMOND. PIPPET. WARDELL. BOCKING. SELKIRK. THOMAS.
A/P/O's MICHELMORE. RILEY. HUTCHINGS. KENDRICK. OLNEY. JUPP. HERIOT-HILL. LESTER. EVANS. DODDS. BANKS. EDINGER.
A/P/O's TODD. EYRES. ROMER. STEVENS. LEACH. HOOK. PELLY-FRY. BARRETT. HAWKINS. YULE. TINNE. LOMBARD. SPENCER.

No. 3 Flying Training School (Bennions top right).

RAF Halton Tug of War team 1931 –
close-up of Bennions.

Bennions in flying gear – Aden posting
with No. 41 Squadron in 1936.

Bennions flying Hawker Demon K4540 in 1937.

Bennions in flying gear besides his Hawker Demon K4525, during the winter of 1937.

Bennions besides his motor car 1938.

Drawing of Bennions by Anne Kennington (courtesy of Anne Kennington).

George, Connie and Avis leaving Buckingham Palace following Bennions' investiture on 18th February 1941.

Hans Ulrich Kettling, Bennions'
victim on 15th August 1940.

Bennions at the controls of Hawker Demon K4525, Catterick, February 1937.

No. 41 Squadron 'Score-board', early 1941. Bennions was materially responsible for the trophy's return to No. 41 Squadron at RAF Coltishall in 2003.

Squadron Leader 'Wally' Wallens taken in 1945.

A devoted Roman Catholic, Lovell used to go to confession following every successful combat. He died in a flying accident weeks after VJ Day.

Flight Commander Norman Ryder. On 1 April 1940, Bennions was acting as Deputy Controller when he vectored Ryder onto an enemy bomber which he successfully destroyed, earning him the DFC.

Eric Lock who won the DSO
DFC and Bar with No. 41
Squadron during 1940.

Squadron Leader Don Finlay.
On 1st October, Finlay failed to
observe the formation of forty
Bf 109s that Bennions reported.
Consequently he went down alone
to the aid of a flight of Hurricanes
which were about to be 'bounced'.

No. 41 Squadron line-up (April to May 1940).

Back row (l-r): Sgts 'Mitzi' Darling (killed), Roy Ford, Jim Sayers, Howitt, Carr–Lewty.

Middle Row (l-r): Plt Off Boret (killed), WO 'Jock' Darrant (Engineering Officer), F'lg Off 'Mac' Mackenzie, Plt Off 'Buck' Murrogh-Ryan (killed), Flg Off 'Lulu' Lovell (killed), Plt Off Bill Stapleton (PoW).

Front Row (l-r): F'lg Off 'Scotty' Scott (killed), F'lg Off Bill Legard (killed), Wg Cdr Guy Carter (Station Commander), Sqn Ldr 'Robin' Hood (killed), Flt Lt Norman Ryder (PoW), Flg Off Steventon (Sqn Adjt),F'lg Off Douglas Gamblen (killed).

No. 41 Squadron Spitfire Mk 1 PN-M, photographed in 1939.

The scattered wreckage of Bennions' last victim, a Bf 109 destroyed on 1st October 1940.

'Ben' Bennions wearing his favoured Guinea Pig Club tie.

Bennions' badges, medal and miniatures. Left top–bottom Irvin Badge, Guinea Pig Club badge, Bullion on Cloth Guinea Pig Club badge, boxed Irvin Caterpillar Club badge. Right Distinguished Flying Cross group with Battle of Britain Bar and MiD Oakleaf, with miniatures below.

In Loving Memory
Of
AVIS BENNIONS
Died 9th June 2000
Aged 84,

Sqn Ldr
GEORGE BENNIONS
DFC, R.A.F (Ret'd)
Died 30th January 2004
Aged 90 Years

TONY BENNIONS
Died 14th August 1951

'Ben' Bennions' headstone, Catterick cemetery. The memorial also commemorates his wife Avis and their son Tony, who died in infancy.

Bennions had noticed that Ryder was not responding to communications from the Sector Controller, and having failed to reach him over the radio, Bennions flew up alongside Ryder's Spitfire, signalling that he would take command; this would be the first time Bennions would lead the squadron into action.

The voice of the Controller came over the radio: '100 bandits on Vector 010.'

Bennions (flying R6604) immediately read the situation and pushed the squadron into a battle climb in order to place them above and up sun of the incoming aircraft; they would attack in the company of No. 607 Squadron, Bennions taking the lead.

The squadron had been in the air for about fifteen minutes when Bennions spotted the most southerly of the enemy formations, over Seaham harbour and heading for Durham. Flying at 13,000ft, the He 111s of KG26 were shadowed by twenty-plus Bf 110s of I./ZG76.

The Bf 110 was a well armed fighter/fighter-bomber. The pilot could fire two cannons and four machine guns in the nose, while sitting back to back with him was the rear-gunner with a single swivel-mounted machine gun.

Bennions later recalled:

The sky seemed full of big black dots and little black dots: the bombers in fives, the fighters in fours. The fighters were positioned some 500 yards behind and about 2,000 feet above, thus creating a dead man's land between the rear guns of the *Heinkels* and the forward guns of the *Messerschmitts.*

The formations were approaching each other head-on. Bennions knew that they would have little opportunity to pick out individual targets at high closing speeds and that his own fighters would be vulnerable to being shot at by half the air gunners in the enemy formation and by the Bf 110s. Quickly assessing the situation, he ordered 'B' Flight to reposition ready to intercept the fighter escort, while leading the seven aircraft of 'A' Flight into echelon starboard to make a beam attack on the He 111s. The bombers maintained formation and Bennions led 'A' Flight under them to avoid the cross-fire from their air gunners and those of the escorting Bf 110s.

At the same time, Flying Officer Lovell, flying as Blue 1, led 'B' Flight into an attack on the fighter escort, latching onto the last Bf 110 in a line of three, opening fire with a concentrated six-second burst that ignited the long-range fuel tanks, before firing off his remaining ammunition into a second which he claimed as probably destroyed.

Lovell's combat report read:

Blue 1 saw three ME110s turn round in line astern and attacked the last of the 3. No.1 attack 250 yds 1 burst 7 secs terrific explosion and flames obviously from tank with partial disintegration of e/a. Attacked another ME110. Many pieces fell away & e/a seemed out of control. 11 sec burst. Total rounds fired 2680. Stoppage in 1 gun due to separated case.

Blue 2, Sergeant Howitt, followed Lovell into the fray and attacked the aircraft next to Lovell's first victim with a short burst. The Bf 110 was badly damaged and dived into cloud at 13,000ft, its path marked by a ghastly trail of smoke.

Ordered to take-on the Bf 110s, Shipman led Green Section into the attack, turning in behind a flight of fighters flying at 18,000ft on the left of the enemy formation, ordering 'echelon port' as they carried-out a No. 3 attack. The Spitfires went in line astern.

Shipman's combat report read:

Before getting into range, the E.A. turned left about quickly and headed straight for me. I engaged the first one with a head on attack at about 400 yards range firing a short burst of 2 seconds. The E.A. broke away to my port at a very close range. No return fire was noticed and no result was seen. The E.A. disappeared behind me.

I then engaged another Me 110 with a series of deflection shots at various ranges, the E.A. evading violently. No effect was seen and no return fire was experienced.

The same E.A. was then attacked from astern position at about 200 yards range. I fired the rest of my ammunition with the result that the starboard engine was put out of action with clouds of smoke. The E.A. then made erratic turns to the left and disappeared into cloud below, apparently out of control.

(signed) E.A. Shipman

The pilot of the stricken Bf 110, Hans Kettling, later wrote of Bennions' attack;

I heard *Obergefreiter* Volk, my radio-operator and rear-gunner, fire his machine gun and on looking back I stared into the flaming guns of four Spitfires in splendid formation. The plane was hit, not severely, but the right engine went dead, lost coolant and the oil temperature rose rapidly. I had to switch off the engine and feather the propeller and tried to reach the protection of the bombers which were overhead in close formation. I was not successful – the plane was slow and I could not gain height. Over the radio I heard the boys in the bombers talking about my plane so I gave my 'Mayday' because the Spits came in for the second attack [Bennions'] and the kill....

Green 3, Pilot Officer Wallens, made a half roll to avoid the head-on attack and, having half-rolled out and dived away, placed himself on the tail of a Bf 110. He was unable to fire before being forced to break, diving onto another fighter. Firing his guns, Wallens made a deflection shot from the quarter, seeing the heavily smoking fighter disappear into clouds. In the confusion a Bf 110 latched onto Wallens but it was spotted and attacked by Sergeant Usmar, Green 2, who fired a short burst at 50 yards before he was forced to break-off due to a He 111 which was flying directly towards him. Usmar turned his attention to the *Heinkel*, which he hit with a well aimed burst at 50 yards and pulled away to starboard; the bomber's pay-load detonated, the shock-wave from the explosion throwing Usmar's aircraft some forty feet higher into the air. During the engagement he claimed one He 111 destroyed and damaged a Bf 110 and a Do 17.

Bennions had led 'A' Flight against the bomber formation, feigning a beam attack before dipping under the enemy, then climbed behind them to attack their escort, one shooting at Bennions who took evasive action, another being caught in Bennions' sights but disappeared in the low cloud; he was only able to claim it as damaged. Bennions then attacked a second Bf 110, which was the one piloted by *Oberleutnant* Hans Ulrich Kettling and which had previously been damaged by Shipman. Bennions hit it in the port wing over Seaham Harbour, seeing smoke streaming from the engine as it descended towards Barnard Castle where it crashed.

Bennions claimed one Me 110 destroyed and another damaged. His combat report read:

As Mitor Yellow 1, leading Mitor Squadron, I first sighted enemy formation in front of several bursts of AA fire, approx 10 miles ahead. I had received orders to attack the bombers but on closing with the enemy, I noticed a large formation of escort fighters about 500 yards astern of the bombers. I dispatched first Green and then Blue Sections to engage the fighters and led Yellow and Red in a Dummy attack on the bomber formation from the beam. The formation of bombers remained intact, so rather than expose the two sections to cross fire from the bombers and forward fire of escort fighters, I broke away with the flight underneath the main formation and turned to starboard, climbing rapidly to position above and astern of the escort formation. The rear 3 E/A were acting as rearguard, so led Yellow Section in to dispose of these. After a burst of approximately 2 seconds, the port engine of the E/A began to smoke and

E/A fell away to port and entered low cloud on a SE course. When E/A entered cloud, I broke off the attack and returned to main formation. I took up position above and astern of formation and dived on a Me 110 which was climbing to rejoin formation.

I opened fire at 250 yards dead astern and after a short burst saw the E/A fall away with the port engine smoking and a red glow on the port side. I followed this aircraft down and saw him gliding down towards Barnard Castle, with either petrol or glycol streaming from the tail, his height was approximately 2,000 feet and he made no effort to climb or turn, so I returned above cloud to endeavour to make contact with remainder of formation.

I could not see anything, so I returned to base and landed.

I had expended about 1,000 rounds with a stoppage in one gun due to a separated case.

Attacks were No. 1 dead astern at range approximately 250–100 yards, bursts of 2 seconds except for preliminary beam attack of approximately 1 second.

(Signed) GH Bennions P/O

Bennions was mid-way between Piercebridge and Barnards Castle when he broke off the attack, fifty miles from where he had picked-up the twin-engine fighter. He radioed to the Controller that he believed that he had shot down a Bf 110 but had not seen it crash.

Oberleutnant Hans Kettling later wrote:

This time they got the left engine, my *Bordfunker* and the front windscreen (the tracer missing me by a fraction of inches). *Obergefreiter* Volk was lying on the floor, covered with blood and unconscious. I had no means of ascertaining whether he was alive or not. Since all flight controls were in perfect order (without the engines of course) and the belly tank empty, I decided to bring the plane down for a belly landing.

I dived away from the fighting, down and down, leaving the lethal Spitfires behind and looking for a suitable landing site. I eased the plane carefully down over a very large meadow but on touching down, I found the speed was still rather high. Finally, it crashed through a low stone wall which was hidden by a hedge, leaving the rear fuselage behind which broke just behind the cockpit.

The plane came to a halt at last. I jumped out, freed Volk and carried him to a safe distance, fearing fire and explosion. I disabled the radio with some shots from my pistol and I tried to set the plane on fire but the two incendiaries we carried for this purpose did not work as expected. One of them burnt my right hand badly....

After that, a lot of people came running armed with stick and stones, threatening and shouting from a distance until some red-capped Military Police took over and transported Volk, who had in some way recovered, and me to the police station of a nearby village where we were locked in two cells.

A doctor came and took care of Volk, who was after all not so very badly wounded, and he took care of my burnt hand too. We got an excellent dinner, with the compliments and good wishes from the local military big-shot. Several RAF officers came and shot me down. I went through these hours as in a trance – I only wanted to sleep....

Meanwhile, Ryder, relegated to Yellow 2, had gone into the attack in line astern of Bennions but was soon under attack from one of the Bf 110 escort. Turning, he fired a burst at his would-be assailant and saw an explosion in its fuselage, confirmed by Mackenzie but only allowed as a probable as no-one saw it crash. Then he sighted and attacked a Ju 88, which was a part of the second wave:

I took off as Yellow One at 12.40 hours. My R/T faded completely, and I handed section to Yellow 3. I took up position as Yellow 2. Large bomber force and escort fighter force was engaged.... I did not fire at bombers but followed Yellow One who was climbing to starboard and attacked a section of escort fighters. I got quarter astern and below a Ju 88 and opened fire [with 800 rounds] at approximately 250 feet. Return fire soon ceased. Large pieces of cowling flew off port side and passed over my port wing. A violent crimson explosion was observed in the centre of the fuselage. I fired all my ammunition and when breaking away the target was losing height and looked as if flaps or dive breaks were down. Small amount of smoke was observed, apart from time of explosion.

Elsewhere during the dogfight, Morrogh-Ryan passed-out while pulling off a tight turn during the pursuit of an enemy aircraft that had stall-turned in front of Ryder, regaining consciousness as his Spitfire hurtled towards the ground.

Red Section broke away from Yellow Section after the initial attack and Pilot Officer Mackenzie, flying as Red 1, selected a Bf 110 which was flying slightly to the starboard of the main formation and opened fire at 200 yards. Streaming smoke from the starboard engine, the raider dived for cloud cover and was allowed as a probable. Red 3, Pilot Officer Eric Lock, was more successful, hitting both engines of a Bf 110 which was seen to crash in Seaham Harbour. This was his first combat victory – Lock would claim twenty-three destroyed and eight probables while flying with the squadron.

Philip Bennion later recalled how his brother, accompanied by Tony Lovell, drove over to see the wreckage of his 'kill':

> While surveying the fuselage they were approached by one of the soldiers assigned to guard duty, who proceeded to give them a blow by blow account of how the Germans had been shot down. At length Lovell stopped the soldier and pointed over to Bennions, explaining that he was the pilot who had shot the *Messerschmitt* Bf 110 down.

Both the pilot, Hans Ulrich Kettling and his wireless operator, *Unteroffizier* Volk, survived the engagement and war.

Kettling contacted Bennions and Shipman in 1980, meeting Shipman later that year. Bennions, however, declined the offer as he felt that somehow it would have been a betrayal of the friends who fought and died maintaining the world's freedom.

Bennions later discovered that six Bf 110s of I./ZG76 had been destroyed without loss, the Squadron's Intelligence Officer writing a summary of the squadron's victories:

> To Intelligence Officer HQ 13 Group
> From Intelligence Officer Catterick
>
> Definite Casualties to enemy 15/8/40
>
> F/O Lovell Blue 1 saw Me 110 explode in flames and partly disintegrate. P/O Bennions Yellow 1 saw Me 110 go down though with engine on fire over Barnard Castle. Wreckage is in field 1 and ½ miles from Barnard Castle.
> P/O Lock attacked Me 110. Saw starboard engine smoke and port engine on fire. Broke away and left E/A in a vertical dive with both engines on fire.
> Sergeant Usmar fired at He 111 saw it explode in mid air and completely disappear.
>
> Squadron Intelligence Report:
>
> A Flight Red and Yellow sections

AD Lovell	Me 110	Confirmed
Bennions	Me 110	Confirmed
Lock	Me 110	Confirmed
Sergeant Usmar	He 111	Confirmed

F/Lt Ryder	Ju 88	Probable
PO Wallens	Me110	Probable
PO Shipman	Me 110	Probable
PO Mackenzie	Ju 88	Probable

Five more e/a were damaged.

Pilot Officer Lock's Spitfire was slightly damaged [a single bullet-hole] in the port wing by return fire from one of the Bf 109 escort.

Bennions felt vindicated as a tactician: he had led his men into a well executed attack giving them the best opportunity of striking the enemy hard, but without placing the pilots in unnecessary danger. He had felt driven to:

Get our own back after 29 July 1940. Then we'd been at Manston and had intercepted a similar number over Dover. But there had been about eighty Me 109 fighters and only twenty Ju 87 dive-bombers. As we attacked the bombers we were bounced by the 109s and lost five aircraft – almost half the squadron – in five minutes. But this was a different kettle of fish.

While No. 41 Squadron had successfully taken on the first wave, a second formation of fifty He 111s crossed the coast over Flamborough Head, bound for Driffield. The Germans' aim was to destroy the northern airfields, with their secondary targets the cities of Newcastle, Middlesborough, and Sunderland. Beyond these bombers was a further formation including Ju 88s of KG 30, ten of which were destroyed off Flamborough Head soon after the attack on Driffield. The combined assault of five Spitfire and Hurricane squadrons scattered the bombers and their fighter escort over a wide area, with a total of forty enemy aircraft destroyed.

No. 41 Squadron flew four more section-strength or solo patrols between 14.10 and 17.30 hours, with Bennions making a forty minute patrol in the Scarborough area at 16.55 hours.

During the first of these, a squadron patrol flown at 25,000ft, three miles south-west of Hornchurch, the squadron engaged a formation of thirty He 111s with their escort of 109s, Lovell attacked a He 111 at 8,000ft without observing any damage, but claimed a Bf 109 as a probable:

We broke up to face the attacking 109s and I peeled away and did a quarter attack on a HE 111, but saw no result. I went into a steep climbing turn and many 109s passed me. I picked out a yellow-nosed ME 109 and attacked him from the rear. I saw much white smoke coming from him and after a few seconds, he did a violent skid and then heeled right over and went towards the clouds. He disappeared into the clouds on his back. I came down through the clouds and saw I was south of the aerodrome. He disappeared through the clouds at 14.35 hours.

During a day when the *Luftwaffe* flew 1,800 sorties, they lost seventy-five aircraft, while the RAF had thirty-four fighters shot-down with eighteen pilots killed or missing.

Between noon and 14.30 hours on the following day, attacks were launched against Portsmouth and targets in Kent and East Anglia, while at 16.30 hours raids began on Dover, the Thames estuary and targets along the south coast between Shoreham and Selsey Bill. There were also raids on airfields in Kent, Hampshire and West Sussex, including Tangmere and Manston, as well as on Biggin Hill, Kenley and North Weald. Tangmere was badly mauled with fourteen aircraft being damaged on the ground. Meanwhile, the Ventnor radar station was hit again and temporarily put out of action.

Further north, No. 13 Group was faced with bad weather conditions and poor visibility which meant there was little flying.

The RAF claimed seventy-two enemy aircraft destroyed, with twenty-nine probables and forty-one damaged. Despite the continued heavy losses, Goering still believed he had the upper hand as German intelligence estimated that Fighter Command had been reduced to 300 operational aircraft with only a further 130 held in reserve.

On 17 August enemy activity was largely limited to reconnaissance flights over Fighter Command's airfields as the *Luftwaffe* tried to gauge the damage inflicted over the previous few days. And with no improvement in the weather conditions, there was very little flying in No. 13 Group's sector, although Bennions made a ten-minute operational flight at 16.00 hours.

Inclement weather and poor visibility in the Catterick area meant that the squadron's aircraft were not called into action on the 18th. Elsewhere, however, the raids intensified on what would become known as 'The Hardest Day'.

A large-scale attack was made at about 12.30 hours, hitting the south-eastern Home Counties, followed by a major assault in the Portsmouth–Southampton area some ninety minutes later. Meanwhile, there were also extensive raids on airfields in the south and south-east as the *Luftwaffe's* campaign to destroy Fighter Command on the ground and in the air continued. Later, at 17.00 hours, heavy raids were experienced over Essex and Kent, while enemy aircraft were plotted off Great Yarmouth, crossing the coast and heading for Birmingham, Worcester, Cardiff and the Weymouth area.

The raids were met with heavy resistance, and losses amongst the enemy bombers were high, resulting in the German *Stuka* units being withdrawn from inland air operations.

RAF fighter pilots claimed 126 enemy aircraft shot down, although the actual figure was closer to 71. The Germans countered these figures with their own, with 147 RAF fighters destroyed for the loss of only 36.

The German press carried the headlines: 'Conclusive Phase of the War Begun' and the 'Closing Act of this Conflict Opens.'

On 19 August, Goering initiated new tactics for his daylight raids, deploying smaller formations of bombers heavily outnumbered by their escort of Bf 109s: their targets were the RAF's airfields.

The *Luftwaffe* flew a small number of isolated raids, while reconnaissance missions were made off the east coast of Scotland and over convoys sailing along the Yorkshire coast. However, No. 41 Squadron was not called upon and was largely limited to night training from RAF Leeming. They did not fly at all on the following day, which saw a few minor raids across the country during the morning, including those against targets near Chelmsford and Lowestoft, while airfields in Kent and Essex were bombed during the afternoon. A convoy sailing to the east of Dunwich was attacked as were Great Yarmouth, Southwold and Wattisham.

Meanwhile, Winston Churchill spoke in the House of Commons:

The great air battle which has been in progress over this Island for the last few weeks has recently attained a high intensity. It is too soon to attempt to assign limits either to its scale or to its duration. We must certainly expect that greater efforts will be made by the enemy than any he has so far put forth. Hostile airfields are still being developed in France and the Low Countries, and the movement of squadrons and material for attacking us is still proceeding....

Concerning his earlier prediction that over English soil Fighter Command would improve their 'kill' ratio to greater than 4:1, he announced that: 'This has certainly come true.' Meanwhile, the stepping up of aircraft production meant that Fighter Command had never been stronger, Churchill adding:

We believe that we shall be able to continue the air struggle indefinitely and as long as the enemy pleases, and the longer it continues the more rapid will be our approach, first towards that parity, and then into that superiority, in the air upon which in a large measure the decision of the war depends.

The gratitude of every home in our Island, in our Empire, and indeed throughout the world, except in the abodes of the guilty, goes out to the

British airmen who, undaunted by odds, unwearied in their constant challenge and mortal danger, are turning the tide of the World War by their prowess and by their devotion. Never in the field of human conflict was so much owed by so many to so few. All hearts go out to the fighter pilots, whose brilliant actions we see with our own eyes day after day....

Dowding's fighter boys were at their zenith. They wore their top buttons undone as a badge of honour and received preferential treatment in bars, dancehalls and just about wherever they were recognized.

Of the Prime Minister's speeches, often quoted at length in BBC Home Service news bulletins and in the press, Bennions later remarked: 'At that desperate time my professional instinct told me that we must be losing the Battle, and it was Winston Churchill's voice on the radio that inspired me and kept me going.'

Bennions was not alone in these sentiments and the Prime Minister's speeches were followed by millions across the country and beyond.

Chapter 10

The Battle Continues

The squadron made two patrols on the afternoon of 21 August, during the second of which Blue Section's Pilot Officers Langley and Shipman, along with Sergeant 'Mitzi' Darling, were scrambled at 16.00 hours and successfully vectored onto a raid. Pilot Officer Shipman lined up a target, shooting down a He 111, which crashed into the sea off Flamborough Head.

Airfields in the east and south of England suffered small raids, while during the following day the *Luftwaffe* flew a number of anti-shipping reconnaissance flights, searching for convoys sailing off the south and east coasts. These led to a major attack on a convoy in the Straits of Dover. A second raid was made in the Manston and Dover area, while the bombardment of Dover began when long-range guns in Cap Gris Nez opened fire.

Reconnaissance sorties were reported off the east coast on 23 August, with a few raids penetrating inland. During the afternoon, these crossed the south coast but were responsible for only minor damage. There was only one report of enemy activity in Catterick's sector when, at 14.00 hours, Bennions was scrambled on an operational patrol but was ordered to return to base after fifteen minutes in the air, the 'bogie' having turned back and was no longer posing a threat.

On 24 August the *Luftwaffe* mounted a series of heavy attacks on airfields, concentrating on No. 11 Group's seven Sector Stations at Tangmere, Debden, Kenley, Biggin Hill, Hornchurch, North Weald and Northolt – it was on these bases that the defence of the whole of the south-east and London depended.

The *Luftwaffe's* raids on RAF Manston were so intense that the base was temporarily evacuated, making it the only Fighter Command airfield to actually be put out of action by the enemy's bombing campaign. Boulton Paul Defiants from No. 264 Squadron were scrambled to meet the raid and managed to destroy three enemy aircraft, but lost the same number – they would soon be confined to night-fighter duties. Elsewhere, there were heavy raids on Southampton and Portsmouth, during which a cinema packed with children received a direct hit with tragic loss of life.

Further north and No. 41 Squadron made a section-strength patrol a little after dawn and a second around dusk, while in the early afternoon Bennions flew to Acklington for thirty minutes' gunnery practice on the ranges. Over the next few evenings, pilots from the squadron practiced night flying out of RAF Leeming. There was little activity in No. 13 Group's area as a whole, and daytime flying was confined to a mere handful of uneventful patrols and scrambles.

German High Command issued a communiqué, claiming successful daylight attacks on Northwood, Hornchurch, Manston, Canterbury, Ramsgate, Great Yarmouth and the Dover army barracks, which led to the German Press claiming '64 enemy planes destroyed' and 'Extensive destruction following surprise attack on England' leaving 'Portsmouth naval base aflame.'

The enemy's claims were, however, wildly inaccurate, as Fighter Command's losses were twenty fighters with six pilots killed in action. Meanwhile, the RAF claimed forty enemy aircraft as destroyed.

That night raids were made against the capital. During the attack a German bomber crew flew slightly off course and their bombs hit a residential area of London, leading to Winston Churchill's order for a retaliatory raid on Berlin. This would have a major impact in the conduct of the war, leading Hitler to change the focus of his air campaign. Earlier the dictator had publicly vowed: 'If they attack out cities, we will rub out their cities from the map; the time will come when one of us will break and it will not be Nazi Germany.'

On 25 August there were a number of minor raids during the morning and early afternoon, with heavy bombing near Warmwell, the Isles of Sheppey and along the Thames estuary.

That night, Bomber Command sent a raid of eighty bombers against industrial targets around the German capital by way of reprisal. These raids continued with attacks on three out of the following four nights. The effects were reported by the American Press:

> The Berliners were stunned. They did not think it could ever happen. Goering assured them that it couldn't. Their disillusionment today is all the greater. You have to see their faces to measure it.

During the morning of 26 August there were raids on the Kent airfields and on targets to the north of the Thames estuary, with No. 12 Group failing to intercept an attack on Debden while its squadrons were in the air. These attacks preceded air raids on Portsmouth and Southampton which began at 16.00 hours.

There was little activity on the following day other than a number of enemy reconnaissance sorties which were made in the Portsmouth–Southampton area and over a convoy sailing off Kinnaird's Head.

The *Luftwaffe* focused their daylight raids against airfields in Kent, Essex and Suffolk on 28 August. During the ensuing dogfights twenty-seven enemy aircraft were destroyed, but twenty RAF aircraft were lost, with nine pilots and three air gunners posted as missing or killed. Poor weather and low visibility meant that there was no enemy activity in No. 41 Squadron's sector.

That night's raids saw the first heavy attack on Liverpool with an estimated 150 aircraft engaged in air operations.

The following morning was relatively quiet, although the *Luftwaffe* launched a major attack on airfields to the south of London, with a later raid on the Rochester area. During a number of combats, nine RAF fighters were lost for the same number of enemy aircraft; two RAF pilots were killed.

The *Luftwaffe* made three major attacks in the east Kent and Thames areas during the afternoon of 30th, with the RAF's airfields once again the main objectives. The RAF claimed fifty-nine enemy aircraft destroyed, twenty-one as probables and twenty-nine damaged, for the loss of twenty-five aircraft and ten pilots killed or missing.

Hornchurch was bombed twice on 31 August, with damage to the apron and across the landing ground and ancillary buildings. The first of the day's raids resulted in damage to No. 54 Squadron's dispersal area, and the full extent of the damage was recorded in their Squadron Diary:

At 13.15 hours A large formation of enemy bombers – most impressive sight in vic formation at 15,000ft – reached the aerodrome and dropped their bombs (probably sixty in all) in a line from the other side of our dispersal pens to the petrol dump and beyond into Elm Park. Perimeter track, dispersals and barrack block windows suffered but no other damage to buildings was caused and the aerodrome, in spite of its ploughed-up condition, remained serviceable. The squadron was ordered off just as the first bombs were beginning to fall and eight of our machines safely cleared the ground. The remaining section, however, just became airborne as the bombs exploded. All the machines were wholly wrecked in the air. The survival of the pilots is a complete miracle. Sergeant Davis, taking-off across the airfield towards the hangars, was thrown back to the other side of the River Ingrebourne, two fields away, and scrambled out of his machine unharmed.

Flight Lieutenant Deere had one wing and his prop torn off: climbing to about a hundred feet he turned over and, coming down, slid along the aerodrome for a hundred yards, upside down. He was rescued from this unenviable position by Pilot Officer Edsall, the third member of the Section, who had suffered a similar fate, except that he had landed the right way up. Rushing across the aerodrome, with bombs still dropping, he extricated Flight Lieutenant Deere from his machine. 'The first and last time - I hope.' Was the verdict of these truly amazing pilots – all of whom were ready for battle again by next morning.

Al Deere later related how, once he had been extricated from the wreckage of his Spitfire, his yellow Mae West attracted the attention of one of the Bf 109 pilots who fired on him as he raced towards cover and one of the hangars, which was sprayed with bullets moments after he arrived.

The second raid arrived at 18.00 hours, with two Spitfires destroyed at dispersals, where one airman was killed.

The air battles in the south led to seventy enemy aircraft being destroyed; a further thirty-four were claimed as probables and thirty-three damaged. The RAF's losses were thirty-seven aircraft destroyed with twelve pilots dead or missing.

Next day three major raids were made on Fighter Command's airfields in Kent causing extensive damage, while in the afternoon the enemy flew reconnaissance sorties between the Humber and Lowerstoft. During these and other operations twenty-five enemy aircraft were destroyed, with a further ten claimed as probables and twenty-four damaged. The RAF lost fifteen aircraft with six pilots killed or missing.

The *Luftwaffe's* efforts were once again focused on airfields in the east Kent–Thames estuary area on 2 September, with a total of five raids during a day when Fighter Command claimed forty-one enemy aircraft as destroyed, with a further eighteen claimed as probables and thirty-two damaged. The RAF lost twenty aircraft with ten pilots safe.

The battle would soon enter a new and decisive phase, one in which Bennions and No. 41 Squadron would play a vital part.

Chapter 11

More Combat and Losses

On 3 September enemy activity began in the south-east of England at 08.30 hours, with a reconnaissance sortie to North Foreland which flew along the Kentish coast to Eastchurch, and out to sea by Dungeness.

Rarely out of action, Nos. 54, 222 and 603 Squadrons, based at Hornchurch, were heavily involved in the day's combats. No. 54 Squadron was scrambled four times and made contact with the enemy on each occasion.

The raids began at 09.15 hours, when twenty-plus enemy aircraft approached Deal but were intercepted off North Foreland, while a further eighty aircraft headed up the Thames estuary. Then came a raid against North Weald involving thirty Do 17s and fifty Bf 110s, which caught a squadron of fighters still refuelling from a previous patrol. Scrambled, the pilots were in the air when the bombs dropped but they were unable to gain sufficient height in time to engage the enemy. Other bombers from this raid flew towards Debden, Hornchurch, Thames Haven and Maidstone, while fifteen aircraft headed for Biggin Hill.

The second main raid of the day developed over France, crossing the Channel and bombing Manston at around 11.15 hours.

At 13.00 hours two raids of over a dozen enemy aircraft flew from Calais towards Foreness, where they were successfully driven off. An hour later six raids were engaged by four squadrons while off Kent, some of the raiders evading the fighters and entered the Thames estuary where they caused several casualties.

During the day's engagements twenty-five enemy aircraft were destroyed, while a further eleven were claimed as probables and ten more damaged. RAF casualties were fifteen aircraft destroyed with seven pilots killed.

Meanwhile, at 13.30 hours Squadron Leader Hood led a formation of No. 41 Squadron's Spitfires, including that flown by Pilot Officer Bennions. Taking off from Catterick, No. 41 Squadron was to relieve No. 54 Squadron who had been in the firestorm since 8 August: all of its pilots were exhausted.

The Hornchurch Station Diary summed up No. 54 Squadron's remarkable record:

> In the late afternoon, 54 Squadron left us for a period of rest and recuperation at Catterick. During the previous fortnight, they had been bearing the brunt of the work in the Sector, for they had to hold the fort, while various new squadrons arrived and settled down into the Sector routine. With the exception of two very short breaks, they had been with us continuously during the first year of the war, and in this period had destroyed ninety-two enemy aircraft.

Before entering No. 11 Group's airspace, No. 41 Squadron's Spitfires landed at Duxford where they were refuelled; a raid was expected in the Hornchurch Sector. It wasn't until 19.10 hours, with the immediate danger passed, that the aircraft took off on the twenty-minute flight to their new base.

It was a very different scene to the one they had left only a few weeks earlier. Bennions later recalled that the pilots experienced great difficulty in finding sufficient landing space due to recent bomb damage; the airfield had been targetted for over a week – there could be little doubt that over the following weeks the squadron would be fighting for its very survival.

At 06.45 hours on 4 September, Flight Lieutenant Ryder led 'A' Flight on a scramble. Once in the air they were vectored onto an enemy aircraft approaching a convoy at 17,000ft. On sighting the lone bomber, Ryder requested the Controller's permission for a section to peel off to engage. The delay meant that the chase proved inconclusive and the enemy aircraft escaped.

On landing 'A' Flight's aircraft were refuelled, the pilots remaining at dispersals ready for a second patrol which wasn't long in coming. Radar picked up a large force building across the Channel and in response the Controller ordered a squadron-strength scramble. Squadron Leader Hood led the Spitfires into the air at 08.45 hours, with orders to patrol. The enemy approached the coast, with one group of around eighty bombers and their escort flying towards the Thames estuary before heading for the airfields at Eastchurch, Hornchurch, North Weald and Debden. A second group of seventy aircraft crossed the coast near Lympne and flew on towards Biggin Hill. With RAF squadrons closing in on the enemy, the raid turned and had recrossed the coast by 09.45 hours.

The next raid didn't develop until 12.35 hours when five bombers were reported over Dover. Meanwhile, a much larger plot was tracked heading across the Channel, and at 13.00 hours the first of 200-plus enemy aircraft crossed the coast between Dover and Littlehampton before flying over Kent and Sussex, with one formation making for the Thames estuary and Gravesend, another for Kenley. At 13.25 hours, fourteen Bf 110s raided the Vickers Works at Brooklands, causing serious damage to the factory.

Squadron Leader Hood led a squadron scramble. In the air by 13.15 hours, the eleven Spitfires headed to intercept a formation which quickly turned back in the face of fighter opposition. The squadron patrolled until 14.30 hours due to the possible threat posed by about eighty enemy aircraft which remained on patrol in the Straits.

Later, between 17.30 and 17.50 hours, several small raids approached the coast near Dungeness but retired before the RAF's fighters could get in amongst them.

In turning back the day's raids the RAF destroyed fifty-two enemy aircraft, while nineteen were claimed as probables, with twenty-two damaged. RAF casualties amounted to seventeen aircraft lost and six pilots killed or missing.

Reich-Führer Adolf Hitler made a speech at the *Sportsplast* in which he signalled the beginning of the all-out night bombing offensive against British cities.

> It is a wonderful thing to see our nation at war, in its fully disciplined state. This is exactly what we are now experiencing at this time, as Mr Churchill is demonstrating to us the aerial night attacks which he has concocted. He is not doing this because these air raids might be particularly effective, but because his Air Force cannot fly over German territory in daylight. Whereas German aviators and German planes fly over English soil daily....
>
> For three months past, I have not ordered any answer to be given, thinking that they would stop this nonsensical behaviour. Mr Churchill has taken this to be a sign of our weakness. You will understand that we shall now give a reply, night for night, and with increasing force.
>
> And if the British Air Force drops two, three or four thousand kilos of bombs, then we will now drop 150,000, 180,000, 230,000, 300,000 or 400,000 kilos, or more, in one night. If they declare that they will attack our cities on a large scale, we will erase theirs!
>
> The English are wondering when the attack is going to begin. The English ask 'Why doesn't he come?' Be calm. Be calm. He's coming. He's coming....

By taking the pressure off the RAF airfields the terror campaigns against the ordinary citizens of Great Britain would prove to be a fatal mistake for the German campaign.

The squadron took off in the early light of 5 September and flew to Manston where they immediately refuelled ready for operations.

During the mid-morning a large enemy formation, estimated at 150 strong, was plotted heading for the coast near Romney. No. 41 Squadron was scrambled and Squadron Leader Hood led twelve aircraft south over Canterbury at 27,000ft, where they were joined by Nos. 501, 603 and 222 Squadrons.

Meanwhile, two enemy formations crossed the coast at around 09.40 hours, each composed of twenty Do 17s flying at 16,000ft, their escort of fifty-plus Bf 109s flying to the rear and side at up to 22,000ft.

Taking the squadron into the attack over Gravesend at 10.10 hours, Hood ordered Ryder to use 'A' Flight to fend off the Bf 109s, while he led 'B' Flight into the rear of the Do 17s, which were flying in tight squadron formation in vics of sections.

Diving down at the head of his section, Hood misjudged the sweep in behind the bombers and instead of being in position to attack the lead formation, and therefore cause the maximum disruption, 'B' Flight found themselves trying to catch up with the rear of the bombers. Gradually overhauling them, Hood and his wingman, Wally Wallens, fired a long burst into one Do17. The attack sent the bombers into confusion, clouds of white smoke emitting from the rear aircraft as pieces flew off. None could be claimed as destroyed as the Spitfires had to break off the attack as a number of Bf 109s from the flank escort were trying to get onto their tails, although Wallens claimed Hood's target crashed at Calais. It had been a daring attack, but when his engine began misfiring, Hood was forced to dive for cloud, limping his way back to Hornchurch.

Flying Officer Boyle, Green 3, had seen his CO in trouble and latched onto one of the 109s that had broken formation to attack the labouring Spitfire. He fired a four to five second burst at close range, sending it spinning down in flames.

Green 2, Flying Officer Wallens, had been flying close behind his CO during the initial attack and fired a quick burst at the bombers before he had to disengage when several 109s tried to get on his tail. Breaking hard to port, Wallens put his Spitfire into a steep dive, losing 8,000–10,000ft before finally pulling out. Climbing back up to the air-battle, Wallens managed to get behind a Bf 109, closing to 250 yards as it approached the coast. Pressing the gun button, he saw the de Wilde ammunition burst in the fighter's fuselage before it went into a steep dive, the pilot using all of his skill and luck to pull out. The Bf 109 was last seen streaming dense smoke as he tried to make for France, where it crashed at St Omer.

Flight Lieutenant Webster, flying as Blue 1, led his section in an attempt to strike at the bombers but their escort prevented a clear attack. He hit one

Bf 109 in the engine, then set the engine of another on fire after three failed attempts to get close to the bombers. Then, out of the corner of one eye, he saw a Spitfire being hotly chased by three 109s. Webster pursued the gaggle of twisting and diving aircraft as they wove their way though the sky, putting a burst of fire into the 109s and forcing them to break-off their attack. Then another Bf 109 presented itself as a target but dived down to tree-top height as Webster closed in for the kill. Using all of his skill, he managed to get a clear shot, damaging the fighter whose pilot was unable to regain altitude and plunged into the ground near Maidstone.

Meanwhile, Flight Lieutenant Ryder had put 'A' Flight into line astern and dived into the Bf 109s, claiming one as a probable. Bennions, flying as Ryder's No. 2, sighted two Bf 109s trying to get onto his tail and shouted a warning as he turned sharply into the enemy.

Bennions used a steep climbing turn to get onto the tail of a Bf 109 which he engaged and claimed as a probable, which was later upgraded to a confirmed kill. His victim was *Oberleutnant* von Werra of Stab II./JG3 whose aircraft was later finished off by Pilot Officer Stapleton of No. 603 Squadron.

Bennions' combat report read:

As Mitor Red 2 [flying X4343] in line astern of Red 1 while acting as rear guard to Blue and Green Sections, I noticed 2 Me 109s above and to the right diving to attack Red 1. I warned Red 1 and we turned right to evade them. We then turned left behind them to engage them. Half way around the turn I noticed another Me 109 about 800 yards astern and to the left. I immediately went into a steep right hand climbing turn at full throttle. The Me 109 tried to follow but after about 2 turns he fell out of the turn completely stalled, and I turned down on to his tail. He carried out a left hand climbing turn and headed S E at full throttle. I immediately closed astern but slightly left and opened fire at approximately 100 yards. After two very short bursts [560 rounds] I observed coolant pouring from the radiator. I was then almost colliding with him so I pulled out to the right and watched him throttle back and go down in a series of steep gliding turns. He appeared certain to go down to ground level since he was then at 6,000 feet 8 miles off Maidstone. So I left him to see if I could catch up with the main force. After heading SE for a few minutes I heard the ground station order all Mitor aircraft to pancake home base, so I returned and landed.

(signed) GH Bennions

Sergeant Carr-Lewty, (flying N3098) Yellow 2, managed to get a good shot at a Bf 109 which was seen to crash. His own aircraft was hit during the engagement, which took place over the Thames estuary at 10.20 hours. Carr-Lewty checked the controls, which remained responsive. He gauged that he had sufficient altitude to make Hornchurch on a dead engine but would need to radio base to prepare them for an emergency landing and so decided against the move: 'Because I might overload the R/T channels which other less experienced pilots, also in need of help, might need....'

Instead Carr-Lewty elected to 'go it alone', ignoring the second option, which was to take to his parachute as there were a number of villages in the close vicinity and he was fearful of his abandoned aircraft causing casualties on the ground. Having decided to search for a suitable landing ground, he spotted a triangular field on an upward slope: 'I had enough height in-hand to make a descending turn around the field for a final inspection, and manage to lower the wheels. I came in to land at 75 mph.

Carr-Lewty narrowly missed a haystack, gate and a hedge-line, touching down some 20 to 30 yards from the edge of the field near Standford-le-Hope. However, the heavy landing caused the undercarriage to collapse and his Spitfire skidded along the ground, causing damage to the underside of his aircraft and propeller.

During what was hectic dogfight, most of the squadron managed to get a shot at the enemy, the squadron's Intelligence Officer reporting:

Enemy Casualties:
2 Me 109   – F/L Webster
1 Me 109   – F/O Boyle
1 He 113 [Bf 109] – F/L Webster

Probable:
3 Me 109 – P/O Wallens, F/L Ryder, P/O Bennions [upgraded to a confirmed]

Damaged:
2 Do 17 – S/L Hood and P/O Wallens

While the Hornchurch squadrons were in the air, their airfield came under attack but was defended by No. 19 Squadron's Spitfires. Led into action by Squadron Leader P C Pinkham, the pilots attacked in flights, one taking on the Do 17s, the other their Bf 109 escort. Climbing into the sun, they were at a major disadvantage and their efforts to defend the airfield cost Pinkham his life, while two Spitfires were damaged but their pilots escaped injury.

Another enemy formation was plotted approaching the coast and at 10.50 hours a dozen Bf 109s attacked barrage balloons protecting Dover. The harbour's guns opened fire, destroying one enemy aircraft and damaging a second. Meanwhile, scattered raids were picked-up by radar heading inland over east Kent, but these petered out a little in the afternoon.

The Squadron's second active patrol of the day came at about 14.50 hours. A large plot was reported to the Controller: two raids composed of up to 120 enemy aircraft were approaching the coast off Kent, some heading for Biggin Hill and the remainder for Hornchurch. The telephone in dispersals rang and someone called-out: 'Squadron scramble!'

Squadron Leader Hood led the race to their aircraft. Also scrambled were the Hurricanes of No. 249 Squadron based at North Weald, along with Debden's Nos. 17 and 73 Squadrons, Northolt's Polish pilots of No. 303 Squadron and No. 46 Squadron from Stapleford.

Once in the air, No. 41 Squadron was vectored onto a large formation of He 111s and Ju 88s and their escort of Bf 109s from I./JG 54, which were reported as flying at 15,000ft over the Thames estuary. A little before 15.30 hours the raid, estimated at fifty-plus enemy aircraft, was intercepted as it crossed the coast near Dungeness.

The squadron had been scrambled too late to gain sufficient altitude to attack from above and was still climbing in close formation when suddenly the CO's voice came over the intercom ordering 'line astern and echelon port'. But before anyone had time to react they had already entered the enemy formation head-on. Bennions, Yellow 1(flying EB-L R6884), had gone into the attack slightly behind 'B' Flight and saw the Bf 109s coming in for the kill: 'Our closing speeds were so high that I only got one second bursts at the enemy aircraft as the raced passed. Although I got a squirt at a few aircraft there was no way of saying if there were any conclusive results.'

Bennions passed through the enemy formation where he found he was alone with no idea what had happened to the rest of the squadron. During the ensuing combat he claimed a Ju 88 destroyed over the Isle of Sheppey, and probably destroyed another.

Pilot Officer Bennions' combat report read:

As Mitor Yellow 1, I led Red Section (sic) to attack three of the formation of Ju 88s. I attacked one and after two bursts of about 2 seconds each the return fire from the Ju 88 cease and the port engine began to smoke. Then seeing an Me 109 diving from above I broke away to port. As the formation turned to starboard I came in again from underneath on to another Ju 88. I fired several short bursts – the wheels were lowered and the port engine exploded. I fired a further burst at the starboard engine and smoke began to pour from that. The e/a was well below the main formation with speed reduced. As my ammunition was exhausted I broke away and circled around one of our pilots descending by parachute north of Southend. I then heard Rival [The Sector Controller] order all Mitor a/c to pancake so I returned to base and landed.

(Signed) G. H. Bennions. P/O.

Flying as cover, above and to the rear, Flight Lieutenant Ryder, Red 1, led 'A' Flight into the attack. Ryder fired a five-second burst at a Bf 109 which had pounced on the rear aircraft in 'B' Flight; he followed it down, streaming flames before it suddenly erupted into a fire-ball.

Somehow, Pilot Officer Eric Lock, Red 2 (flying N3162), managed to pass through the fighter escort and fire a burst at close range, sending one He 111 into the Thames estuary.

I was Red 2 flying in formation with the rest of the squadron. When we intercepted a formation of enemy aircraft we attacked the bombers first. After we engaged we broke away to port, and then I saw Red 1 shoot down an Me 109 which exploded in mid-air. It then developed into a dogfight. I then attacked an enemy *Heinkel* 111 which crashed into the river and followed it down.

I climbed back to 8,000 feet and saw another *Heinkel,* which had left the main formation. I attacked and set his starboard engine on fire. I closed in to about 75 yards and after two long bursts, smoke began to emerge from the fuselage.

The enemy aircraft then put his wheels down and started to glide; I stopped firing and followed him down. I was then attacked by a Me 109 who fired at me from below, wounding me in the leg. As he banked away he stalled turned; I fired at him and he exploded in mid-air.

I then followed the bomber down; it landed on the sea about ten miles from the first one in the mouth of the river. I circled around a boat which was at hand. I also flashed my downward light, and saw the boat go to the enemy aircraft. I was then joined by Red 3; on our return up river we saw the first bomber still floating, and a small rubber dingy.

Lock joined-up with Pilot Officer Morrogh-Ryan, Red 3, before landing back at base at 15.30 hours. Morrogh-Ryan had witnessed Lock's victories, also claiming a Bf 109 destroyed, while Sergeant Ford claimed a Bf 109 as probably destroyed.

The Bf 109s, meanwhile, attacked 'B' Flight, which lost four out of six aircraft. It is believed that Squadron Leader Hood's Spitfire may have been shot down by Timmerman of I./JG54 and that he attempted to bail out but his parachute deployed early and became entangled with his aircraft. His Spitfire (P9428) crashed in several large sections near Nevendon, its ammunition expended in combat. It is not know if Hood's body was recovered, although the Barking & Dagenham burial register records on 12 September the internment at Becontree Cemetery in Grave B1:684 of a '*Hauptman* Walter Heatz'. This body was never reinterned on Cannock Chase, Staffordshire, with all of the other German casualties of the two World Wars as his name does not tally with any *Luftwaffe* records. It remains a possibility that the misidentified body might be that of Squadron Leader Hood.

When Hood failed to return he was posted as missing and his name was, with particular regret, wiped from the duty board.

During the engagement Webster (flying R6635) may have collided with a Hurricane of No. 73 Squadron flown by Flight Lieutenant R E Lovett, the wreckage crashing near Markham Chase School, Laindon, Essex, at 13.25 hours. A blood-stained parachute pack marked 'Webster' was later discovered by schoolboy Roland Wilson on his father's land at Framptons Farm, near Nevendon Church. The parachute had not been used, while the webbing harness straps had been ripped to pieces in the crash impact.

'Wally' Wallens, flying as Blue 2, later recorded the head-on attack:

> As usual I was flying Number 2 on 'Robin' Hood leading 'B' Flight and, being unable to gain height advantage and position in time, 'Robin' put us in line-astern and open echelon port and attacked head-on, a desperate manoeuvre that could age one very prematurely. Within seconds all hell broke loose and, as the action developed, 'B' Flight was overwhelming attacked by the 109s.

> Four Spitfires from 41 Squadron failed to return this engagement. Pilot Officer Tony Lovell had parachuted out of his burning aircraft over South Benfleet and returned to Hornchurch.

Wallens recalled the combat that occurred at 15.30 hours:

> After opening fire at the bomber coming so rapidly towards us, I had broke away violently and escaped the attacking 109s, diving vertically to 10,000 feet and climbing nearly as steeply back up sun. Turning, with the westering sun behind me, I searched for the action which, as ever, had moved away.

> On a south-easterly heading, and jinking, I caught up with two 109s below returning home in open formation and, seeing no cover, attacked one with long burst, which destroyed it. Then, like a foolish virgin, the most simple of novices, I committed the cardinal error and, instead of breaking violently away, slid across after the other.

So [as] I lined the 109 up in my reflector sight the roof fell in on me, and I cursed the stupidity that would probably cost me my life. Of course, the Jerries were not fools, keeping a tail cover for protection, and I had fallen for it.

The 109, which I glimpsed screaming down had opened up, luckily at maximum range, and raked me with heavy and concentrated fire before I could move. The din was indescribable.

Wallens felt the hits as the 109's cannon and machine gun fire tore great chunks out of his aircraft's wings. One round exploded within the cockpit and his instrument panel disintegrated while the armoured glass windscreen was scored on the inside but remained intact: 'My leg went numb with a hammer blow that, strangely, did not seem to hurt at all, as a cannon shell tore it apart.'

Wallens had frozen for a second but suddenly reacted and broke violently to port. Despite suffering severe damage, he was able to maintain control and level out, but he could hear that the engine was misfiring and thought it was about to seize or disintegrate. He gingerly tried the controls to measure the aircraft's responses: they were not good and he decided that his only chance was to bail out. Pulling for the canopy jettison, Wallens found it didn't work. Reaching up for the handle to pull to back manually he discovered that it was jammed.

Forced to stay with his crippled Spitfire, Wallens headed for Hornchurch, searching for a field in which to make a crash landing; he was losing height rapidly. Wallens was four miles from safety when the Merlin finally failed and, too low to glide to base, he dropped it down in the nearest flat stretch of ground, crashing through a fence before flying across an open ditch and ending up in the next field.

Wallens was trapped in his shattered Spitfire (X4021) and had to be rescued by two farm workers who had seen his descent and raced across the fields to his aid.

'Wally' Wallens was taken to Orsett Hospital with serious leg injuries. While the squadron remained in the Sector his pals were able to drop by when they were off-duty, or quite literally pay a flying visit if they were on duty: 'Sometimes they'd fly past my window and wave to me. Some days, someone wouldn't come past the window and I knew he'd gone and I'd never see him again.'

Following a spell on Air Sea Rescue, Wallens would return to combat in 1944, flying operations over France and Holland, earning the DFC.

Meanwhile, another aircraft, that flown by Flying Officer Lovell, was badly hit while in combat over the Thames estuary at 15.30 hours. Disconnecting the oxygen and radio, Lovell undid his safety harness, closed the throttle and pulled the canopy back before bailing out dangerously low, his mad rush earthwards abruptly halted as his Irvin parachute deployed, leaving him gently swaying in the harness. A heavy landing led to a twisted ankle as the ground raced up to meet him. Lovell's aircraft (R6885) crashed and burned out relatively harmlessly in Kimberly Road, South Benfleet. Distressed at the possibility that the wreckage might have claimed casualties on the ground, Lovell, insisted on being taken to the scene of the crash before his own injuries were treated.

Bennions recalled how Lovell, who was a devout Roman Catholic, would go to visit the station padre after shooting down one of the enemy. He would be seen ploughing a lonely furrow at dispersals, pacing up and down deep in his own thoughts and prayers and with no malice towards the *Luftwaffe* air crew.

The remnants of the patrol made their way back to base where they reported to the Intelligence Officer and filed their combat reports. All were anxious to find out what had happened to Hood and Webster. Meanwhile, the ground crew refuelled and rearmed their aircraft in preparation for further combat.

Wallens reported having heard an explosion within the formation and it was at first believed the pair might have collided – it remained a possibility that they might have bailed out.

Following the air battle a strong enemy formation numbering some seventy-plus aircraft patrolled the Straits of Dover, while a seaplane rescued a German air crew off Ramsgate. Meanwhile, Nos. 10 and 12 Groups provided patrols over Tangmere and North Weald.

The Squadron was scrambled at 16.15 hours and ordered to patrol. With the failure of Hood and Webster to return from the last mission, it was Ryder who took temporary charge of the squadron, leading nine Spitfires into the air. After patrolling for nearly an hour they were ordered to land at 17.20 hours.

The squadron's claims for the day were four Bf 109s destroyed and three allowed as probables, with two Do17s damaged.

The Air Ministry claimed thirty-six enemy aircraft destroyed, with twenty-two probably destroyed and a further seventeen damaged. Twenty-three RAF fighters were lost, with eleven pilots killed or missing, two of these from Bennions' No. 41 Squadron,

Squadron Leader (26110) Hilary Richard 'Robin' Hood, DFC, RAF, was the son of John L B Hood and Helene M Hood (*née* Lessel). He was 32. Hood's body was never recovered and he is remembered on the Runnymede Memorial, Panel 4.

Squadron Leader Hood was awarded the DFC, the announcement appearing in the *London Gazette* of 29 March 1941:

Air Ministry 27 May 1941
Royal Air Force.
The King has been graciously pleased to approve the following awards:-

Award of the Distinguished Flying Cross

Squadron Leader Hilary Richard Lionel HOOD (26110) (deceased) – with effect from 11th August 1940.
The above awards are for gallantry and devotion to duty in the execution of air operations.

Flight Lieutenant (37436) John Terence 'Terry' Webster, RAF, was cremated and is remembered on the Darlington Memorial in Durham, Panel 4. Webster was born in Liverpool and had served with the squadron since 11 April 1938.

Webster had been awarded the DFC in 1940, having destroyed eleven enemy aircraft with two shared destroyed, and had one unconfirmed destroyed. The award was announced in the *London Gazette* of 30 August 1940:

The King has been graciously pleased to approve the under-mentioned appointments and awards, in recognition of gallantry displayed in flying operations against the enemy:

Award of the Distinguished Flying Cross
Acting Flight Lieutenant John Terrance WEBSTER (37436)
Flight Lieutenant Webster has led his flight in innumerable offensive patrols during the latter part of the Dunkirk operations and during the intensive air fighting over the English Channel and Dover area in protection of shipping. With great skill and gallantry he has personally destroyed seven enemy aircraft and assisted in the destruction of two others. One day in August, 1940, he and another pilot of his section engaged considerably superior numbers of enemy fighters. Three were destroyed by this officer. Not content with this, he also attacked an enemy torpedo boat with considerable success. His faculty for seeking out and engaging the enemy has been outstanding.

Webster's finally tally was eleven destroyed, two shared destroyed, one probably destroyed and five damaged.

With the loss of both Squadron Leader Hood and Flight Lieutenant Webster, the obvious choice was to make Ryder acting CO. Many of the pilots, including Frank Usmar, however, hoped that Lovell and Bennions would be promoted in the field and that Bennions would become commander of 'A' Flight. In the event, Flight Lieutenant Ryder remained as acting CO while awaiting a new commander; Bennions would continue to act as a flight commander but without the rank.

Ryder had already led the squadron on numerous combat missions. He recalled:

> As a leader of the Squadron, I felt it was my duty to get the boys into the scrap on the best terms I could squeeze out of the situation; not to charge off personally and let things sort themselves out as fate dictated. Perhaps the most debilitating aspect was not the air combat, but the 'combat waiting'. This really sorted out the weaker spirits. We were up in the dark and groping around our aircraft before dawn. Then into our Mae Wests and the long day commenced. A fighter pilot's role is quite unique. Once the hood was closed, he was alone with his thoughts and fears. If he turned away from trouble and took on the lonely smoking target, he alone knew about it and all of us can be hard on ourselves. Another thought for him to carry during the long wait on the ground. Knowing that if he failed again, then all self-respect would be gone and the Squadron had a weak link.
>
> I made it a rule when in charge of the Squadron that the newest or weakest pilot flew as wingman to myself, or Tony Lovell if in 'B' Flight. We could both do our jobs and look after the new boy. Your eyes definitely became 'skinned' in time and you could see things you had no hope of doing during the early stages. Some would come home with bullet holes in their aircraft, yet professed to having seen nothing or felt nothing. Perhaps the worst handicap was having to fight with only one side of the cockpit hood clear of ice, the other opaque and useless. This was due to the torque sweeping the hood in a corkscrew fashion. It did not always occur, but often enough at 30,000 feet plus. I had the Hornchurch Wing above 30,000 feet, a number of times and the Squadron up to 36,000 feet – quite high with no body heating and probably four pairs of gloves. Frostbite was not that uncommon.

The air campaign continued to intensify and on 6 September RAF Stations in the south-east received a signal placing them on No. 2 Alert – which meant an 'attack probable within the next three days.' Meanwhile, Air Vice Marshal Keith Park relayed instructions to his squadrons ordering them to ensure they protected the aircraft factories, which were believed to be the *Luftwaffe's* next target of choice.

There were three major attacks launched against the south coast of England and the Thames estuary area during the day, the enemy also targeting aircraft production by bombing the Supermarine factory at Southampton and the Hawker factories at Kingston-on-Thames.

The first attack began at 08.40 to 09.50 hours with 300 enemy aircraft crossing the coast in a wide fan between Dover and Dungeness, parts of the raid penetrating as far as Biggin Hill and North Weald.

No. 41 Squadron was scrambled, with Flight Lieutenant Ryder receiving instructions to lead the ten Spitfires on a patrol of base at 20,000ft.

They were close to their operational altitude when Pilot Officer Lock passed out due to oxygen failure. His aircraft peeled off the formation and plummeted 12,000ft before he recovered consciousness and somehow wrestled his Spitfire out of its steep dive. Now flying alone, he sighted a Ju 88 over the English Channel, which he chased back over France and shot down. The aircraft was seen to dive nearly vertically, leaving a streak of smoke and flames before crashing twenty miles behind Calais. This was in flagrant breach of Keith Park's order that no enemy aircraft should be pursued over the Channel. Meanwhile, the rest of formation returned to Hornchurch without anything further to report.

A second raid, numbering 200-plus hostiles, was plotted massing over France, and at 12.50 hours No. 41 Squadron was scrambled and ordered to patrol over Hornchurch, the enemy crossing the coast between Dover and Dungeness five minutes later. The raid was followed by a number of other smaller formations, focusing on targets in Kent and Sussex, some reaching as far as Debden and Hornchurch. Four squadrons from No. 12 Group were called upon to support No. 11 Group's fighters.

The Spitfires of No. 41 Squadron patrolled but were unable to engage the enemy and Flight Lieutenant Ryder led them to their forward base at Rochford, where they landed at 13.45 hours and were refuelled. The last of the raids had recrossed the Channel by 14.00 hours.

The third phase of the day's attack began at 17.45 hours and lasted for about an hour. Fifty enemy aircraft crossed the coast between Maidstone and the Thames estuary heading for Hornchurch.

No. 41 Squadron was scrambled at 17.35 hours when Ryder led eight Spitfires on a patrol. Ryder detailed Bennions (flying R6884) and Sergeant Usmar of Green Section to act as rear cover, patrolling 5,000ft above the main formation and keeping as best they could to the cloud cover. Twenty minutes into the patrol and while flying east of Eastchurch, Bennions sighted two formations of four Bf 109s emerging from cloud some 500ft above 'B' Flight and diving onto Ryder's Red and Yellow Sections. Bennions called out a warning, which came just in time and the Spitfires had precious seconds to take evasive action. Turning the tables on the enemy, Ryder doggedly pursued one Bf 109, lining it up in his sights and firing short bursts before finally seeing it explode and fall into the sea off Southend pier. Flying Officer Mackenzie sent a Bf 109 down smoking, firing the remainder of his ammunition into another which was flying at low altitude. The enemy fighter was badly damaged and made a forced landing in a cornfield near Canterbury.

During the same engagement Flying Officer Lovell, flying as Yellow 2, claimed a Bf 109 destroyed. This aircraft was probably Bf 109E (3225) of III./JG27, which came down by the Nore boom at 16.15 hours after combat over the Thames estuary. The pilot, *Oberleutnant* Scheuller, was captured.

The engagement took place at 4,000ft, 15 miles north of Manston, Lovell's Combat Report reading:

> We attacked several ME 109s and I chose one that was flying fast. I chased him for 25 miles and gave him a four seconds burst. His left wheel came down, white fumes came out of his engine and he dived for the sea. He turned south and started climbing, so I closed in again and gave him a 7 seconds burst, whereon he blew up and spun into the sea. I returned to forward base.

Meanwhile, Flying Officer Scott and Sergeant Darling were both awarded one Bf 109 as probably destroyed.

Flying top cover, at around 19,000ft, Bennions (flying R6884) had singled-out the rearmost aircraft of a formation of Bf 109s as they were about to dive down on the remainder of the squadron. Switching on his gunsight, he positioned himself behind the enemy aircraft for the kill before pressing the firing button, unleashing the eight 0.303 Brownings with an almost deafening roar. Moments later he attacked and destroyed the rear fighter of a second formation, sending it crashing in flames into the marshes on the Thames estuary.

Bennions' combat report confirmed the details:

> Blue section was ordered to act as rearguard to Red and Yellow section. In company with Sergeant Usmar, I remained above and behind when Red and Yellow sections went down to attack and I carried out turns above them and saw two groups of five Me 109s turn down towards Red and Yellow sections. I turned in behind the last one of the second and opened fire from astern and slightly left at about 150 yards range. The aircraft burst into flames and the hood came back towards my aircraft, the remainder of the enemy aircraft went down in flames and black smoke pouring from it. I turned about to starboard and attacked No. 5 of another

formation of Me 109s. I closed to approx. 150 yards again slightly left and astern. I fired another short burst of approx. 2 secs [fired 880 rounds in two 2 second bursts closing to 75 yards]. And the Me 109 burst into flames. Again the hood of the machine came back towards me and I saw the pilot make a parachute jump out of the left side of the aircraft. The aircraft went down in flames.

(signed) G.H. Bennions P/O

One of Bennions' victims was Bf 109 E-4 (1129), flown by *Unteroffizier* Hempel who was killed when his aircraft exploded; both victories were confirmed by Sergeant Usmar, who also claimed a Bf 110 as damaged.

The Squadron Operations Record Book recorded their haul as five Bf 109s destroyed, including Lock's destroyed during the earlier patrol, with a further three claimed as probably destroyed. During the day's engagements the RAF claimed forty-four enemy aircraft destroyed, with twenty as probables and seventeen damaged. RAF losses included twenty-two aircraft with seven pilots killed or missing.

Despite the combined efforts of eighteen squadrons, including one drawn from No. 12 Group, many of the bombers found their targets, including the oil storage tanks at Thameshaven. The resulting fires could not be put out and remained as a beacon for the night's raids.

That evening, at 8 pm an ENSA Concert Party performed at Hornchurch. A raid came overhead during the show, the workshop venue being peppered by spent shrapnel which showered down throughout the evening from the ack-ack guns. In the best theatre tradition, however, the performance continued albeit in heavily subdued lighting.

Saturday 7 September saw the beginning of a new phase of the Battle of Britain, with the *Luftwaffe's* daylight raids transferring their main focus to London, while night raids were aimed at the East End and the Docks.

At readiness since before dawn, the squadron had a tense morning with two false alarms, the first of which came when Flight Lieutenant Ryder led eleven Spitfires on a scramble at 09.25 hours with orders to patrol. The raid turned back early and the squadron was ordered back down to conserve fuel.

On landing twenty minutes later, the Spitfires were immediately refuelled, their pilots sitting in the cockpits on standby awaiting another scramble. The Controller telephoned dispersals at 10.00 hours, scrambling one section, Bennions leading Sergeants Howitt and Usmar on a patrol which landed twenty-five minutes later, the danger averted.

The first main raid of the day began at about 11.00 hours. After building up over the French coast, a force of seventy-plus enemy aircraft approached

Folkestone, attacking Dover and Hawkinge, with a part of the raid flying further along the coast towards Hastings.

In response to the raid the squadron received the order to scramble and Flight Lieutenant Ryder took off at the head of eleven Spitfires. Airborne by 11.05 hours, the squadron was ordered to patrol. The Spitfires landed back at base at 12.15 hours without results.

It continued to be a busy day and two flight-strength patrols were made in the Calais–Boulogne district between 13.00 and 15.00 hours.

At 15.15 hours ten enemy aircraft were reported patrolling the Straits and appeared to cross the coast near Lympne. No. 41 Squadron was scrambled and lifted off at 15.45 hours when they were vectored onto the enemy. During the engagement Bennions' aircraft (EB-L serial No. R6884) was hit by enemy fire and he was forced to make a belly-landing at Rochford at 16.15 hours. His aircraft's undercarriage collapsed due to combat damage and he was unable to take any further part in the day's combats.

A second raid of 100-plus enemy aircraft began to arrive over Kent coast at 16.25 hours, with a further wave of around 250 aircraft following forty-five minutes later, targeting the Thames estuary, the east of London and the airfields both to the north and south of the capital. Nos. 222 and 603 Squadrons were in the air at 16.50 hours and were vectored onto the enemy. With No. 11 Group already stretched, five fighter squadrons from No. 12 Group were brought into the battle. The raid, by then estimated at nearly 1,000 enemy aircraft, was met by twenty squadrons in the biggest air battle thus far in the war.

Flight Lieutenant Ryder had led eight Spitfires on a scramble at 16.30 hours, with orders to patrol home base when they came up against a formation of thirty-plus Do 17s with their forty Bf 109 escort.

Leaving two aircraft as top cover, Ryder led six fighters in a line astern attack against the bombers, making a single pass before dividing to make individual combats as suddenly friend and foe became embroiled in a wild melée, vying for position.

Ryder hit one Do 17 before breaking away to strike at the fighters, engaging the Bf 109s, firing short bursts at three, leaving the last with smoke pouring out: he was awarded one probable. Climbing back up to 20,000ft, Ryder made several more passes, firing on the bombers and exhausting the remainder of his ammunition before peeling off and heading for base where he re-armed and refuelled ready for the next scramble.

Flying Officer Scott, Yellow 1, attacked one Bf 109 and set its engine on fire before running out of ammunition. As he came alongside the enemy fighter, the German pilot signalled his surrender and made as if he were preparing to affect a forced landing near Dover, but was last seen flying at 200ft and still heading for the coast.

Sergeant McAdam, Yellow 2, experienced engine trouble and fell back but, looking for a target, found a Bf 109 which he hit and saw trailing smoke as it plunged in a vertical dive. He claimed it as destroyed. Regaining altitude, McAdam flew over London where he sighted and attacked a formation of Do 17s, destroying one and damaging a second. During the combat his aircraft was damaged and was set alight. He force-landed at Leonard Drive, Drakes Farm, Rayleigh, at 18.08 hours. McAdam escaped unhurt but his Spitfire (P9430) was partly destroyed by fire.

Another casualty was Sergeant Ford (flying N3266), who force landed between Confield Tye and Tinsleys Farm at West Hanningfield, Essex, at 17.45 hours, following combat. Ford was unhurt.

Pilot Officer Morrogh-Ryan's Spitfire (X4318) was damaged during combat. Shot down over Hornchurch, he forced landed in Kemsleys Field, Star Lane, Brickfields, Great Wakering at 18.20 hours.

The squadron's Intelligence Officer recorded their tally of one Bf 109 destroyed and two damaged, along with one Do 17 probably destroyed and another damaged, with two Do 215s damaged.

Of the Hornchurch Squadrons, the pilots of No. 222 Squadron had claimed six enemy aircraft as destroyed with a further five probably destroyed. Two of their Spitfires received slight damage. No. 603 Squadron lost one Spitfire with three more damaged, but without injury to any of their pilots.

A total of seventy-four enemy aircraft were destroyed with a further thirty-four claimed as probables and thirty-three damaged. The RAF's losses were twenty-seven aircraft destroyed with fourteen pilots killed.

The sirens had sounded across London at 16.45 hours, and within minutes the air was filled with the drone of enemy bombers, punctuated only by the pounding of ack-ack guns, before the first of thousands of 25kg and 250kg high explosive bombs – each He III could carry 40 x 25kg bombs or 4 x 250kg bombs – and incendiary bombs began to fall. Wave after wave of bombers followed throughout the night and the all-clear was not given until 05.30 hours the following morning, by which time an estimated 300 tons of high explosive bombs had fallen on the capital, causing around 2,000 deaths or serious injuries amongst the civilian population. This was the beginning of the London Blitz.

The ferocity of the raids had not been seen over Great Britain before and severely tested the capital's defences. Ninety-two guns protected London that night but within four days there would be nearly 200 batteries working with searchlight crews who scoured the skies for the enemy. Their beams, however, only penetrated to 12,000ft and so they were of very limited use. Without the aid of direction-finding technology, the gunners pointed their guns skywards and fired blindly, at a rate of ten rounds per minute; the shells set to explode at a pre-determined altitude rained down shrapnel on the streets and buildings below. Although the guns caused few casualties, the sound of their fire served to help maintain morale.

German radio reported the heavy bombing of London by day and night on what became known as 'Black Saturday', claiming that a thousand-plus bombers had flown over the East End of London during the raids:

> The streets in these quarters of London are torn up, many buildings have collapsed. Some subway stretches also fell in. Two gas works blew up and a large number of warehouses were destroyed....
>
> All this combined to create the impression of a blazing inferno, ghastly beyond human imagination....

Meanwhile Goering announced, on air, that he had personally taken charge of the *Luftwaffe's* campaign and that he had given the order to turn their attention from the airfields to the city of London.

The following morning, Winston Churchill visited the East End of London to see for himself the damage caused by the previous night's Blitz, the first of a campaign which would not end until 10 May 1941, with only a single night without air attacks. In all some 50,000 civilians were killed and many more injured.

Squadron Leader Robert Charles Franklin Lister was posted to command No. 41 Squadron on 8 September. Lister had won the DFC for his role in ground support operations flown against the Fakir of Ipi during the operations in Waziristan in 1937. He had suffered a fractured spine in a flying accident while adjutant of No. 614 Squadron, AAF, Cardiff. Following nine months in plaster, he was only allowed back onto flying duties in August 1940, and was posted following his conversion onto Spitfires at 7 OTU Hawarden.

Due to Lister's obvious lack of combat experience, Flight Lieutenant Ryder took the lead in the air until their new CO had a sufficient grasp of modern air combat to take over tactical control. Meanwhile, towards the end of the month Lovell would be made flight commander.

Under Squadron Leader Hood the NCOs and officers were free to play chequers or cards at dispersals without the restraints of rank. Lister, however, was less relaxed and called the NCOs into his office where he warned them that they would be court-martialed if they played cards at dispersals. The decision made the waiting for combat all the more intolerable and there would be no games, they just sat around looking glum and the pilots universally agreed that the waiting was far worse than combat itself.

There was little activity until around 11.00 hours when 100-plus enemy aircraft crossed the Kent coast. Twenty minutes later the Sector Controller scrambled No. 41 Squadron, and Flight Lieutenant Ryder led eleven Spitfires into the air with orders to patrol Dover, where they were 'bounced' by Bf 109s at 12.15 hours.

Flying Officer W J Scott (Flying R6756) was shot down in flames; no parachute was seen and his log book was annotated with the simple but very final words 'killed in action'. The remainder of the squadron somehow managed to escape the onslaught and returned to Hornchurch from their advanced airfield at Rochford at 15.20 hours.

A second raid began at about 19.30 hours, with thirty-plus enemy aircraft crossing the coast near Shoreham, while around 100 bombers of *Luftflotte 3* targeted London as a prelude to that night's bombing.

During the day's daylight raids the RAF claimed four enemy aircraft destroyed with three more claimed as probables and a further eight damaged. The RAF lost four aircraft with two pilots killed. Included in these casualty figures was 'Jack' or 'Scotty' Scott.

Flying Officer (70611) William John Moir Scott, RAFVR, was the son of William Moir Scott and Katherine Ellen Scott, of South Kensington, London. He was buried in his birthplace at Dundee Western Cemetery, Angus, Scotland, Section 19, Grave 25c. He was 25 and had attained a BA at Canterbury.

German radio reported the heavy bombing of London and the development of the aerial assault: 'For weeks the British people have been deluded into believing that the German raids on London had been repulsed. In reality no such raids took place. They did not begin until yesterday.'

There were minor raids hitting Clacton and targets from Beachy Head to Central London during the following morning. While at around 16.15 hours radar located a formation of enemy aircraft building in the vicinity of Calais/Boulogne, and twenty minutes later the plot was monitored crossing the Channel.

No. 41 Squadron was already at a high state of readiness and at 16.44 hours the Controller ordered a squadron scramble. Flight Lieutenant Ryder led the formation. Once in the air, they were ordered to patrol between Maidstone and south of London. The squadron climbed to around 20,000ft. Bennions and Ryder had earlier discussed how they had rarely met the enemy on their own terms and this time they were determined to get the upper-hand. Meanwhile, at 16.55 hours, the enemy, numbering some 300 aircraft, crossed the coast between North Foreland and Dover, heading for the Thames estuary and south London, their targets including the aircraft factories.

Following the Controller's vector, No. 41 Squadron located a formation of He 111s and their Bf 109 escort at around 17.50 hours, on the homeward leg over Brighton and flying some 2–4,000ft below. Ryder immediately put the squadron into position and gave the order to attack.

During the ensuing combat Ryder shot down one Bf 109 and claimed a second damaged, while Lock destroyed two Bf 109s over Maidstone.

Bennions (flying X4343) attacked two Bf 109s, one of which he destroyed between Maidstone and south London, the engagement taking place at 15,000ft. His combat report read:

> After Red Section broke away I took my lead of Mitor Squadron and asked for pip squeak zero – I did not get into communication with Rival so I maintained patrol with remainder of Squadron and climbed to 31,000 feet. While patrolling there I noticed a large formation of aircraft approximately 10 miles to the North west.
>
> I turned in to attack from the sun and ordered Blue Section to attack the highest section of Me 109s, and the remainder to attack the aircraft below.
>
> I engaged the outermost of the Me 109s and after 3 bursts of approximately 3 seconds each [opening fire at 200 yards and closing to 75 yards], the enemy aircraft burst into flames with black smoke pouring from the side, rolled over to the left and went down.
>
> I then took avoiding action from an aircraft in the rear, and eventually discovered it to be a Hurricane.
>
> (Signed) G.H. Bennions

Bennions landed back at base at 18.15 hours.

Sergeant Usmar shot at one Bf 109, which was already in a dive, while a second fighter peeled off to the right and climbed into the sun ready to come down behind him. This was something he later confessed that his former flight commander, Terry Webster, had warned him against doing, because the enemy fought in pairs and a second Bf 109 was sure to pick him off. Firing a long burst, Usmar saw blue-black smoke emerging from the enemy aircraft. Just at that moment the second enemy fighter began firing on him and Usmar took avoiding action by flicking the Spitfire over and diving vertically from 20,000ft to sea-level over the beach before tree-hopping back to Hornchurch. Despite observing damage to the 109, Usmar's claim was reduced to a probable. The blue-black smoke could have been caused by the pilot ramming the throttle and mixture levers forward, over-boosting in order to make his escape.

No. 41 Squadron's combat claims were seven Bf 109s destroyed and one damaged, with one Bf 109 probably destroyed. In attacking the bombers, they destroyed one He 111 damaged; all without loss.

Meanwhile, No. 222 Squadron had attacked the same raid, claiming two Bf 109s destroyed and another allowed as a probable, while one He 111 was damaged. Twenty-four squadrons had been involved in combating the enemy, although there was widespread damage, with one bomb falling close to the Operations Room at Hornchurch.

During the day's air operations the RAF claimed fifty enemy aircraft destroyed with another nine probables and thirteen damaged, for the loss of twenty aircraft and five pilots killed or posted as missing. The Germans, meanwhile, had grossly over-estimated their successes, claiming twice the number actually destroyed.

The weather across the whole of the country was poor on 10 September, resulting in low visibility. After waiting at dispersals for most of the morning, Flight Lieutenant Ryder flew a weather reconnaissance at 10.50 hours. It was clear that there would be little enemy activity, although there remained the possibility of lone-raiders and reconnaissance missions.

The weather had improved towards the late afternoon and soon a raid began to develop, and at 15.30 hours some 250 enemy aircraft were plotted crossing the Kent coast, about thirty reaching central London and others bombing the Brooklands aviation factory. Meanwhile, Portsmouth was also targeted by another attack.

At 15.45 hours, a second wave of 100 enemy aircraft crossed the coast between Dungeness and Dover. Sixteen squadrons were scrambled to patrol the airfields and to intercept the enemy before they reached the capital. Some of the bomber formations attacked Dover, which was once again shelled by German long-range shore batteries based in France. During the day the RAF claimed two enemy aircraft destroyed and one probably destroyed.

Tension was high due to an increase in the invasion alert level and the warning bells were rung in some churches in the south of England, initiating defensive manoeuvres amongst both army and Home Guard units.

The sirens sounded across London in the late evening, heralding the beginning of another night of raids. Around 150 enemy bombers pounded the capital, while smaller raids hit Merseyside, Portsmouth, Poling, Tangmere and targets in north Wales.

The *Luftwaffe* flew a number of reconnaissance missions throughout the morning of 11 September, including sorties made over east Kent and the Thames estuary.

At readiness since early light, No. 41 Squadron's first scramble was made at 15.15 hours when Squadron Leader Lister flew in the company of Flight Lieutenant Ryder and nine others. The eleven Spitfires took off in squadron formation to deal with two raids consisting of twenty aircraft at 25,000ft and six-plus at 11,000ft, which crossed the coast near Dover and flew towards the Thames estuary and to Essex.

Once airborne, Sergeant I E Howitt (flying N3059) peeled off, detailed by the Sector Controller to act as a spotter in the Deal–Dover coastal area. Howitt reported a dozen Bf 109s at 15,000ft before sighting a second enemy formation, this time flying at 32,000ft over Dungeness and then, later, another approaching Folkestone. At this point he was attacked by a Bf 109. Howitt shook off the fighter and was able to resume his role, locating two more raids before his Merlin engine seized, as a result of combat damage to the oil cooling system. Using all of his flying skills Howitt was able to make a safe landing back at base at 16.30 hours.

Meanwhile, at 16.15 hours, the squadron was vectored onto the enemy, making contact with a formation of seventy to eighty Ju 88s and their Bf 109 escort flying at 20,000ft.

Flight Lieutenant Ryder led the squadron into the attack, peeling off to port in single file and diving 5,000ft out of the sun onto the centre of the Ju 88s, successfully dispersing the formation, claiming one as damaged.

Lock made several attacking passes on a Ju 88 which he followed down, seeing it crash in a field seventeen miles south of Maidstone. Then, while climbing back up to the battle he was attacked by a Bf 110, which he out-manoeuvred, placing it in his sights and using the last of his ammunition to send it down ten miles south-east of his earlier kill, a stream of acrid smoke marking its descent. By now Lock was running low on fuel and made for West Malling.

Pilot Officer Langley (flying X4325) attacked the bombers which were by this time over Sevenoaks, seeing his rounds strike a Ju 88 before his aircraft was hit from the rear and, with loss of control of his aircraft, he was forced to bail out at 16.35 hours.

Mackenzie had passed through the Ju 88s without getting a clean shot and so he pulled back hard on the controls and took his Spitfire up to 30,000ft. Spotting a lone He 111 making for the coast, he pounced giving it a long burst from astern and sending the bomber into a shallow dive. Losing altitude, Mackenzie tried to evade another fighter, which turned out to be Lock, who had witnessed the victory.[1]

Bennions (flying X4343) was attacking one of the Bf 110s escort over Maidstone when suddenly his cockpit was filled with a blinding flash as he was hit by a cannon shell.

Bennions' combat report read:

Leading Blue Section, 41 Squadron Red and Blue Sections dived on to the main formation of bombers and Me 110 escort fighters in an attempt to break the formation. I attacked a section of 6 Me 110s. The first one that I fired at turned over on its left side and dived away. My closing speed was so great that I could not see what damage if any had been inflicted. I continued to fire at the a/c in front, firing short bursts [2-second bursts at 200 yards, closing to 50 yards] and then climbing slightly and diving on to the next one.

After the third attack I received a good burst in the starboard side of my a/c and felt a short sharp pain in my left heel. I broke away and found that my guns would not fire owing to the air bottle having been pierced by bullets. My brakes, flaps and guns would not function and my top petrol tank was pierced, so I returned to base and landed.

(Signed) G.H. Bennions.

With his shoe full of blood, Bennions hobbled to see the MO who extracted the shell splinter and put a few stitches into the wound. Despite the obvious pain, he was flying again the following day.

The Squadron's Intelligence Officer filed the following report on the engagement:

Most of the Squadron got in a burst. Just prior to the break through and during which time they were under heavy return fire they actually broke the rear half of the main formation and the Squadron, now dispersed continued to attack individual targets. About 25 Ju 88s formed a defensive circle and F/Lt Ryder saw several Spitfire a/c diving through and firing short bursts at any e/a that presented a target.

The Squadron was ordered to preserve its ammunition and about 10 minutes after the initial attack was told to patrol Home Base to engage about 50 e/a approaching from the south east. Squadron a/c was reforming over Home Base angels 15 but were then given the order to 'pancake'.

Our casualties: 2 aircraft Category 3 and 2
                   Pilot P/O Bennions slightly wounded
Enemy Casualties: 1 He 111 K destroyed – landed
                   1 Ju 88 damaged (port engine)

Meanwhile No. 603 Squadron's 'B' Flight had joined other No. 11 Group squadrons in engaging an enemy formation of 100-plus Bf 109s, Bf 110s and He 111s over south London, making several claims.

During the day's engagements the RAF claimed eighty enemy aircraft destroyed and a further thirty-four probably destroyed, with forty-four damaged. Nine enemy aircraft were credited to ack-ack batteries, with the same number damaged. RAF losses were twenty-eight destroyed with seventeen pilots killed or missing.

A German High Command communiqué claimed fifty-four RAF fighters destroyed, for the loss of only eighteen *Luftwaffe* aircraft.

That night the bombers returned to London and Merseyside, the German *New British Broadcasting Service* warning the capital's population to: 'Leave London now. The central districts are marked down for destruction as surely as was the riverside.'

Bad weather intervened. There was heavy rain throughout much of the following morning and it wasn't until 12.10 hours that ten of the squadron's Spitfires flew through the rain to their advanced base at Rochford. Here Bennions and the other pilots waited for the day's raids to develop. However, while the *Luftwaffe* flew a number of reconnaissance missions, including those in the Dover area and over the Thames estuary, there were few raids, and after a tense few hours at dispersals the squadron returned to Hornchurch where they were stood down. The situation was the same for much of Fighter Command and as a whole, the RAF's claims for the day were one enemy aircraft destroyed and three damaged.

The poor weather of the previous day continued on 13th and there was further welcome respite for Fighter Command's battle-weary pilots and ground crews.

There was, however, a window in the thick cloud and at 10.50 hours one section flew to their forward base at Rochford but no operational patrols were made, although a number of small raids were flown over Kent and the south London area, targets including Dover, Rochford and Biggin Hill. During one attack Buckingham Palace was straddled by bombs, two landing eighty yards from the King and Queen who were meeting the King's Secretary, Sir Alexander Hardinge. The Queen later remarked: 'I'm glad we've been bombed. It makes me feel I can look the East End in the face.'

The weather improved as the day went on and towards the early evening London was once again subjected to raiders.

Adolf Hitler met with his High Command in Berlin on 14th, further postponing the invasion. Goering had insisted that all he needed to destroy Fighter Command was 'five consecutive days of bombing', but he had grossly underestimated the British resolve and that of Dowding's 'Fighter Boys'.

On the same day Lock was flying at 32,000ft, acting as spotter when he saw a dozen Bf 109s at 25,000ft near Dover and dived to attack the rear of the formation.

Lock's combat report, which was not timed, read:

I attacked the last section of the formation, which were flying in a diamond shape. I was just about to close in, when I was attacked from above by some Me 109s. They peeled off from about 3,000 feet above and carried out a head-on attack on me. I waited till one of them was in range, and gave him a long burst of fire. He passed a few feet above me. I carried out a sharp turn to the right and saw him in flames. Just then I was attacked again from head on. I waited till he was at point blank range. I saw my bullets go into the enemy aircraft, and as he was about to go underneath me I gave him another burst.

I then saw more enemy aircraft coming down on me, so I half rolled and dived through the clouds. I had just passed through the clouds when I saw someone who had bailed out; I followed him down to the ground. I am pretty certain it was a Me 109 pilot, as I saw he was wearing a tin hat. I saw some of our troops rush up to him, and he appeared to be holding up his arms. I flew low over the field and he waved back. This was afterwards confirmed by the police.

At 13.40 hours the squadron took off for their forward base at Rochford, where No. 222 had landed only a few minutes earlier. Here they remained at readiness, despite the lack of activity in the squadron's sector. At 15.20 hours, however, around 150 enemy aircraft crossed the coast between Deal and Dungeness. One formation headed to attack the capital via the Thames estuary and another from the south-east. Ten minutes later Nos. 222 and 603 Squadrons were scrambled to intercept a formation of Bf 109s approaching the Canterbury area, the former losing three Spitfires with one pilot killed.

No. 41 Squadron was scrambled at 15.50 hours, when Flight Lieutenant Ryder was at the head of ten aircraft, including one flown by Squadron Leader Lister.

During the engagement Squadron Leader Lister was wounded and bailed out of Spitfire R6605 – he had been flying at the rear of the formation and had been jumped by a high-flying Bf 109 which came down from out of the sun. Once more Norman Ryder would assume command, now until the arrival of Squadron Leader Don Finlay.

A second raid began to develop at 18.10 hours, when the first of seven formations, each consisting of between a dozen to thirty aircraft, crossed the coast at Dover and Lympne. The enemy's targets were the capital along with the airfields at Kenley, Biggin Hill, Northolt and Hornchurch.

Ten fighter squadrons were scrambled, including No. 41 Squadron, with Flight Lieutenant Ryder leading. In the air with orders to intercept, they were vectored onto the enemy, which had just crossed the coast. The squadron sighted and engaged a formation of seven Bf 109s flying at 31,000ft. During the combat that followed, the squadron was able to claim two Bf 109s as destroyed. Meanwhile, Hornchurch's Nos. 222 and 603 Squadrons also engaged the enemy, the latter claiming one Bf 109 as destroyed.

During the day, raids struck Cardiff, Ipswich, Farnham and Gloucester, the RAF claiming fifteen enemy aircraft destroyed, three as probably destroyed and a further twelve as damaged, for the loss of twelve fighters with eight pilots safe.

That night the *Luftwaffe* returned to attack London.

Notes

1. Mackenzie later shot down *Messerschmitt* Bf 109s on 5 and 30 October and again on 17 and 27 November 1940, and was awarded the DFC before becoming a Fighter Controller at Catterick in April the following year.

   Mackenzie's DFC was promulgated in the *London Gazette* of 15 November 1940:

   Air Ministry 15 November, 1940
   Royal Air Force

   The King has been graciously pleased to approve the following awards in recognition of gallantry displayed in flying operations against the enemy:

   Awarded the Distinguished Flying Cross

   Flying Officer John Noble MACKENZIE (40547), No. 41 Squadron.

   Flying Officer Mackenzie has flown with the squadron since the war began and has on numerous occasions led his squadron. He took part in the intensive air fighting covering the Dunkirk operations, and has since led his section with conspicuous success. Since 6 September, 1940, this officer has destroyed at least seven enemy aircraft and has at all times shown great skill, courage and determination in pressing home his attacks against superior numbers of the enemy.

Chapter 12

A Decisive Battle

A cloudless sky greeted the pilots as they were awakened with a mug of coffee at around 04.30 hours on the morning of 15 September. Dowding had already studied the RAF's meteorological reports and knew there was likely to be renewed heavy activity.

The early morning, however, remained quiet and it wasn't until about 11.00 hours that radar began to pick up plots around Calais, where a large number of enemy aircraft were gathering in preparation for a raid. Climbing through cloud the Do 17s lost their tight formation, and had to re-group before rendezvousing with their escort, twenty Bf 109s from three *Gruppen*. Winston Churchill, who was paying a surprise visit to the control room at Group Headquarters, Uxbridge, looked on as the raid developed and as Keith Park ordered two of the Biggin Hill squadrons into the air before the first enemy crossed the French coast. Meanwhile, on a separate plot, a hit and run raid of twenty bomb-carrying 109s and their escort crossed the Channel.

At 11.20 hours the order was given for the Kenley, Hendon, Middle Wallop and Hornchurch squadrons to scramble as the bombers and their escort crossed the south-east coast, while Observer Corps reports led to a request for No. 10 Group to scramble a squadron to protect London from an attack from the south west. Five of the Duxford squadrons were ordered into the air to form a 'Big Wing' at 20,000ft and to patrol a line from Debden to Hornchurch. And finally, ten more fighter squadrons joined the ring around the capital, bringing No. 11 Group's commitment to sixteen squadrons. When Churchill asked what squadrons were held in reserve, he was informed that there were none.

With the fighters limited to under two hour's flying time, they would have to be used sparingly in combat and their return to base staggered in order to ensure that sufficient aircraft were refuelled, rearmed and ready to meet the next wave of attacks – it was an extremely delicate balance and failure to protect the airfields and Fighter Command's infrastructure could prove fatal.

The first wave of enemy aircraft numbered around 100 Do 17s of KG3 and III./KG76 along with 400 Bf 109s acting as their fighter escort. They crossed the Kent coast at 11.30 hours, with the Biggin Hill squadrons the first to engage the enemy. The Spitfires from Nos. 72 and 92 Squadrons had been scrambled early enough to gain altitude and were some 6,000ft above the bombers and 3,000ft above the enemy fighters when they caught up with the 109s. Meanwhile, the Spitfires of No. 603 Squadron were vectored onto the bombers. Next into combat were the Hurricanes of Nos. 501 and 253 Squadrons based at Kenley. As the bombers continued on their path, they were further hit by the Hurricanes of No. 229, while those of the Polish No. 303 Squadron closed in on their target.

Meanwhile, the Bf 109 fighter-bombers had overtaken the main force and were attacking targets of opportunity in and around London.

As the raid progressed, the bombers were closing in on London. Having fought their way through to the capital, the Bf 109 escorts were already running low on fuel and many were faced with a choice of either sticking with the bombers, which were being hit by a further wave of RAF fighters, or recrossing the Channel while they could still reach their home airfields.

The fire from the ack-ack batteries died down ahead of the next, and overwhelming fighter attack made by Nos. 17, 66, 73, 257, 504 Squadrons, closely followed by No. 41 Squadron, with No. 609 Squadron patrolling to the west.

Scrambled at 11.40 hours, Flight Lieutenant Ryder led ten Spitfires into the air with orders to patrol Gravesend at 20,000ft. Here they sighted and intercepted a formation of thirty Do 17s. While they closed to attack the bombers, an unseen formation of Bf 109s attacked them from above. Taking evasive action, Bennions (flying X4343) in 'B' Flight briefly got onto the tail of one fighter just west of Ashford. The pilot half-rolled and dived away with Bennions' Spitfire in hot pursuit. Firing three bursts of 2 seconds from 250 yards and closing to 75 yards, Bennions saw his rounds strike the Bf 109 which erupted into flames as the pilot, *Leutnant* Bertel, bailed out.

Bennions' combat report, timed at 11.50 hours, read:

Leader Blue Section I was attacked by Me 109. After a steep right hand climbing turn the Me 109 with a Yellow nose fell out of the turn and I turned on to his tail. He rolled over and went vertically downwards and pulled out heading south east as soon as he straightened up. I gave him three short bursts. He burst into flames and after knocking off his roof bailed out. The a/c hit the ground alongside a large wood north of the Railway line running west from Ashford. The pilot was still floating down when I left to try and pick up the enemy again.

(Signed) G. H. Bennions

Lovell also avoided the fighters as the Spitfires dived down to make their surprise attack. He managed to get onto the tail of one Bf 109, firing a decisive burst and seeing the canopy fly off moments before the pilot bailed out.

Meanwhile, Darling, who had also evaded the attacking Bf 109s and was patrolling around the Dover area, climbed up to 20,000ft from where he sighted and attacked a Do 17, one of a formation which was already heading for home. Lining up the bomber, Darling switched the gunsight on, the luminous spot seeming to travel along his target as he jammed his thumb on the gun button. The wings of his Spitfire shuddered as the eight Browning 0.303 machine guns burst into life, Mitchell's creation earning its name. Darling set the port engine alight before a Bf 109 intervened and he was forced to break off the attack.

As No. 41 Squadron left the conflict, five squadrons from Duxford's 'Big Wing' launched their attack. With few of the Bf 109s remaining close to the bombers, they proved easy targets, but the large number of fighters engaging them meant that they got in each other's way and multiple claims were made against the same enemy aircraft.

Despite Fighter Command throwing 167 fighters into the battle, around 100 enemy bombers successfully reached London. The British fighters did, however, cause mayhem among the returning aircraft, a pattern which would be repeated.

No. 41 Squadron had successfully destroyed two Bf 109s in flames with one Do 215 claimed as damaged, but at the height of the dogfight Pilot Officer G A Langley (flying P9324) was shot down by a Bf 109. His Spitfire crashed and burnt out at Wick House, Bulphan, near Thurrock at 12.30 hours.

Pilot Officer (81641) Gerald Archibald Langley, RAFVR, was the son of Archibald Frank Martin and Mary Elizabeth Langley, of Northampton. Langley was 24. He was buried at Abington (SS Peter and Paul) Churchyard, Northampton, Grave 13.00.

With another raid approaching, eight squadrons were scrambled at 14.00 hours. Once in the air they were ordered to patrol over Chelmsford, Hornchurch, Kenley and Sheerness in order to counter the threat.

Around 150 enemy aircraft crossed the coast near Dover, a second wave of 100 enemy aircraft following close behind, targeting south London and rail infrastructure around London and Kent.

Five minutes after the first RAF fighter aircraft took to the air and just as the second wave approached four more squadrons were scrambled to be joined by another eight, making twenty in total. Once again the Duxford 'Big Wing' was called upon to assist in the defence of London, while fighters from No. 10 Group were scrambled to the west of the capital – between them they would take a heavy toll on the enemy who had been told that Fighter Command was on the verge of extinction.

No. 41 Squadron took off at 14.10 hours, Flight Lieutenant Ryder leading, with orders to patrol at 25,000ft. Climbing rapidly in squadron formation, they joined Nos. 92 and 222 Squadrons in making the first contact with the enemy, engaging them over Romney Marsh. The enemy formation included up to thirty Do 17s and He 111s and their Bf 109 escort flying at 19,000ft. As the Spitfires prepared to go into the attack, Keith Park called upon Nos. 603 and 303 Squadrons, the only No. 11 Group units left in reserve – a total of 276 RAF fighters would be engaged.

Flight Lieutenant Ryder put the squadron in line astern before diving into the enemy fighters which were providing close cover; this tactic dispersed the bombers which headed into cloud. Ryder singled out one Do 17 which had been forced to break formation. This was also attacked by Pilot Officer Boyle and by several Hurricanes and came down near the Isle of Sheppey; the Bf 109s did not intervene.

Meanwhile, Boyle, who had been flying as 'Tail-end-Charlie', sighted three Bf 109s diving out of the sun as the initial engagement began. Attacking one head-on at 500 yards, he left it spinning down, trailing flames and smoke, before he made an attack on the bombers, sharing a Do 17 with Ryder.

Pilot Officer Baker, who had been flying in the company of Boyle, spun out of the first attack before joining Sergeant Darling, and together they passed through the He 111s, meeting the enemy head-on. Baker, having damaged one bomber, sighted a lone He 111 under attack from a number of Hurricanes and joined the chase and soon overhauled the *Heinkel*, closing to effective firing range. He gave the bomber a burst of fire and saw it descend onto mudflats on the Thames estuary. Baker, who had joined the squadron earlier that month, had already destroyed two enemy aircraft while flying with No. 610 Squadron based at Biggin Hill.

At about the same time, Darling witnessed one of the He 111s he had shot at fall away. Chasing the enemy he finished off his ammunition and last saw the bomber losing power in both engines and with its wheels down, either trying to land or having lost hydraulics.

During the same engagement, Pilot Officer Mackenzie hit a Bf 110 in the port engine sending it diving for cloud. Pilot Officer Lock joined three Hurricanes heading for the same number of Do 17s, which were closely escorted by a similar number of Bf 109s, all of which were flying above the cloud base. He assisted in the destruction of one of the enemy fighters before making stern and quarter attacks on a bomber, setting its starboard engine on fire. The Do 17 was seen to dive into the sea, breaking-up on impact. The bomber was awarded to Lock as a 'shared'.

As the dogfight developed, Lovell got a shot at a He 111 but without results. Then, placing himself close behind a Bf 109, he fired a more accurate burst, seeing it emit a plume of white smoke before disappearing into cloud; he was able to claim one Bf 109 destroyed. Lovell would destroy another Bf 109 on 20 October and on 17th and 27th November, while he was credited with a Ju 88 on 30 March 1941 before being posted away from the squadron. He flew throughout the hostilities, destroying eighteen enemy aircraft in the air and was five-times decorated for gallantry (DFC 1940, Bar 1942, DSO 1942, Bar 1945, US DFC 1944). Sadly, he was killed in a flying accident on 17 August 1945, two days after the end of the war with Japan.

Bennions (flying X4343) who reported seeing Bf 109s, Do 17s, and Bf 110s east of London flying at 30,000ft, engaged a Do 17, expending all of his ammunition [2,640 rounds], while chasing it half way back cross the Channel. He was frustrated to see it limp on despite obvious damage. The combat took place at about 14.30 hours.

Bennions' combat report read:

> After intercepting enemy aircraft, I engaged several Me 109s, eventually putting a short burst into one of them, which immediately pulled up and spun down into the clouds beneath. I could not see any sign of smoke or flames.
>
> Looking around, I found a large formation of 110s diving towards the cloud layer over Ashford. I attacked one but had to break away when attacked by an Me 109. After breaking away, I sighted a Do 17 and followed him over the coast near Dungeness.
>
> I closed to about 300 yards and fired 3 bursts of about 4 seconds each into the enemy aircraft [firing from 300 yards, closing to 100 yards]. The first burst was seen to strike the port side of the enemy aircraft and the second caused the starboard engine to start smoking. When I left the aircraft, it was at 2,000 feet, 4 miles south of Dungeness. Another friendly aircraft was attacking it.

(Signed) G.H. Bennions

On landing back at Hornchurch the pilots gathered round the squadron's Intelligence Officer and filed their individual combat reports. No. 41 Squadron claimed five enemy aircraft destroyed, two of which were *Messerschmitt* Bf 109 fighters. Three more aircraft were claimed as probables and a further two damaged; all without loss.

Of the other Hornchurch squadrons, No. 222 Squadron claimed three enemy aircraft destroyed, two probables and one damaged, while the attack was a disaster for No. 603 Squadron. They claimed one Bf 109 but lost two pilots killed, including their CO, Squadron Leader George Denholm.

The remaining bombers flew on past Maidstone and Gravesend and turned towards the docklands. A third wave of fighters, which included the Spitfires of No. 66 Squadron, attacked, striking at the bombers which were by then only ten minutes from their target. Seventy bombers reached London and dropped their payloads.

Meanwhile, a formation of Bf 109s flew out from France to escort the bombers on their return leg as another raid developed, with twenty-five aircraft targeting Portland at 15.30 hours. The raiders were engaged and successfully driven off.

At 17.25 hours a raid of fifty-plus enemy aircraft crossed over the Isle of Wight, heading for targets around Southampton. Six squadrons and one flight were scrambled and made a successful interception, driving off the bombers.

During the day the pre-war fighter pilot and former Olympian, Don Finlay arrived at No. 41 Squadron to take over command. Squadron Leader Finlay had been assigned to a desk job, but circumstances demanded that he be posted to command No. 54 Squadron on 26 August. He had been shot down and wounded the following day and at the time of his posting to No. 41 Squadron was still recovering from his wounds. Ryder and Bennions would continued to lead in the air.[1]

It had been a momentous day for the RAF and that night the BBC News announced *Luftwaffe* losses of 185 aircraft, although post-war research has reduced this figure to fifty-six, partly due to exaggerated claims made by No. 12 Group. What was certain was that the RAF had lost twenty Hurricanes and seven Spitfires, with twelve pilots killed and another four wounded, while another was taken as a PoW.

Despite heavy loses among its own pilots the RAF had won what would prove to be a decisive victory.

Many of Fighter Command's best pilots had already been in combat since mid-July, while others had borne the brunt of the *Luftwaffe's* assault since the air operations over France eight months earlier – many would soon need to be rested or would become casualties.

Note

1. Finlay was born in 1909 and was thirty-one when he took command of No. 41 Squadron – this made him one of the oldest squadron leaders engaged in the Battle of Britain. Initially Finlay acted as Ryder's wingman until he gained more combat experience. On 23 August he claimed a Bf 109, sharing a Bf 109 on 1 October and a Do 215 on 7 October. On 9 October he damaged a Bf 109 and another on the 20th. Sharing a Bf 109 on 27 October, he claimed a Bf 109 on both 23 and 27 November.

Finlay was posted away to become No. 11 Group Engineering Officer and destroyed a Bf 109 on 3 March 1942, while flying with No. 485 Squadron, and a Focke-Wulf FW 190 on 30 July with the Hornchurch Wing. Finlay was awarded the DFC, *London Gazette* 10 April 1942:

Air Ministry,
10 April, 1942
Royal Air Force

The King has been graciously pleased to approve the following awards in recognition of gallantry displayed in flying operations against the enemy:-

Distinguished Flying Cross
Acting Wing Commander Donald Osborne FINLAY (36031)
From September, 1940 to August, Wing Commander Finlay was commanding officer of No. 41 Squadron. He participaterd in many sorties during which he destroyed at least 3 enemy aircraft in combat. On one sortie, he attacked a German ship, leaving it a mass of flames. During the period his squadron destroyed 66 enemy aircraft. Since joining his present unit, Wing Commander Finlay has participated in several sorties. On 3rd March, 1942, he destroyed a *Messerschmitt* 109 following a courageous head-on attack, this bringing his victories to 4. This officer has always shown great keenness and he has set a splendid example to all.

He later commanded No. 608 Squadron before becoming Senior Air Staff Officer (SASO) 210 Group and later commanding No. 906 Wing in Burma. He retired from the RAF as a Group Captain on 1950, having been awarded the AFC in September 1944.

Chapter 13

The Battle Rages On

No. 41 Squadron had been at readiness since dawn on 16 September, while two British spotter aircraft flew a patrol at 07.00 hours. They had not long been in the air when radar reported the first of several waves of enemy aircraft, totalling some 350 bombers and their escort, crossing the Kent coast between Dover, Rye and the Isle of Sheppey from 07.35 hours, one raid heading up the Thames estuary for London.

No. 11 Group scrambled twenty-one squadrons, including No. 41 Squadron, which met the attack with eight Spitfires led by Flight Lieutenant Ryder.

Taking off at 07.30 hours, they were vectored onto one of the enemy formations and the squadron successfully engaged, with Bennions destroying one Bf 109 between Canterbury and Herne Bay. During the melée his own aircraft was hit by six rounds:

> You felt every emotion under the sun, from elation to panic, during that chaotic period. The adrenalin was flowing, but you had to be frightened, hearing explosions and seeing bits falling off your own aeroplane. Getting up at four o'clock in the morning and being on readiness sometimes until 10 o'clock at night creeps up on you! I became so tired that towards the end of September I could fall asleep instantly and anywhere, even on the floor.

As a seasoned pilot, Bennions found that combat was a natural extension of flying:

> I aimed to destroy the enemy machine. There was no animosity towards the German pilot. I never feared combat. I had every faith in Mitchell's Spitfire and the ground crew who serviced it under incredibly difficult conditions.

Back on the ground, Bennions joined the pilots at dispersals where they sat around waiting for the next scramble. Bennions never feared the combat, but hated every moment at dispersals: 'More nerve–racking was the time spent on the ground between sorties; waiting and waiting and waiting for orders to take off for the next sortie.'

The squadron was in the air again later that day when, at 18.30 hours, a plot of around thirty aircraft was reported approaching Dover. Fifteen minutes later the Controller scrambled No. 41 Squadron. Flight Lieutenant Ryder led a formation of nine aircraft into the air. The raid turned back before crossing the coast and Ryder was ordered to pancake, the squadron landing at Hawkinge twenty minutes later. There would be several more hours at readiness before they were finally allowed to stand down.

The squadron was at their advanced airfield from early light on the 17th, and at 07.45 hours Pilot Officer Lock was ordered to patrol Hornchurch below cloud base in response to reports of a lone reconnaissance aircraft which was flying over the east Kent area. Despite following updated courses, Lock was unable to make contact with the enemy and returned to Manston.

The morning, which remained quiet, saw the arrival from No. 610 Squadron of Sergeant Cyril Stanley Bamberger but there would be no time for the new pilot to settle in, he would be flying operations later that day.

A plot estimated at 300-plus hostile aircraft began building-up on the other side of the Channel at around 15.00 hours, when eleven aircraft from No. 41 Squadron were scrambled.

With Bennions (flying X4317) leading the squadron, they were ordered to patrol Manston before being vectored onto the enemy bombers and their escort which crossed the coast at Lympne, Dover and Deal. Two formations of Bf 109s were spotted, but while Bennions was still leading the squadron in a battle-climb they sighted a third formation of Bf 109s and made an interception.

Pilot Officer Bennions' combat report as Mitor Leader read:

After the commencement of the engagement, I found myself about 2,000 feet below a section of 5 Me 109s. Two of the Me 109 dived down on to me and I evaded by turning sharply right; then one dived away and as I turned to follow, 3 more came down on me. After turning and twisting violently, I spun out and on pulling-out I found that one only had followed me down. I turned to engage and he disappeared in the clouds. I climbed back to 15,000 feet and sighted a loose formation of 4 Me 109s circling. I attacked the rear one from the inside of a left-hand turn and after a short burst [firing a two second burst between 200 yards, closing to 75 yards], I saw pieces fly off the aircraft, which then rolled over and spun inverted for about 8,000 feet and then dived straight into the ground midway between

Canterbury and Herne Bay near a very large wood [crashing at Bishopden Wood nr Dunkirk, at 15.40 hours].

(Signed) G H Bennions

Flying Officer Boyle attacked the higher-flying 109s, which turned towards France: two of them collided and spun out of control. Boyle, who was credited with the destroyed 109s, then returned to Hornchurch, his Spitfire (X4178) having been damaged during the combat, which took place over Maidstone at 15.35 hours.

During the same engagement Sergeant 'Jock' Norwell, only recently posted from No. 54 Squadron, dived onto a formation of three Bf 109s which were heading for home, successfully damaging one.

However, Pilot Officer Harold H Chalder, who had arrived on the squadron only two days earlier, was shot up by Bf 109s off Dover at 15.45 hours while flying Spitfire N3366. He managed to evade his attackers and landed without further damage. During the same combat Pilot Officer Henry C Baker's Spitfire (X4409) force-landed at Stelling Minnis after being 'badly shot-up' by Bf 109s over Manston.

Also hit during the combat with Bf 109s over Dover at 15.40 hours was Spitfire R6867, flown by Pilot Officer J N Mackenzie, which crash-landed at Hornchurch.

The squadron had claimed three Bf 109s destroyed and one damaged, for two aircraft Category 2 and one Category 3. More importantly, all of the pilots returned to Hornchurch uninjured while the new pilots had gained valuable combat experience and had survived to tell the tale.

Far from being on its knees, as Goering had believed, Fighter Command had been able to scramble twenty-eight squadrons to face the enemy; No. 11 Group deploying twenty-three, while a further five squadrons from No. 12 Group had patrolled north of the Thames estuary, beyond the limits of the raid. The RAF destroyed five enemy fighters, along with four claimed as probables, with two more damaged. To add to this tally the ack–ack batteries also claimed two destroyed. The RAF lost one pilot killed.

With the RAF still able to meet every raid in force, the *Luftwaffe* had failed to materially damage Fighter Command, let alone destroy it. Adolf Hitler was forced to postpone Operation Sealion indefinitely, and two days later the invasion barges and troop concentrations, which included 20 divisions, begin to disperse. The air campaign against Great Britain, however, continued.

The first big raid of the following day saw a formation of some 150 aircraft building up over Calais with Nos. 222 and 603 Squadrons being scrambled and ordered to patrol Maidstone at 20,000ft. Minutes later, at 09.10 hours, No. 41 Squadron was scrambled when Bennions commanded a formation which was ordered to orbit Maidstone with the Spitfires of No. 603 Squadron.

The first enemy formation crossed the coast near Hythe, the second flew over north Foreland and headed up the Thames estuary. A part of the raid headed north-west over Kent but was forced to turn back, with only a few bombers reaching the capital. Meanwhile, one element of the raid crossed over Herne Bay and on to Essex; another formation focused their attack on Hornchurch.

At 10.10 hours Bennions' 'A' Flight sighted a formation of fifty-plus Bf 109s flying some 7,000ft above them and he ordered line astern and put them into a battle-climb, just as the enemy fighters split into groups of five and dived onto the Spitfires. Bennions ordered the Spitfires to take evasive action but several aircraft were nevertheless damaged. The enemy's tactics appeared to be for one or two aircraft of each group to attack while the remaining three waited above, to come down as required.

During the dogfight, Bennions (flying X4317) claimed a Bf 109 probably destroyed south of Maidstone – west of Gravesend, with a second claimed as damaged. His own aircraft suffered minor combat damage but he managed to return to Hornchurch where he made a safe landing.

Bennions' combat report:

After being ordered to patrol Maidstone at 20,000 feet and then to vector 130 degrees, Angels 25, the Squadron commenced to climb and arrived at 25,000 feet, when they were ordered to orbit. I then sighted a large loose formation of 109s about 5–7,000 feet above. I ordered all 41 Squadron aircraft to form line astern and commence climbing. The enemy aircraft split into groups of approximately five, and dived down to attack us. We took violent evasive action and eventually I managed to get my sights on an Me 109. I gave a burst of approximately 2 seconds [firing from 250 yards, closing to 100 yards and firing 640 rounds] and saw pieces breaking off the side of the 109. The enemy aircraft then went down in a very flat spin with two streams of white petrol or glycol pouring from either side of the fuselage and black smoke coming from the tail. I could not definitely destroy the enemy aircraft, because I was being attacked by a further section of five 109s.

(Signed) G.H. Bennions

Meanwhile, Pilot Officer Lock probably destroyed another Bf 109 and Sergeant Usmar claimed two more but one was downgraded to a damaged.

Usmar had dived through cloud and emerged to find himself about 500 yards behind two Bf 109s but was travelling too fast. Throttling back, he fired a long burst at the aircraft to his left which rolled over and span down in flames. Now almost overtaking the second, Usmar fired without using his sights – he was almost on top of the enemy when it fell away. Pulling out of the attack and putting his fighter into a tight right-hand turn, Usmar half-expected a gaggle of Bf 109s to be on his tail, but there were none. Looking down he could still see his two victims falling out of control towards marshland. Having fired the remainder of his ammunition with inconclusive bursts at aircraft that crossed his path, Usmar returned to base.

Taxiing to dispersals the pilots reported to the squadron's Intelligence Officer who awaited their return, unused combat forms in-hand. Having filed their reports, they waited impatiently for the next scramble. Bennions had led the squadron on another successful encounter and despite being attacked by a higher flying formation of deadly 109s, they had managed to claim a brace of Bf 109s as probably destroyed and the same number as damaged; all without loss.

Enemy aircraft began massing in the Calais area again at around 12.15 hours, and at 12.37 hours 100-plus aircraft crossed the coast to the north of Dover, heading towards Maidstone. A second formation of fifty-plus raiders followed, with another passing over Deal; together these formed the first wave, while at 12.45 hours the second wave, consisting of three raids of fifty-plus aircraft, passed over Dover, with a dozen Bf 109s left circling the Straits. Fifteen minutes later, two raids totalling approximately sixty-plus aircraft were in the London area with another 120-plus between Rye and the mouth of the Thames.

No. 41 Squadron was scrambled at 12.35 hours and Bennions led the formation with orders to link-up with No. 603 Squadron and patrol Maidstone at 20,000 feet. No. 222 Squadron had already taken-off from Rochford and engaged the enemy, with Sergeant Hutchinson being forced to bail out of his damaged Spitfire.

Fifteen minutes into their patrol and before they could rendezvous, No. 41 Squadron was bounced by a formation of Bf 109s estimated at sixty strong while flying between Maidstone and Gravesend. The squadron quickly lost its formation and individual dogfights ensued. Bennions, flying Spitfire X4317, turned the tables on his would-be assailants and destroyed one, claiming another as probably destroyed and damaging a third, firing several two second bursts from 250 yards, closing to around 75 yards, and firing all 2,820 rounds.

Bennions' combat report read:

Intercepted large loose formation of Me 109s, the lowest of which was 500 feet above [and to port]. I ordered the Squadron into line astern and turned in to attack, but had to break away [and ordered squadron to take evasive action] when attacked from above and behind.

I climbed up to 32,000 feet and attacked a formation of 5 Me 109s circling in open echelon formation. I closed with No. 5 and after two short bursts, the machine exploded in front of me and everything was obscured. I pulled up and saw an aircraft firing at me from astern. I turned about after feeling a burst hit the port side of the aircraft and attacked the 109 which was attacking me. I gave him two short bursts and saw bits flying off the starboard plane and thick black smoke pouring from what seemed to be the oil cooler under the starboard main plane. He then half-rolled and my attention was distracted by a further formation of 109s coming towards me from the port rear quarter. I turned about to starboard and attacked No. 4, who immediately showed signs of being hit and half-rolled. I half-rolled after him and when he levelled out, I gave him a long burst, which caused a stream of white smoke to pour out in large quantities from a position about 1 yard from the fuselage on the port main plane. I had exhausted my ammunition and the 109 was going down towards Dover, leaving a long trail of white smoke behind, so after looking at the damage to my aircraft, I decided to return to base and land.

(Signed) G. H. Bennions.

Pilot Officer Lock claimed a Bf 109 destroyed with a second as a probable, while Sergeant Darling shot at one Bf 109 which fell into the sea. Several of the Spitfires, including Bennions', were damaged, but none of the pilots injured. The squadron landed at about 13.45 hours and the aircraft were quickly checked over before being either taken off strength for repair or refuelled and rearmed, ready for the next sortie.

The day's third major raid began at about 15.45 hours when a formation of 100 enemy aircraft flew over east Kent, while another of the same strength crossed the coast in the Dover/Deal area. By 17.00 hours seven more raids of two hundred-plus aircraft were over the Isle of Sheppey, mid-Kent and the Medway areas.

At around 16.12 hours, nine of the squadron's Spitfires were scrambled and ordered to patrol base at 20,000ft. Once in the air they were vectored onto enemy aircraft flying in the Thames estuary area at 25,000ft.

Acting as 'weaver', Sergeant Darling sighted a formation of enemy bombers escorted by Bf 109s at 17.15 hours. Calling out a warning, he dived down and destroyed one Ju 88. Sergeant Beardsley claimed two Bf 109s as damaged while Pilot Officer Aldous claimed another. Both Beardsley and Aldous had only recently transferred from No. 610 Squadron.

There were no large-scale raids during 19th, although a series of lone raiders bombed targets in London and Liverpool. No. 41 Squadron flew several sorties between 09.25 and 13.30 hours in response to enemy reconnaissance missions. Meanwhile, flight and section-strength patrols were made of the Rochford area between 13.40 and 17.40 hours. No enemy aircraft were engaged.

Despite the lack of contact with the enemy, this was a Red Letter Day for the squadron. In the late afternoon Bennions was called into the Station Commander's office, where Wing Commander Guy Carter greeted him with a warm handshake, offering his personal congratulations as he read aloud the message which had been received from RAF Tangmere. Timed at 16.00 hours, the text read: 'PILOT OFFICER BENNIONS, CONGRATULATIONS ON THE AWARD OF THE DISTINGUISHED FLYING CROSS.'

The award had some additional significance for Guy Carter who had commanded No. 41 Squadron during the Great War; he could be rightly proud of the way his successors had equipped themselves during the Battle.

Bennions later recalled his feelings at the news of his richly deserved award:

There was no time to think about it at the time – we were in the middle of a battle that was still to be won. But it was recognition for the squadron as a whole, because you were always acutely aware that you owed everything to the men who kept you in the air and gave you every last bit of performance out of your aircraft – without them you'd have been finished.

Bennions was, of course, quite right. There was no time for celebrations or complacency, as the squadron could be called-upon at any minute to engage the enemy. Although Bennions was confident in his own abilities and in his ground crew, he still knew that fate could play its hand and he could be killed – there were no guarantees.

On the following day the enemy flew a number of reconnaissance missions over the Thames estuary and around Foreland and Dover between 06.00 and 10.30 hours, Bennions' squadron flying patrols against these lone aircraft.

Meanwhile, at 09.30 hours, Bennions crossed the Channel to make a weather reconnaissance, flying at low level over the icy waters in order to try to avoid detection. On his return flight Bennions looked up and saw anti-aircraft fire at about 20,000 ft while flying near Ashford in Kent. Just ahead of the line of shell bursts he saw a tiny speck which he believed to be a single German aircraft. Lacking altitude, he decided to climb at maximum power while flying towards Dungeness where he believed the aircraft's paths would cross and he would be best positioned to make an interception.

This he did, but to Bennions' dismay, although he had reached 20,000 feet, the enemy was flying above him. Bennions, still climbing, decided to put himself on the same course and waited for the enemy aircraft to come overhead, but ended up some 20ft below and 200ft astern of the Bf 110. Lifting his nose, Bennions put his thumb on the gun-button but the German fired at the same time, the bullets registering. Breaking off the combat, Bennions made a forced landing at Lympne. Climbing out of his Spitfire, he counted nearly 200 bullet holes and considered himself to have had a lucky escape.

Radar located a large raid starting to mass in the area around Calais at 10.40 hours, with the first formation of twenty-plus arriving over Dungeness at 11.00 hours. This raid was followed by upwards of a dozen enemy aircraft, which crossed the coast at Dover, Lympne and Deal. Another formation flew up the Thames estuary, converging on east London, with bombers hitting Biggin Hill, Kenley, Hornchurch and the inner Thames estuary. Twenty squadrons, including No. 41 Squadron, were scrambled to meet the raid, while another four were already on patrol.

Flight Lieutenant Ryder led ten Spitfires on a scramble at 11.20 hours to patrol the Manston area. They landed at 12.35 hours without having entered into combat with the enemy. No. 222 Squadron's 'B' Flight was also in the air and engaged the enemy over the Thames estuary at 11.30 hours, loosing two Spitfires, with Pilot Officer Whitbread killed.

The enemy flew a number of reconnaissance sorties over Sussex, Kent and in the Straits of Dover between 13.00 and 17.00 hours. No. 41 Squadron was scrambled twice, sending up section-strength patrols. At 16.05 hours Bennions took off on an hour-long patrol during which he claimed a Ju 88 as damaged, his combat report not surviving.

Meanwhile Lock flew a solo reconnaissance mission over the Channel, during which he sighted and destroyed a *Henschel* Hs 126 army co-operation aircraft, and a Bf 109, which crashed into the Channel.[1]

Although spared any major attacks on London, the aircraft factories or Fighter Command's infrastructure, nevertheless it had not been a good day for the RAF, losing seven aircraft with four pilots killed, claiming four enemy aircraft with another probably destroyed and two damaged.

During the early morning of 21 September a number of enemy aircraft bombed Weybridge and targets near Ramsgate and Rye. No. 41 Squadron was not called into action until the late afternoon, when a medium size raid of 200-plus enemy aircraft was plotted approaching the coast, which they crossed at 18.00 hours. Flight Lieutenant Ryder led the scramble, with orders to patrol in conjunction with No. 222 Squadron.

The RAF scrambled twenty squadrons across the south of England, while other squadrons were already patrolling the Hornchurch and North Weald areas. Despite the numbers of aircraft in the air there were few combats, and during the day the RAF only claimed two enemy aircraft as destroyed, plus another probably destroyed, with a further six damaged. No RAF fighters were lost.

Between 07.00 and 11.00 hours and 13.00 and 15.00 hours on the 22nd, reconnaissance aircraft flew in the Straits of Dover and over the Channel convoys, while later a number of lone raiders flew over Biggin Hill, Northolt and parts of London.

No. 41 Squadron flew to Rochford at 19.05 hours, just as three raids crossed the coast heading for the London. These were followed by widespread raids against targets in the south-east. The squadron was unable to claim any enemy aircraft as damaged or destroyed. While they were in the air, however, a 1,000lb bomb was dropped on Hornchurch, the blast blowing in windows over a large area, but otherwise causing little damage. For Bennions it was a salutary reminder of why he preferred to face the enemy in the air.

A little before 09.00 hours on 23 September a raid was seen massing over the other side of the Channel, and ten minutes later. Flight Lieutenant Ryder was at the head of twelve Spitfires on a scramble in the company of No. 222 Squadron with orders to rendezvous over Rochford with No. 603 Squadron; No. 222 Squadron was to act as rear cover. Their target was an enemy formation estimated at 200 enemy aircraft, mainly Bf 109s, the first of which crossed the coast near Dover at 09.26 hours. A section of nine enemy aircraft detached itself from the main attack and flew west along the south coast towards Hastings. The remainder were in a spread formation between Dover to Maidstone with others over the Thames estuary. The counters on the operation room table mounted up as the raid developed and a total of twenty-four squadrons were eventually scrambled to meet the enemy.

Bennions tried to communicate with Ryder who was commanding the squadron in the air. It quickly became apparent that he was having difficulties with his radio.

Twenty minutes into the patrol and with Bennions now leading the squadron, twelve Bf 109s were seen in line echelon over Dover flying slightly below at 33,000ft and to starboard side; there were no bombers in sight. Engaging the enemy, Bennions (flying EB-J R6619) sent one down into the Channel, his log book further recording that his victim *Unteroffizier* K Elbing bailed out to become a PoW.

Bennions' combat report read:

After R/T failure of Mitor Red 1 [Flight Lieutenant Ryder]. I took over lead of Squadron and after several vectors on which I sighted several formations of friendly fighters I eventually sighted E/A slightly below on our starboard side. I ordered line astern and turned in to attack and a series of dog fights ensued in the course of which I succeeded in shooting down one Me 109 [opening fire with three 3-second bursts from 250 yards, closing to 100 yards], which landed on the sea N. of Dover; about one mile from the shore, and nosed in – the tail remained visible for approximately 3 minutes and had a yellow strip down the rudder at its extremity.

(Signed) G H Bennions

During the engagement two more Bf 109s were claimed as probably destroyed, with two damaged, while several others were shot at but without results. One enemy pilot was seen to bail out but his aircraft remained unclaimed by either Nos. 41 or 603 Squadron.

At around 12.30 to 13.00 hours three aircraft piloted by Pilot Officers Baker and Mackenzie, along with Sergeant Bamberger, flew to Hawkinge from where they escorted an Avro Anson on a reconnaissance mission over Calais. The Anson, which was acting as spotter for heavy guns firing from Dover, was attacked by nine Bf 109s, one of which was awarded to Bamberger as a probable, while a second was damaged.

Bennions' log book records an eighty minute patrol flown at 15.15 hours, which was not confirmed by the Squadron Operations Book. He later explained that at the height of the Battle of Britain his and other log books were often kept up-to-date by office staff:

Throughout the latter half of the Battle of Britain, I simply did not have time or the inclination to fill in my log book. The office staff did that for you from the flight authorization book – which again was not always completed – there simply was not sufficient time for such niceties. We really began to earn our pay then.

At around 17.00 hours advanced radar detected a plot building-up over France. Half an hour later forty enemy aircraft flew over the Thames estuary and the Isle of Sheppey before heading south towards Rye. Meanwhile, a formation of fifty-plus enemy aircraft crossed the coast between Folkestone and Dover; the attack was limited to an area east of the line between the Isle of Sheppey and Rye.

Twelve squadrons were scrambled to counter the threat, including ten aircraft from No. 41 Squadron. Once in the air the Spitfires were vectored onto the enemy but no casualties were reported on either side.

There were two late afternoon raids made by lone aircraft, one of which dropped bombs on Northolt at 19.30 hours.

During the day the RAF destroyed eleven enemy aircraft with a further six probably destroyed and six damaged. The Dover barrage shot down one more with another credited as a probable. Eleven RAF fighters were shot down with the loss of three pilots killed or posted as missing.

The first raid of the day on 24 September began at 08.30 hours when 200 aircraft, the bombers out-numbered by their escort by a ratio of 2:1, crossed the coast between Dover and Dungeness, their targets, Gravesend and the Tilbury Docks. At the same time a diversionary raid of fighters headed towards the Isle of Sheppey. No. 11 Group scrambled fifteen squadrons to engage the bombers, destroying one with five more claimed as probables and another seven damaged.

A second raid developed when 100 enemy aircraft crossed the coast in the Dover area at 11.15 hours. In response eighteen squadrons were scrambled, including No. 41 Squadron. Ryder commanded the formation, which got into the air by 11.50 hours. Thirty minutes later the raid turned back and the Controller ordered No. 41 Squadron to 'pancake'.

Another wave, which consisted of eighty-plus aircraft, flew in over the Estuary, turning southwards towards their targets in Kent. No. 41 Squadron's Spitfires were waiting, refuelled and with their pilots still strapped in. The order came for a Squadron Scramble and Ryder led them off at 12.50 hours. Once in the air the formation was vectored onto the bombers but before they could engage they were 'bounced' by Bf 109s.

Sergeant McAdam was forced to bail out of Spitfire N3118 wounded, following combat over Dover at 13.45 hours. He landed in the English Channel and was picked up and taken to Dover Hospital. He discharged himself and had returned to the squadron by the end of the day. McAdam claimed a Bf 109 on 25 October but was killed in action while still with the squadron. He was shot down by *Major* Mölders on 20 February 1941, while flying Spitfire P7302, and picked up from the sea dead.

Another victim of the same combat was Sergeant Darling. His Spitfire, R6604, crash-landed outside Dover having been hit while over the Channel. Darling emerged from the Spitfire unhurt. The remnants of the squadron landed at 14.30 hours.

In the squadron's last mission of what had been a busy day, Flight Lieutenant Ryder and Pilot Officer Mackenzie flew an uneventful patrol between 16.30 and 18.10 hours.

During the day the RAF claimed seven enemy aircraft, with eight probables and another thirteen as damaged. The RAF's losses were five aircraft destroyed with two pilots killed or missing.

The enemy flew single aircraft reconnaissance sorties throughout the 25th, targeting the Straits, the south and south-east, as well as the capital.

Radar detected a formation of 100 aircraft massing in the Calais area at about 09.00 hours. No. 41 Squadron was among the squadrons scrambled in response to the alert. Bennions taking off at 08.50 hours at the head of twelve Spitfires. Bennions followed the Controller's vectors but they were unable to get to grips with the enemy and landed at 10.05 hours.

While the squadron flew to their forward base in the early afternoon, they were not scrambled.

In No. 10 Group's area a raid of around sixty enemy aircraft was launched on the Bristol Aeroplane Company's factory at Filton at 11.45 hours, while the oil storage facility at Portland was bombed by Ju 88s. Later, at 16.45 hours, an attack was launched on the Plymouth area by twenty-four bombers and their escort of twelve Bf 110s. The enemy was intercepted by two sections which dispersed the formation. One bomber was shot down, with two more claimed as probables, and another damaged; all without loss.

During the day as a whole, the RAF destroyed twenty-two enemy aircraft, with a further eight probables and ten damaged. Ack-ack batteries, meanwhile, were credited with three enemy aircraft destroyed while a further two were damaged. The RAF lost four aircraft, with one pilot killed and second posted as missing.

Meanwhile, news of Bennions' awarded had been published in the Staffordshire press and as a result he received a letter of congratulations from the head master of his old school:

Longton High School, Stoke-on-Trent
25th September, 1940

Dear Mr Bennion (sic),
May I extend to you on behalf of the School, our heartiest congratulations on the award to you of the Distinguished Flying Cross, and our sincere appreciation of the service for which the award was made.

You had already left the school before I came in 1935, but there are still several of the older members of staff who well remember you. We are delighted with the vast strides you have made since you became an Aircraft Apprentice and wish you every success in the career on which you are so happily embarked.

Yours sincerely,

(Signed) M. V. Gregory
Head Master.
Pilot Officer G. Bennion (sic), DFC

Most of the following day's raids were directed against Bristol and Portsmouth and the Hornchurch squadrons were able to enjoy a relatively quiet period.

No. 41 Squadron was at their forward landing ground at Rochford early in the morning, but while the *Luftwaffe* made reconnaissance sorties over Kent, the capital and along the Thames estuary, and while enemy formations flew over the Straits of Dover, no raid materialized. During the afternoon the enemy flew lone sorties bombing coastal towns, while a number of aircraft flew over London. Interceptions were made.

The first real attack came in No. 10 Group's area, when 100-plus bombers severely damaged the Supermarine factory at Southampton, the raid beginning at 16.30 hours.

Meanwhile, the enemy threatened No. 41 Squadron's sector and they were scrambled and were ordered to patrol between 16.30 and 17.20 hours, Flight Lieutenant Ryder taking off at the head of the squadron formation. No claims were made.

An early evening raid saw twenty-five enemy aircraft over Crewe, while that night's raids once again focused on the capital.

The RAF claimed thirty-two enemy aircraft destroyed with ten probably destroyed and a further eleven damaged. The ack-ack batteries meanwhile claimed one destroyed, one probable and two damaged. RAF losses included ten aircraft destroyed with three pilots killed or posted as missing.

A major attack was launched at 09.00 hours on 27 September, when 180 enemy aircraft, comprising 100 fighters and eighty bombers, crossed the coast between Dover and Folkestone. No. 11 Group scrambled thirteen squadrons, with eleven being successfully vectored onto targets. Meanwhile, four squadrons from No. 12 Group were ordered to patrol North Weald and Hornchurch against possible raiders.

No. 41 Squadron was scrambled at 09.50 hours, with Flight Lieutenant Ryder taking off at the head of twelve Spitfires. Once in the air the squadron was ordered to patrol. Despite Fighter Command's best efforts, a few bombers broke through to central and west London.

Elsewhere, at 11.20 hours, twenty-five bombers with their escort of forty-five Bf 110s failed in their attack on the Bristol Aeroplane Company's factory but had more success against the RAF Station at Filton.

Six formations, totaling some 300 enemy aircraft, crossed the coast between Dover and Lympne from 11.45 until 12.15 hours. The main force headed for Chatham, and both Nos. 41 and 222 Squadrons were scrambled and vectored onto enemy aircraft over Maidstone. In total some twenty fighter squadrons were scrambled, engaging the enemy over east Kent and Sussex.

No. 41 Squadron was in the air by 11.35 hours, with Flight Lieutenant Ryder commanding a formation of twelve Spitfires. At 12.15 hours they sighted the enemy and engaged a formation of Bf 109s. During the combat Sergeant Usmar (flying EB-S, serial R6884) was hit and his aircraft caught on fire, the flames quickly spreading to the cockpit. Despite being wounded and losing blood, he managed to bail out over West Malling, his Spitfire crashing at Swanton Lane, Mereworth. Usmar intended making a drop before pulling the ripcord but deployed his parachute almost as soon as he was clear and had to beat his flaming clothes out during the descent, before using his wireless cable to make a tourniquet to stem the flow of blood from his right leg. Usmar landed in an apple-orchard where he was nearly set upon by hop pickers who thought he was a German. Finally convinced that he was British, they took him to a doctor in Yalding, and he was admitted to Preston Hall Hospital – Usmar's parents lived at West Malling and had witnessed his descent without realizing who he was.

Meanwhile, Sergeant Darling (flying X4409), wounded in the shoulder, was forced to bail out. He was also admitted to Preston Hall Hospital. The Squadron could claim one victory, with Sergeant Norwell destroying a Bf 109, before landing back at base at 12.40 hours.

During the same engagement No. 222 Squadron claimed two Bf 109s destroyed for the loss of one Spitfire.

The next raid began at 15.00 hours with nine formations totaling 160 aircraft crossing the coast between Dover and Brighton, flying towards south London. RAF fighters dispersed the raid, although twenty bombers reached the capital. Scrambled at 15.10 hours, Ryder led the squadron into the air where they joined No. 603 Squadron to patrol at 5,000ft.

A little over half an hour into their patrol the squadron was 'bounced' by Bf 109s, and Flight Lieutenant Ryder's Spitfire (R6755), was hit twice and fatally damaged. Ryder disconnected the oxygen and R/T, undid his Sutton harness, closed the throttle and pulled the canopy back. He bailed out, hurtling head over heels towards the tail plane, which he thankfully missed as his flailing hand grabbed for the 'D' ring. The mad rush earthwards was abruptly halted as the canopy deployed with a loud 'bang'. Ryder swayed gently in the parachute harness as he floated down, landing at East Malling, uninjured. His Spitfire crashed nearby, a cloud of black smoke billowing up into the air marking the point of impact. Sergeant Bamberger had more luck and claimed one Bf 109 as damaged. The squadron landed at 16.10 hours.

Also engaged were the pilots of No. 603 Squadron, which lost Pilot Officer Philip Cardell who was shot down by a Bf 109. Meanwhile, No. 222 Squadron lost Sergeant Ernest Scott whose Spitfire wreckage was only finally located in the 1970s, at Greenway Court, Hollingbourne, Kent. The landowner was initially reluctant to allow its recovery, which did not take place until 1991, following an appeal by Sergeant Scott's brother and sister to Prince Charles who was able to lend his support to the cause. Scott was buried with full military honours at St John's Cemetery, Margate.

The *Luftwaffe* continued to fly sorties over the Channel, south-east coast and along the Thames estuary, while anti-shipping reconnaissance sorties were made over convoys along the coast of East Anglia.

Bennions' log book records a sixty minute patrol flown at 17.55 hours which is omitted from the Squadron Record.

The RAF claimed 131 enemy aircraft, with a further thirty-three probably destroyed and fifty-two damaged. Ack-ack batteries claimed two enemy aircraft with two more as probably destroyed. Meanwhile, the RAF lost twenty-seven aircraft, with eighteen pilots killed or posted as missing.

Night raids focused on London, Merseyside and the Midlands.

On the morning of the 28th, large formations of enemy aircraft were plotted approaching the coast and at 09.40 hours ten Spitfires from No. 41 Squadron patrolled with No. 603 Squadron.

At 09.55 hours the raid, totaling 120 aircraft, approached the Kent coast, seventy making their way further inland in two waves. The first wave of thirty aircraft flew to Biggin Hill and about six of these reached central London. The second wave reached Maidstone.

The enemy was engaged over Charing, Kent, and at 10.30 hours, Pilot Officer H H Chalder was shot down while piloting Spitfire X4409. He bailed out moments ahead of an explosion which ripped his aircraft to pieces over East Stour Farm, Chilham. Chalder landed at Garlinge Green, Kent, but died of his wounds at Chartham Military Hospital on November 10th. He was buried at St Nicholas Cemetery, Newcastle-upon-Tyne.

Other casualties included Flying Officer Boyle (flying X4426) who was shot down over Charing. His Spitfire crashed and burned out on Erriotts Farm, Dadmans, Lynstead at 10.37 hours.

Flying Officer (40204) John Greer 'Beryl' Boyle, RAF, was the son of Dr Joseph P Boyle and Catherine Greer Boyle, of Ottawa, Ontario, Canada. He was buried in St Peter & Paul New Churchyard, Lynsted, Kent, Row F, Grave 1. Boyle joined the squadron on 5 May 1940, since when he had claimed five destroyed and a further two shared destroyed, but did not receive a gallantry award. He was 26.

Meanwhile, Pilot Officer E S Aldous was more fortunate. His Spitfire (X4345) was damaged in combat over Charing at 10.40 hours and was written off after making a forced landing at Pluckley. Aldous was injured and was taken off squadron strength and given sick leave.

Of the other Hornchurch Squadrons, No. 603 lost Flight Lieutenant Harold MacDonald, bounced by Bf 109s at 10.20 hours over Gillingham. His Spitfire crashed at Brompton Barracks.

A total of seventeen squadrons had been scrambled to intercept these raids which finally dispersed at about 10.40 hours. Enemy patrols were unusually active in the Straits.

The squadron could only muster eight Spitfires for a scramble flown at 12.30 hours, when Flight Lieutenant Ryder led a patrol from Hornchurch from where they were vectored onto a raid approaching over Kent. However, they were bounced by Bf 109s which came down from 27,000ft, damaging two Spitfires, including Bennions'.

The second main raid of the day began at 13.30 hours when about thirty to forty bombers, escorted by around 120 Bf 109s, crossed the coast between Dungeness and Lympne, heading for Maidstone and the Thames estuary. The raid spread out over Kent but did not penetrate further west than a line from Beachy Head–Maidstone–Isle of Sheppey. All operational squadrons of No. 11 Group were employed against this attack, along with five squadrons from No. 12 Group which patrolled Hornchurch and North Weald. By 14.10 hours, the enemy aircraft were flying back towards France.

No. 41 Squadron was vectored onto the enemy, which they engaged. Bennions, firing several 2-second bursts from 300 yards, closing to 100 yards, claimed two Bf 109s as probably destroyed; one over Canterbury and the other four miles south of Brighton. During the air battle his Spitfire (R6619) was hit in the fuselage by 20 mm cannon shells. The engagement took place at 13.45 hours.

Bennions flying as 'A' Flight's Yellow 1, filed the following combat report:

While proceeding on a vector of 100 degrees, the squadron was attacked by part of a large formation of Me 109s and had to split up.

I followed Red 1 around and eventually we sighted several groups of 109s about 2,000 feet above on the port side.

I allowed about 25 to pass and then turned in to attack. I closed with one of the rear ones and after a short burst I saw bits fly off the port main plain near the fuselage and coolant pouring back from the port wing radiator, together with black smoke pouring from the tail. I re-sighted and was about to fire again when I was hit by cannon shell on the port side and had to break away. I climbed up again and sighted another formation of approximately 15 Me 109s diving down. I turned down after the last 109 and after a short burst he slowed down and turned right to a southerly course. I fired a few more bursts from dead astern and black smoke and white streams poured back from the tail. I left him 4 miles S of Brighton at 4,000 feet, gliding down, because I was short of petrol and miles away from my home base.

(Signed) G.H. Bennions.

The last of the squadron's aircraft landed at 14.00 hours and were immediately checked-over and refuelled and rearmed, Bennions' Spitfire being taken off-strength for repairs.

At 14.15 hours, some sixty enemy aircraft flew from Cherbourg towards Portsmouth; this would prove to be the third main attack of the day. The raids were met by five squadrons of No. 11 Group which were diverted from the Kent attack, and by four squadrons of No. 10 Group; the enemy jettisoned their bombs into the sea and turned back.

Later a convoy sailing near the Thames estuary was attacked between 17.30 and 19.30 hours, while the enemy was active in the Straits. Meanwhile, a lone enemy aircraft launched a surprise attack on Dover.

RAF fighters destroyed six enemy aircraft, with a further four only allowed as probables with one damaged. The RAF lost sixteen fighters with seven pilots safe.

No. 41 Squadron was once again at readiness before dawn on 29 September. Bennions was scrambled at 07.00 hours, making a thirty-minute patrol in search of an enemy reconnaissance sortie over the Thames estuary. This was one of a number of lone enemy aircraft active from the Estuary to Beachy Head, with other sorties flown over Farnborough and Worthing.

Bennions made his second operational patrol of the day between 13.55 and 14.40 hours, when Flight Lieutenant Ryder led ten Spitfires on a patrol. No enemy aircraft were engaged and the squadron landed without incident. Tension, however, remained high and the pilots stayed close to their aircraft awaiting a further scramble.

A raid developed at 16.10 hours when three formations of fifty, twenty and twenty Bf 109 fighters and fighter-bombers crossed the coast west of Dungeness at 10 minute intervals, while a further twelve aircraft flew inland at Dover. The first raid headed west of the London area before wheeling to the south, with one formation breaking away and heading towards central London. The remainder penetrated only some twenty-five miles inland; all flew close to their ceiling height.

Flight Lieutenant Ryder led ten aircraft on an operational patrol at 16.25 hours. The Squadron Diary recorded that they were vectored onto the high flying enemy fighters but without results. Bennions' recollections prove more revealing and demonstrate that the Spitfire did have some failings.

The *Luftwaffe* had begun to fly missions at a very high altitude, their Bf 109 operating at over 30,000ft, making the Hurricane and Spitfire pilots' job all the more difficult. During this sortie Bennions tried to take on two Bf 109s flying at 37,500ft, their superchargers compressing the air to supply their engines with sufficient oxygen.

After a prolonged battle–climb, Bennions found himself a thousand feet below the fighters, his aircraft's Merlin engine misfiring as it gasped for air at the rarified altitude. He had hit a 'glass ceiling' and struggled to keep his nose up in the air, the slightest movement causing his aircraft to dive 200 or 300ft: 'I thought I would just get up behind them to shoot them out of the sky, but I couldn't.'

Meanwhile, the Bf 109s remained just out of range, but swept down towards Bennions' Spitfire. Despite their height advantage, they did not close to within firing range:

> Once I got into their slipstream, and my Perspex iced up instantly and I could not see anything at all. My screen became quite opaque and I had to open the hood to see where the two Huns had got to. I felt like kite balloon being dived upon as my aircraft stood up at a ridiculous angle. In opening the hood I lost 1,000 feet, so I had to break off and come down without firing a shot. They were still patrolling when I went home.

Between 17.00 and 18.00 hours the enemy flew reconnaissances sorties over Kent, Eastchurch and Detling.

Meanwhile, there were number of new faces in the Officer's Mess that evening following the arrival from No. 611 (West Lancashire) Squadron of Flying Officers D A Adams, D H O'Neill and James Richard Walker, while posted from No. 610 (County of Chester) Squadron were Flying Officer M P Brown and Pilot Officers D E Mileham, G G F Draper and J G Lecky.[2]

The first heavy raid of 30th September materialized at 09.00 hours when two formations totalling thirty bombers and 100 Bf 109s crossed the coast around Dungeness. Their targets were Biggin Hill and Kenley. A dozen aircraft patrolled just inland near Dungeness, while another fifty patrolled off Dover ready to give cover to the withdrawal of the bombing force.

A little over an hour later a second raid developed when seventy-five enemy aircraft composed of bombers with fighter escort crossed at Dungeness, again heading for the Biggin Hill and Kenley areas. Twenty-five Bf 109s were left patrolling the Straits ready to give protection for the returning bombers which recrossed the Channel at 10.30 hours. Although at readiness, No. 41 Squadron was not scrambled to intercept.

Advanced radar began to pick up another raid which was developing over the other side of the Channel. At 13.10 hours the Sector Controller telephoned No. 41 Squadron's dispersals at Rochford and ordered a squadron scramble.

Squadron Leader Finlay led the formation with orders to patrol the Thames estuary between Rochford and Chatham at 30,000ft. Meanwhile, No. 222 Squadron was also in the air and was vectored to fly over south eastern London where they engaged twenty He 111s and their escort. They claimed two Bf 109s but Sergeant Hutchinson's aircraft was hit and he bailed out badly burnt.

As the raid developed, the Observer Corps reported some 100-plus enemy aircraft flying over Lympne. A second wave, numbering sixty-plus, crossed the coast only minutes later, while forty Bf 109s patrolled at Dover.

Lovell, flying at the rear of the squadron which was flying at 24,000ft, sighted thirty-plus Do 17s flying to the west of Dungeness, some 7,000ft below. The squadron was ordered into the attack line astern. Lovell, firing at close range, recording hits on the fuselage of a bomber at the rear of the formation, but became entangled with the bomber's Bf 109s escort. During the ensuing dogfight, Flying Officer Lovell's Spitfire (X4344) was damaged in the starboard wing by a 20 mm cannon shell and he was forced to make a wheels-up landing at Hornchurch at a little after 14.25 hours.

Lovell's combat report read:

...informed Mitor leader, who put the Squadron into line astern and followed me down. A number of Hurricane aircraft were attacking the formation. I chose one of the rear Do 215's and gave a short burst to kill the rear gunner, and then closed right in to 20 yards, firing the whole time. I saw bits come off the aircraft and when I was close up, I could see the riddled fuselage. The rear gunner was dead.

Then there was a loud report and a cannon shell entered my starboard wing and bits entered the cockpit. I broke away and returned to base. The undercarriage was jammed, so I had to land with it up.

During the same engagement Pilot Officer Brown claimed a second Do 17 damaged.

Meanwhile, Sergeant Beardsley (flying P9394), who had joined the squadron on the 18th, made beam and stern attacks on a Do 17 which he last saw at 1,000ft gliding towards the French coast. Pulling up, he attacked a Bf 109 which was flying at 2,000ft, firing off the last of his ammunition. The enemy aircraft went into a steep dive with smoke pouring out. Then suddenly he sighted six Bf 109s who were bearing down on him. Out of ammunition, Beardsley had to fly for his life trying to shake off the enemy, but they made several successful passes, setting his engine on fire. Losing glycol and with fumes entering his cockpit, he somehow managed to evade the enemy and nurse his badly damaged Spitfire back towards the coast.

Despite the flames and the engine seizing while near Folkestone, Beardsley calmly worked out a course and was able to stretch his glide and put down at Hawkinge at 14.20 hours:

> Having crash-landed, I scrambled out of my still burning Spitfire as the fire tender and ambulance raced across the landing-ground. There was no transport to take me back to Hornchurch, so I had to make my own way via the Tube, in my flying gear and lugging my heavy parachute. I was absolutely exhausted when I arrived, only to be asked: 'and where the bloody hell 'ave you been!?'

Pilot Officer Baker had been assigned to spotter duties. While flying over Dungeness at about 25,000ft he reported seeing a bomber formation flying some 10,000ft below. Meanwhile, the leader of the bomber's escort of sixty Bf 109s, which was flying 3,000ft above him, sent down a few fighters to attack the lone Spitfire. Having shaken off the attack, Baker later sighted a damaged Bf 109 heading for home. He latched onto the lone fighter which he sent down into the sea ten miles off Dungeness.

Nine enemy aircraft, Ju 88s and Bf 109s, managed to penetrate London's defences, while others reached the south-western suburbs. The aircraft were observed re-crossing the coast at 13.45 hours, some of them obviously damaged and limping home.

The *Luftwaffe's* forth attack of the day began at 16.08 hours when four raids totalling about 200-plus enemy aircraft crossed the Kent coast at ten minute intervals and flew from Dungeness to Biggin Hill and over east Kent from Kenley to Hornchurch. Some flew west and approached Weybridge from the south, turning west down the Thames Valley as far as Reading.

No. 41 Squadron was scrambled at 16.04 hours, when Squadron Leader Finlay took off at the head of the squadron. The squadron was ordered to patrol Maidstone and was vectored to Hornchurch at 30,000ft where they engaged a formation of thirty-eight Bf 109s which were flying to the south of London some 500ft below. The combat took place at around 16.45 hours.

Bennions, flying EB-B, became detached from the rest of the squadron and was flying in the company of No. 603 Squadron when he claimed a Bf 109, opening fire at 100 yards and firing a 2-second burst, closing to 50 yards. Bennions' combat report explains:

> After leaving Rochford to return to Hornchurch, 41 Squadron was ordered on patrol. I had to land at Hornchurch to obtain a parachute, as the one I was wearing had been damaged by an enemy A.P incendiary bullet.

I took off again immediately, with the Controller's permission and eventually joined up with 603 Squadron, in the rear.

The squadron intercepted and turned in to attack a loose formation of Me 109s slightly above on the right.

I noticed 2 enemy aircraft on my left diving down towards the formation of Spitfires, so I turned to engage them. They pulled out of the dive and commenced circling and crossing over alternately one behind the other. I waited until one crossed from left to right and closed right in on a climbing quarter, firing with full deflection and allowing the enemy aircraft to run through the sight. The enemy aircraft rolled over onto its back, the nose went up and it spun down inverted. I followed the other one round, occasionally glancing at the first one, which continued spinning until it disappeared below the clouds. As soon as the 1st aircraft had disappeared, the 2nd one dived way on a southerly course and although I followed at full throttle until I had crossed the coast at Brighton, I could not catch him.

G.H.B.

Bennions' Combat Report was later annotated by the Squadron's Intelligence Officer: 'P/O Bennions seriously wounded 1/10/40 certified copy.'

Meanwhile, Lovell selected a Bf 109 as his target and dived down to make the attack, his combat report read:

...fired all my ammunition in short bursts into it, starting at 250 yards and closing to 50 yards. At my first burst, white vapour came out from the wing roots on both sides. The 109 continued down to the cloud and home....'

Having run out of ammunition, Lovell flew in line astern of the aircraft and noted the number of bullet holes along the fuselage. The Bf 109 (No 5814, 9+) of I./JG1, which Lovell was only able to claim as damaged, crashed at Chequers, Shadoxhurst, south of Ashford; its pilot, *Unteroffizier* Edward Garnith, bailed out and was captured.

The RAF claimed forty-five enemy aircraft destroyed, plus thirty-two as probably destroyed, with twenty-nine damaged, with one destroyed by ground-fire. Meanwhile, twenty RAF fighters were lost, with eight pilots killed or posted as missing.

Lovell's name was put forward for the award of the DFC in early November. The recommendation read:

Flight Lieutenant LOVELL has flown with his Squadron in active operations against the enemy continuously since the War began. In the early days, whilst operating from his home base at CATTERICK, he destroyed 1 Ju 88 and 1 Me 110, and later from HORNCHURCH, during the DUNKIRK operations, he, in company with another pilot, destroyed 2 He 111s. Since then he has himself destroyed a further 4 Me 109s and 1 Me 109 probably destroyed, making a personal total of 7 destroyed and 1 probably destroyed.

This gallant young Officer has led his Flight, and on occasion his Squadron with great courage, coolness, and determination, and his successes are the reward of hard fighting over a long period.

Air Officer Commanding No. 11 Group, Air Vice Marshal Park, added his endorsement in similar terms, the award being approved by Air Chief Marshall H C T Dowding.

Lovell's DFC was promulgated in the *London Gazette* of 26 November 1940:

Air Ministry 26 November 1940

The King has been graciously pleased to approve the under-mentioned appointments and awards, in recognition of gallantry displayed in flying operations against the enemy:

Award of the Distinguished Flying Cross
Acting Flight Lieutenant Anthony Desmond Joseph LOVELL (40402) – No. 41 Squadron
    This officer has flown continuously on active operations against the enemy since war began. He has shown a fine fighting spirit and has led his flight and on occasions his squadron with great courage, coolness and determination. He has destroyed seven enemy aircraft.

Notes
1. Lock would destroy Bf 109s on 5th, 9th, 11th, 20th October and two Bf 109s on 17 November, before being shot-down and wounded. Lock was awarded the DFC (*London Gazette* 1 November 1940) and Bar (*London Gazette* 22 November 1940), and the DSO (*London Gazette* 17 December 1940).

   London Gazette 1 November 1940
   Air Ministry 1 November, 1940

   Royal Air Force
   The King has been graciously pleased to approve the following awards in recognition of gallantry displayed in flying operations against the enemy:

Pilot Officer Eric Stanley LOCK (81642), Royal Air Force Volunteer Reserve.
This officer has destroyed nine enemy aircraft, eight of these within a period of one week. He has displayed great vigour and determination in pressing home his attacks.
London Gazette 22 November 1940
Air Ministry 22 November, 1940

Royal Air Force
The King has been graciously pleased to approve the following awards in recognition of gallantry displayed in flying operations against the enemy:

Awarded a Bar to the Distinguished Flying Cross
Pilot Officer Eric Stanley LOCK, DFC (81642), Royal Air Force Volunteer Reserve.
In September, 1940, while engaged on a patrol over the Dover area, Pilot Officer Lock engaged three *Heinkel* 113s one of which he shot down into the sea. Immediately afterwards he engaged a *Henschel* 126 and destroyed it. He has displayed great courage in the face of heavy odds, and his skill and coolness in combat have enabled him to destroy fifteen enemy aircraft within a period of nineteen days.

London Gazette 17 December 1940
Air Ministry 17 December, 1940

Royal Air Force
The King has been graciously pleased to approve the following appointments and awards in recognition of gallantry displayed in flying operations against the enemy:

Appointed a Companion of the Distinguished Service Order.
Pilot Officer Eric Stanley LOCK, DFC (81642), Royal Air Force Volunteer Reserve, No. 41 Squadron.
This officer has shown exceptional keenness and courage in his attacks against the enemy. In November, 1940, whilst engaged with his squadron in attacking a superior number of enemy forces, he destroyed two *Messerschmitt* 109s, thus bringing his total to at least twenty-two. His magnificent fighting spirit and personal example have been within the highest traditions of the Service.

2. Flying Officer Dennis Arthur 'Fanny' Adams, AAF, had served with No. 611 Squadron since 1938, training on Hawker Hind light bombers. On 1 January 1939, the squadron became a part of No. 12 Group, Fighter Command and on 19 May they received their first Spitfires. Adams had flown numerous convoy patrols before making his first sortie with the squadron over Dunkirk on 23 May, probably destroying a Ju 87 over the beaches on 2 June. When 'A' Flight was detached to Ternhill, Adam must have felt that he would miss all of the action, the remainder of the squadron flying stints at Digby and Duxford, where throughout September they took part in 'Big Wing' operations. Adams, however, was able to destroy a Do 215 reconnaissance aircraft of 2 (F)/121 on 21 September.
   Serving with No. 41 Squadron, Adams was shot down by return fire from a Do 17 on 17 October while over Folkestone, while flying N 3267. Forced to take to his parachute, he landed at Douglas Farm, Postling. He survived the Battle and was posted away in the following April, tour expired.
   Flying Officer Desmond Hugh O'Neill (40638) joined the RAF on a short service commission in January 1938 and trained at No. 10 FTS Ternhill before serving with

No. 2 Anti-Aircraft Co-operation Unit at Lee-on-Solent. Having converted to Spitfires, O'Neill was flying with No. 611 Squadron at RAF Digby by August 1940, before being posted to No. 41 Squadron. Flying Officer O'Neill was killed in a flying accident on 11 October 1940, when he collided with Sergeant L R Carter during a battle climb to engage Bf 109s. He bailed out of his Spitfire (X4042), which fell near the Crooked Billet, Ash, but he died when his parachute failed to open. O'Neill was the son of Lieutenant Colonel Edward M M and Ethel M O'Neill of Glasnevin, Dublin, Ireland and husband of Muriel O'Neill. He was buried in Streatham Park Cemetery, Surrey, Square 7A, Grave 12104. He was 25.

Flying Officer James Richard Walker, a Canadian, had joined the RAF on a short service commission in October 1938 and had completed his training in time to join No. 611 Squadron at Ternhill on 27 July 1940. With No. 41 Squadron he would claim Bf 109s destroyed on 7 and 9 October, before volunteering to serve in Malta. Sadly, he was lost with five other Hurricane pilots when they took off from the deck of HMS *Argus* with a Fleet Air Arm (FAA) Skua acting at navigator – the Hurricanes ran out of fuel and all six pilots were killed. He is remembered on the Runnymede Memorial.

Flying Officer Maurice Peter Brown joined the RAF in March 1938 and had joined No. 610 Squadron by the Battle of Britain. He shared in the destruction of a Do 17 before being posted to No. 41 Squadron, claiming a Bf 109 on 20 October. Brown later won the AFC (*London Gazette* 1/1/1946) and retired from the RAF as a squadron leader later that year.

Pilot Officer Denys Edgar Mileham had joined No. 610 Squadron at Acklington on 3 September 1940. Flying with No. 41 Squadron, Mileham destroyed a Bf 109 on 5 October but later transferred to No. 234 Squadron, with whom he was serving when he was killed in action as a flight lieutenant, on 15 April 1942. He is remembered on the Runnymede Memorial, Panel 66. He was 22.

Pilot Officer Gilbert Graham Fairley Draper joined the RAF in August 1939 and having gained his 'wings' was with No. 2 Squadron when he volunteered for Fighter Command in August the following year. He joined No. 610 Squadron at Acklington on 3 September, following a conversion course at No. 7 OTU Hawarden. Flying with No. 41 Squadron, Draper was shot down while in combat over Ashford on 30 October. His Spitfire (P7282) crashed at New Barn Farm, Postling, Draper was slightly injured and taken to Willesborough Hospital, where he was admitted. Draper was later shot down again on 7 August 1941, while over Fruge, near Lille. He spent the remainder of the war as a PoW.

Pilot Officer John Gage Lecky entered RAF College Cranwell in April 1939 and received his commission in March the following year, his course having been shortened due to the outbreak of hostilities. Initially serving with an Army Co-operation Unit, Lecky joined No. 610 Squadron at Biggin Hill in August, before transferring to No. 41 Squadron.

Lecky was shot down by Bf 109s on 11 October and bailed out but was killed. His Spitfire (P9447) crashed at Preston Hall, Maidstone. He was buried in All Saint's churchyard, Tilford, Surrey. He was 19.

Chapter 14

Against All Odds

With a raid plotted heading for Dover, No. 41 Squadron was scrambled at 13.05 hours on 1 October, when Flight Lieutenant Ryder led twelve Spitfires with orders to patrol a line between Hornchurch and Rochford at 28,000ft.

The raid crossed the coast and the Observer Corps reported two formations of fifty enemy aircraft, one heading for Maidstone and Biggin Hill. Vectored onto the enemy, No. 41 Squadron located a number of Bf 109s flying several thousand feet below them. Ryder, who remained in command of the squadron in the air, gave the order and the squadron dived down into the attack. In the ensuing melée Finlay, acting as Blue 2, together with Pilot Officer Adams, managed to damage a Bf 109 before the squadron broke off the attack and landed at 14.40 hours. The aircraft were immediately refuelled and rearmed ready for another patrol.

The second heavy raid didn't materialize until later that afternoon when fifty enemy aircraft appeared flying north-west towards Biggin Hill. Another formation of the same strength followed but very soon both withdrew. In all, some thirteen squadrons were detailed to the attack.

At 16.10 hours seventy enemy aircraft flew in three successive waves towards Kenley, in what would be the third large raid of the day. Forty raiders approached the south-east edge of London's Inner Artillery Zone but immediately turned south-east. The remainder turned away before reaching London. All of the enemy aircraft had re-crossed the coast by 16.40 hours.

Due to go on leave and travel home that evening, Bennions was wearing his best blue uniform when No. 41 Squadron was scrambled against a force of Bf 109s flying at 20,000ft just north of Brighton. Bennions had remained at dispersals rather than collect his things and wait out the afternoon in the Officer's Mess so he decided to fly one last sortie and try to make his total of kills an even twelve: 'I thought I'd like to shoot one more Hun down before going for a rest.'

It was at about 15.50 hours that the squadron was scrambled and nine Spitfires were ordered to patrol the Maidstone area flying at 30,500ft where they intercepted raid No. 15, which consisted of about twenty-five Bf 109s flying some 500ft below.

'A' Flight followed Flight Lieutenant Lovell into the attack. The enemy dived off into clouds as Lovell pursued one Bf 109, firing off all of his ammunition, claiming it as damaged. Low on oxygen and unable to engage the fleeing enemy fighters, the remainder of the squadron reformed on Lovell at 12,000ft and made for base.

It was at about 16.55 hours when Bennions (flying EB-J X4559), who still had half of his oxygen remaining, saw a formation of Hurricanes about to be attacked by around forty Bf 109s.

Radioing a warning to his CO, Bennions followed the set routine of flying along side Finlay's Spitfire, indicating the direction of the enemy. However, the inexperienced Finlay saw the Hurricanes but not the Bf 109s flying some 500ft above them and ready to pounce. Unheard by Bennions, he had radioed that the aircraft were 'friendly'.

Bennions, meanwhile, had continued his dive towards the Bf 109s, suddenly realizing that he was alone and heading into the Bf 109s against impossible odds. He decided to latch onto the last aircraft in the formation and make a hit and run attack, hoping to distract the enemy long enough for the Hurricanes to escape the danger or at least to reposition ready to take on the *Messerschmitts.*

Pressing the gun button, Bennions fired two concentrated bursts, which struck the Bf 109 in the engine and fuselage. The enemy fighter caught fire and Bennions saw the canopy fly off as the pilot bailed out over Henfield. At that moment a cannon shell exploded in Bennions' cockpit, red-hot shell splinters piercing his skull, destroying his left eye and damaging the other, causing deep burns and multiple lacerations.

Bennions' Spitfire went into a steep dive, but somehow he managed to pull the nose up, but the pain in his right arm and his leg told him that his wounds were more extensive than the obvious head and eye injuries: 'I cleared my other eye with my glove and found I was able to see vaguely. I could see that the hood and cockpit were shattered, so I decided to bail out.'

Bleeding heavily from his wounds and with the median nerve to his right hand severed, Bennions struggled to extricate himself from the crippled fighter: 'I undid the oxygen tube, disconnected the wireless plug, slid back the hood, opened the door and fell over the side. I don't know what altitude the aircraft was at – I couldn't see.'

He had never made a parachute descent – while the theory was covered in pilot training, there were no facilities for pilots to practice the drill that might well save their life: 'When I felt myself clear and falling through space, I put my left thumb through the ring of my ripcord and gave a slight pull. I felt a terrific jerk as my parachute opened, then I lost consciousness.'

Looking on in awe as Bennions had taken on forty Bf 109s single-handed was farm-hand Mr. J Shepherd of Dunstall Farm, Henfield. Following the developing combat he witnessed Bennions destroy one Bf 109 before his own aircraft was hit and fell in flames at Heathenthorn Farm, near Aldborne.

Shepherd saw the limp body of the semi-conscious pilot floating down and raced to the scene where he discovered the badly injured Bennions, burnt and bleeding heavily from the head, face arm and leg. Bennions opened his right eye but could not see and believed he was blind: 'The thing I remember is lying on the ground telling my name and Squadron to someone attending me.'

The farm workers had already sent for help and administered what first aid they could, but Bennions was in great pain and slipping in and out of consciousness: 'Everything faded completely.'

Using a five-bar gate as a stretcher, Shepherd and another farmhand carried Bennions to an ambulance which took him to Horsham Cottage Base Hospital. Weakened through loss of blood he received five pints of plasma on arrival, while doctors tried to stabilize his condition and worked to save the full use of his right hand and his right eye.

On 2 October the following signal was received at 14.05 at hours RAF Catterick:

ADVISE MRS BENNIONS MOWBRAY ROAD CATTERICK P/O BENNIONS SERIOUSLY WOUNDED AT PRESENT AT HORSHAM COTTAGE HOSPITAL

Avis rushed to be by her husband's side, as did his mother. Philip, however, was kept away owing to the severity of his brother's injuries. His immediate reaction had been to enlist but he was turned away as he was still underage; it would be another three years before he joined his brother in the Services.

Meanwhile, doctors had told Bennions that he had lost the sight in his left eye. It would have to be removed if they were to have any chance of saving the other, which otherwise would develop cataracts and he would lose his sight. Understanding that this would mean the end of his flying career, Bennions initially refused but after a forty-eight-hour delay he finally had to agree. Emergency surgery saved his right eye, although for weeks afterwards Bennions could barely distinguish light from shade.

Plastic surgeon, Sir Archibald McIndoe visited Bennions at Horsham, where he assessed his facial and head wounds. The shell splinters had damaged Bennions' skull, leaving his brain partly exposed. It was decided that the best place to treat these injuries was at the specialist unit at The Queen Victoria Hospital, East Grinstead.

As with so many of the patients who had suffered traumatic head and facial burns, or who had lost their sight or suffered other injuries that they knew would result in them being grounded, Bennions had physiological issues to address and conquer before he could truly begin on the recovery process:

> I was very concerned, very upset, feeling rather annoyed with myself for having been shot down so decisively and for having sort of put myself out of contention. I felt, I don't know, awful feelings really, terribly isolated. I couldn't see, I couldn't hear very well. I couldn't recognize people unless it was someone really close to me.
>
> My wife came down and my mother came down. But I was feeling extremely sorry for myself which is a very bad thing for anybody. I felt so deflated just as though half my life had been taken and the half wasn't worth bothering with. It was, I think, the worst period of my life, but you get over it.
>
> I think the people in the hospital; one person in particular, put me on a much more even footing. I think he was a South African, Godfrey Edmunds was his name. He'd been badly burnt.

Another of those whose stoicism deeply effected Bennions was a patient in Ward 3:

> ...my friend, the chap I'd joined up with from school. He was in Ward 3 in East Grinstead. He'd been shot down flying Hurricanes. He had heard that I'd been admitted to the hospital. He'd sent a message along, 'Could I go and see him?' he couldn't get out of bed, his legs were badly burnt. Would I go and see him?
>
> I was on crutches at the time, but I managed to get over there with a hell of a lot of a struggle and self pity. As I opened the door in Ward 3, I saw what I can only describe now as the most horrifying thing I had ever seen in my life. That was this chap who had been badly burnt, really badly burnt. His hair was burnt off, his eyebrows were burnt off, his eyelids were burnt off, you could just see his staring eyes. His nose was burnt, there were just two holes in his face. His lips were badly burnt. I looked down at his feet also. His feet were burnt.
>
> I got through the door on crutches with a bit of a struggle. This chap started propelling a wheelchair down the ward. Halfway down he picked up a chair with his teeth. That's when I noticed how badly his lips were burnt. I mean, his lips were badly burned but he caught hold of the back of the chair with his teeth, and he rested the back legs on the little platform on the front of his wheelchair and he came on towards me, the new boy, at the entrance to the ward.
>
> He stopped beside me, slung the chair off along side, and said: 'Have a seat, old boy.'

And I thought: 'What have I got to complain about?' And, from then on, I started to recover.

The patient in Ward 3 was Sergeant Ralph Carnall of No. 111 (F) Squadron. Bennions and Carnall had been boyhood friends, both enlisting in the RAF at the same time. Ralph Carnall had flown Hawker Hurricanes over Dunkirk and was later shot down on the first day of the Battle of Britain and again on 16 August, on the second occasion being badly burned.

The dedicated staff were kindness itself as Bennions had already discovered. During his eighteen-week stay he underwent a programme of plastic surgery and became one of Archie McIndoe's 'Guinea Pigs'. Bennions recalled that his facial injuries were considered so distressing that for the first month he was not permitted to see a mirror – not that at that time he would have been able to see anything bar the barest outlines.

Bennions later recalled how the Guinea Pigs were immensely proud of wearing their Service uniform and air crew brevets and despite their injuries, refused to wear Hospital Blues, the traditional uniform of convalescing Servicemen. Their protests were eventually heard and they were permitted to wear their RAF uniforms, including most importantly, their wings. McIndoe would use the threat of wearing 'Blues' to try to check some of the men's livelier antics.

Of course, alcohol was forbidden in the hospital, but somehow it got onto the wards and there were impromptu parties and personal celebrations, all of which helped the men along their individual road to recovery.

Of Sir Archibald Hector McIndoe FRCS, Bennions wrote:

He was a god. Really. A remarkable man. Nothing was too much trouble for him when he was caring for the needs of the aircrew he was looking after. He could have got us to do anything.

He hated red tape. He used to cut through it – and that didn't make him popular in Whitehall. He frequently had arguments over his insistence that we, and he, had the facilities that he needed. Once, he threatened that, if he didn't have more money and equipment, he'd mobilize all of us, wheelchairs, crutches, and all, and march us down Whitehall to shame the powers-that-be. We'd have done it for him, too.

Flying had meant everything to me. I had lost an eye, couldn't even write or walk, and felt that my whole life was finished. But Archie was such a marvellous man, and seeing people around me who were much worse off than I was gave me a sense of proportion.

Bennions' injuries had thrown his and his family's lives into turmoil. After the initial fears that he might not survive his head wounds, they had to face the possibility that he might have been permanently blinded. Now with the sight in his right eye saved, Bennions had began the long process of undergoing facial reconstruction operations. Gradually he made a steady recovery and practical matters had to be dealt with.

Avis spent her time between Catterick and East Grinstead. With Bennions still on No. 41 Squadron's strength, the family was able to remain amidst their friends in their long-term home, which provided some stability both for Avis and Connie.

The farmer whose prompt actions helped save Bennions' life was moved to write to his CO explaining the circumstances surrounding his injuries. The letter was marked 'Confidential for background information only!' by the squadron's Intelligence Officer, Lord Gisborough:

1.10.40
P/O Bennions
'Missing – B[aled] O[ut]
Dunstalls Farm
Henfield
Sussex
3rd October, 1940
To OC 41 Squadron RAF

Dear Sir,
    Pardon me for writing, but you may like to hear of one of your Pilot Officers – I think he said his name was Pilot Officer Bennelles? (DFC)? of the above Squadron.
    I was watching the air battle, when your Pilot Officer shot down a *Messerschmitt* 109 – then about 40 Germans dived on to him and he was hit with a cannon shell. He must have been nearly blind before he bailed out, coming down half a mile from the above address. I and others bandaged him up as well as we could before he was taken to Hospital at Horsham.
    He is a brave Pilot and a credit to his Squadron and may God help him to get well, as I being an ex RAF man I am proud to think we have such brave lads in the RAF.
    Please forgive me for writing, but I thought you would like to know.

I remain, Sir,
Yours faithfully,
(Signed) C. J. Shepherd

A copy was forwarded to Bennions who, once he was able to focus well enough to write, penned a letter thanking Shepherd for all he and his friends had done.

Chapter 15

An Appointment at the Palace

One of the many stages along Bennions' path to recovery was socializing with his fellow pilots beyond the walls of The Queen Victoria Hospital and becoming a part of the wider RAF family once more. An opportunity to re-enter the scene came as a result of his award of the DFC, which had been promulgated in the Supplement to the *London Gazette* published on 1 October 1940, the date of his fateful combat. The entry read:

Air Ministry 1st October, 1940.

Royal Air Force
The King has been graciously pleased to approve the under-mentioned appointment and awards in recognition of gallantry displayed in flying operations against the enemy:-

Pilot Officer George Herman BENNIONS (43354).
Pilot Officer Bennions has led his section with great distinction. He has destroyed seven enemy aircraft and possibly several others. His determination and coolness have had a splendid influence on his squadron as a whole.

By the time Bennions' award had been officially announced, he had already destroyed another four enemy aircraft, claiming a fifth in dramatic fashion when single-handedly taking on forty Bf 109s in order to save a formation of Hurricanes. Meanwhile, he had probably damaged another five.

It was generally accepted that four to five kills warranted the award of the DFC, a similar number triggering a second award or Bar, although it may be noted that Lock had nine confirmed kills before he was recommended for the DFC, and had scored fifteen victories in nineteen days, before Finlay got around to recommending him for a Bar.

Towards the end of the year, with the Battle of Britain won, Fighter Command was no longer on the back-foot and had already begun flying offensive sorties over enemy occupied Europe. There was time to re-assess some of the events of the summer, when all that had stood between Hitler and invasion had been the English Channel and the 'Few'. Some 544 men had died during the air battles and many more, like Bennions, suffered terrible injuries. The successes of many pilots had been acknowledged with gallantry awards, promotions, or with a Mention-in-Despatches. But the pace of the campaign had been rapid and it had often proved difficult for the paperwork to keep up with the events as they unfolded, while the subsequent deaths of material witnesses meant that many individual acts of heroism were never reported and prolonged gallantry often went unrewarded. In this respect, No. 41 Squadron stood out, with the loss of four squadron leaders or flight commanders in the space of a few short weeks.

Consequently, Bennions' case is not the only instance of No. 41 Squadron's pilots being overlooked for gallantry awards. Other names which spring to mind include Boyle, who destroyed five enemy aircraft, with two shared destroyed, and Carr-Lewty who flew during the Dunkirk operations and made 100 sorties during the Battle of Britain. As a flight commander, Ryder had continued to lead from the front and had shot down another five enemy aircraft before the end of November, while Usmar and Wallens both got close to five confirmed kills. Even their former CO's award of a DFC was not promulgated until the end of March 1941.

There was, however, the opportunity to make amends, when presumably on the instigation of Air Vice Marshal Saul, who was evidently concerned at the lack of a recommendation for a second gallantry award, No. 13 Group took the unusual step of writing to Squadron Leader Finlay requesting details of Bennions' flying record and his total 'score'. The letter was dated 27 December 1940.

Clearly, Bennions should have received more adulation and a second gallantry award; his tally had nearly doubled since the recommendation for the DFC was submitted. The reply from Finlay, however, was late in coming, woefully so considering that its contents were already known at the time of the original enquiry four months earlier – Bennion's tally had been chalked-up on the squadron's unofficial scoreboard, while a twenty-minute scan through the Squadron Operations Book and a glance at Bennions' DFC recommendation or citation, followed by a conversation with Lovell or Ryder, would have provided all of the relevant information. In Finlay's defence, he was increasingly involved in patrols and combats during October and November 1940.

The reply, when finally composed, read:

From No 41 Squadron, Catterick
To RAF Station, Catterick
Date 4 May, 1941
(Marked) Confidential, for background information only!
A/F/Lt G H Bennions DFC

1. With reference to Headquarters, No. 13 Group letter 13G/ S.3014/Int. Dated 27th December, 1940, the following details concerning the above mentioned officer have been consolidated from information recently compiled and are submitted with the recommendation as stated for further recognition.
2. PO Bennions was an operational pilot in No. 41 Squadron since the outbreak of war until October, 1940, when he was seriously wounded and shot down. On September 17th, 1940, he was awarded the DFC having at the time of the award destroyed 7 enemy aircraft.
3. Subsequent to this award P/O Bennions destroyed a further 5 enemy aircraft and probably destroyed 5 more. His operational fighting ended when he was shot down in a big battle over Sussex, which culminated in the loss of one eye, on October, 1st 1940. A letter received from a farmer who witnessed the battle stated that P/O Bennions fought a large formation of enemy fighters single-handed. During the latter half of September when 41 Squadron was in a depleted state, with the Commanding Officer wounded and only one Flight Commander available, P/O Bennions led the Squadron on several occasions.
4. Throughout the whole of his operational career, this officer displayed a fine offensive spirit and great courage. When the necessity arose, he took over leadership of the squadron with equal skill and determination and was a great factor in the success of the Squadron through this difficult period.

(signed) D Finlay S/Ldr
Commanding No. 41 Squadron, Catterick

The tardy reply was sent months after Air Vice Marshal Saul's departure from No. 13 Group in January 1941, and evidently failed to result in action from his successor. The letter was not a 'recommendation' for a particular award in itself and, perhaps, should have been accompanied by the appropriate recommendation form – there would be no Bar to Bennions' DFC.

Finlay, of course, had been present at the outset of Bennion's fateful sortie, but was left behind when he dived into the formation of Bf 109s to save a flight of Hurricane pilots from annihilation. He had not observed the enemy fighters bearing down on the Hurricanes, even when their presence had been pointed out to him by a more experienced fighter pilot. Furthermore, when Bennions, who had come alongside his leader's Spitfire and signalled the location of the enemy before peeling off into the attack, Finlay had failed to follow Bennions' descent and its outcome.

Shepherd's testimony tells us that the sky was clear enough for the farm worker to appreciate that Bennions had initiated the attack by diving down into the formation of around forty Bf 109s in order to save the Hurricanes. Meanwhile, Bennions was also able to appreciate the scene below him from his own initial vantage-point and Finlay had evidently seen the Hurricanes but not the Bf 109s just above them.

The act of supreme gallantry which ultimately led to the end of Bennions' combat role in the Battle of Britain is underplayed in Finlay's letter. There is no mention of the figure of forty enemy aircraft, given by Bennions and corroborated by an independent witness on the ground, nor of the fact that in making his attack he saved a much smaller formation of Hurricane pilots who would otherwise have been 'bounced' by the 109s. The omissions were most regretable.

Recovering from his wounds and with no thoughts of medals and recognition, Bennions wrote to C J Shepherd, whose prompt actions undoubtedly helped to save the sight of his other eye. He kept Shepherd's reply, which echoed many people's sentiments at the lack of a Bar to Bennions' DFC:

Dunstalls Farm
Henfield
Sussex
22 Jan 41

Dear Sir
How pleased I was & surprised to hear from you but I am very sorry indeed to hear you have lost your eye although I thought you would when I bandaged it up for you.

I have been looking in the papers to see if you got a bar to your DFC as God knows you should have as many a Pilot would have set for home when they saw they were out numbered as you were that day as I have seen since where a pilot went into 40 alone and he got the DFC. Still, I suppose it was because only a few people saw it, had an officer in the Navy or Army seen it and wrote as I did, you would no doubt have got it, but thank God you are still alive as the Rev (indecipherable) of Henfield asked us all to pray for you in church the next Sunday. I hope you are quite well again now and again thanking you for letting me know how you got on.

I remain
Yours Sincerely
C J Shepherd

An article appeared in the press later in the year, which evidently quoted Shepherd's account of the incident under the headline 'One Against Forty':

Shot-down pilot got *Messerschmitt* first.

Standing on a Suffolk farm, an ex-RAF man saw a Spitfire pilot attack a formation of 40 *Messerschmitts* single-handed and send one diving to the earth in flames before he himself was shot down.

The onlooker wrote to the CO of the Fighter Squadron: 'He is a brave pilot and a credit to his squadron. May God help him to get well. I am proud to think we have such brave lads in the RAF.'

The pilot, badly injured, landed by parachute in a field half a mile from the farm.

He told his story in hospital, and yesterday it was released by the Air Ministry news service: 'Everything faded out.'

Homeward bound after a patrol the pilot sighted a formation of Hurricanes, and to the east a large formation of *Messerschmitt* 109s, he decided to attack.

'I chose what I thought to be the last of a series and attacked the nearest one,' he said. After two short bursts from the starboard quarter the enemy aircraft caught fire, and the pilot opened his hood.

'Just then I was struck by cannon fire in the cockpit. Everything faded out completely, and I vaguely remember pulling the aircraft out of a steep dive.

'I undid the straps and cleared my right eye with my glove, and remembered seeing the hood shattered.

'I slid back the sliding portion and climbed out, and after a short interval pulled the rip cord. I lost consciousness several times on the way down and eventually landed in a field. I tried to stand up after a few minutes but could not. Later someone came along and attended to me.'

The ex RAF man, who with others, bandaged him before he was taken to hospital, confirmed his victory over one *Messerschmitt*. He saw about 40 Germans dive on the Spitfire.

The pilot, who was awarded the DFC some time ago, is now out of hospital.

Bennions' injuries meant that he was unable to attend Buckingham Palace to receive his award until February 1941, when he received the award from the hands of the King. The letter informing Bennions of the ceremony read:

Central Chancery of
The Order of Knighthood
St James's Palace SW1
3rd February, 1941

Sir,

The King will hold an Investiture at Buckingham Palace on Tuesday the 18th February, at which your attendance is requested.

It is requested that you should be at the Palace not later than 10.15 o'clock a.m.

Dress – Service Dress, Morning Dress or Civil Defence Uniform.

This letter should be produced on entering the Palace, as no further card or admission will be issued.

Two tickets for relations or friends to witness the Investiture may be obtained on application to this Office and it is urgently requested that the application should bear the same reference number as on the card enclosed.

Please send an <u>immediate acknowledgment</u> to the Secretary, Central Chancery of the Orders of the Knighthood, St James's Palace, London, SW1, on the enclosed card.

I am, Sir,
Your obedient Servant
(Signed) Secretary.

Pilot Officer George H. Bennions DFC, RAF

Bennions duly replied, requesting tickets for Avis and their daughter Connie, who was old enough to appreciate the ceremony without being overawed by the day. The beige tickets arrived a few days later: 'Buckingham Palace. Admit one to witness the Investiture Central Chancery of the Order of the Knighthood 18th February, 1941.'

The family travelled down from Catterick by rail, stopping overnight in the war-torn capital. The atmosphere in London had changed. This was not the Buckingham Palace of pre-war picture-books: the guardsmen with their bright red tunics and tall bearskins had given way to khaki-clad soldiers in their tin helmets and sandbagged sentry-posts, while the windows were either shuttered or criss-crossed with brown paper strips to prevent splintering. After five months of relentless *Luftwaffe* night raids, much of London was bomb-damaged. The Palace had suffered several direct hits. Indeed, at least one investiture in 1940 had had to take place in a shelter, due to the imminent threat of a raid.

On arrival at Buckingham Palace, George saw Avis and Connie to the friends' and relatives' gallery from where they were ushered into the Investiture room and sat down on the gilded chairs awaiting the beginning of the award ceremony. Meanwhile, Bennions was shown to an ante-room, where many of those due to receive their awards were already gathering. After a brief wait and time to become acquainted with some of the other RAF personnel, a number of Palace staff entered the room and gathered the medal recipients together, before a senior official gave them a run through the proceedings, reminding them of the etiquette which had to be observed by all ranks: they were instructed not to speak to the King unless spoken to first, not to look the King in the eyes, not to initiate a conversation, and to give simple answers to any question the King asked before retiring when dismissed.

Everyone was issued a hooked clasp to attach to their uniform's breast pocket and onto which His Majesty would hang their award.

As the appointed hour approached, the servicemen were lined up in order of seniority both in rank and their awards. All arose for the National Anthem as King George VI entered the Investiture room. The King stood before them in the full dress uniform of an Admiral of the Fleet, while the aides-de-camp of the three Services and the Lord Chamberlain were in close attendance. Adjacent stood the Gentlemen at Arms.

The ceremony had begun and one by one the recipients were called forward to receive their awards. At length Bennions found himself on the threshold of the Investiture room, waiting for his name to be called out, upon which an officer indicated for him to march into the room and up to the Lord Chamberlain where he halted, turned left and faced the King. He couldn't help being surprised at the slight appearance of the monarch. Pausing now, Bennions heard his name announced: 'To receive the Distinguished Flying Cross, Flying Officer George Herman Bennions, Royal Air Force.' He bowed from the neck before taking three steps forward. The King placed the DFC onto its hook before shaking his hand firmly and offered his congratulations with a warm smile. Bennions took three steps backwards and bowed, turned and marched out of the room.

Avis and Connie who had witnessed the ceremony with the other friends and families waited for Bennions to reappear. There had been a number of honours and awards and it took a while for remaining presentations to be made and the ceremony concluded, the NCOs receiving their awards last of all. Bennions didn't like the class distinction which extended even as far as how the medals were presented: the officers receiving the DFC were given a plush box for their crosses, while the NCOs were handed a plain cardboard box for their DFMs.

As they left the Palace, the Press descended on the award-winners and their families and guests, taking photographs and asking for quotes for the next day's newspapers. George, Avis and Connie were photographed as they strode off out of the gates and into the Mall. The family were able to take in some of the sights and sounds of the capital, enjoying a meal and buying a few souvenirs of the day before making the return journey north to Catterick. It had been a tiring day but it was an important landmark both in Bennions' career but also in his fight back to a full recovery.

Chapter 16

The Long Road Back

Returning to duty with No. 41 Squadron, still based at Catterick, Bennions found many of his fellow officers were sympathetic to his plight and he managed to wangle the occasional unofficial flight in a Spitfire, but the Air Ministry were less willing to allow a one-eyed pilot to fly, no matter who he was. Bennions was sent to Central Flying School to be assessed for flying duties. Their verdict was that he had lost none of his flying abilities but they could not pass him without a medical, which resulted in an A2B Non-Operational rating. This meant that Bennions could fly but not operationally, nor was he permitted to fly at night, and he had to have a passenger acting as a spotter and to assist with judging distance particularly on landing etc.

Promoted to the rank of flying officer on 1 April 1941, Bennions resumed his pre-war duties in the Control Room at Catterick where he became Fighter Controller, later being promoted to Senior Controller. But Bennions' thoughts were on flying again and he asked his Wing Commander to sponsor his efforts to get back behind the controls of an aircraft, resulting in the following letter to HQ No. 13 Group:

From RAF Station Catterick
To Headquarters, No 13 Group
23rd November 1941

Squadron Leader G. H. Bennions, DFC
Enclosed herewith for your consideration is an application from S/L Bennions for permission to keep flying practice or to transfer to the GD (General Duties) Branch of the RAF.

On several occasions S/L Bennions has piloted me in a dual control aircraft. There is no doubt from my personal experience that he is an exceptional pilot and in spite of the loss of one eye he always seems to know the position of other aircraft which may be in the air at the same time.

In the circumstances it is recommended that this matter should be referred to the Air Ministry with the request that authority should be given for S/L Bennions to fly any type of aircraft for the purpose of keeping himself in flying practice and to enable him to use aeroplanes for communications purposes.

At the time of writing, S/L Bennions is employed as Chief Controller in the Sector Operations Room at Catterick. He has complete knowledge of his job together with organization ability and in my opinion is very well employed for the benefit of the Service.

(Signed) G F Wood
Wing Commander Commanding,
RAF Station, Catterick

With time, Bennions was permitted to continue flying practice and during April 1942, he flew both Tiger Moths and the Miles Master, making local solo flights. Initially he flew on little more than a wide circuit of the aerodrome, spending just ten minutes in the air, but soon he was making flights of twenty and forty minutes' duration, eventually being sanctioned to make a longer trip. Officially, however, he could only fly with a second pilot in case he experienced difficulties, particularly in judging distances on landing.

Bennions was promoted to the rank of flight lieutenant on 1 June and seven days later achieved one of his personal goals when he flew a Spitfire on a seventy-five minute gunnery exercise. Still hoping to serve in combat role, no doubt Bennions saw this as a further step towards operational sorties. More flights in a Spitfire followed over the next weeks and months, while during October and November he made five air to air gunnery flights. When, on 7 December, a barrage balloon came adrift from its mooring and threatened to damage power and telephone lines, Bennions was scrambled and successfully shot the balloon down. More air to air gunnery practice was to follow in December, while on the 23rd and 28th Bennions flew interception patrols.

Bennions' continued devotion to duty, despite his wounds, was acknowledged by an official 'Mention-in-Despatches', which was promulgated in the New Year's Honours List of January 1943. Later in the year the official parchment arrived, which read:

By the King's order the name of A/Squadron Leader G H Bennions DFC, Royal Air Force was published in the *London Gazette* 1 January, 1943, is Mentioned-in-Despatch for distinguished service. I am charged to record His Majesty's high appreciation.

(Signed) Archibald Sinclair
Secretary of State for Air

More co-operation and low flying exercises followed, while on 5 February Bennions carried out a convoy patrol, something which had become painfully mundane in early 1940, but which was another important marker along his personal road to recovery. Bennions was to make a further eight air-firing flights during the coming weeks and on 1 March practiced air attacks, 'bouncing' an 'enemy' formation. Making his approaches from behind and slightly above, he checked his mirror for 'the Hun in the sun' before lining-up the last aircraft in the formation. Waiting until it filled the sight, he pressed the gun-button and gave it a 'short burst' – he felt exhilarated.

Bennions remained keen to get the opportunity to fly operationally, that much was plain for all to see. He was delighted to learn of a posting to North Africa where he was put in charge of a party of ground crew belonging to No. 219 Squadron. It was a first step, although his role was only ever meant to be temporary. Bennions' next appointment was as RAF Liaison Officer in the Mediterranean, working with the Spitfire-flying pilots of the US 31st and 52nd Fighter Groups. Respected by all ranks, Bennions found the Americans were more liberal when it came to allowing him to fly solo and he was soon on Spitfires once more and made a number of flights. However, he was not officially permitted to take part in offensive sweeps or scrambles.

On 5 February 1943, Bennions made a forty-five minute convoy patrol, later undertaking low flying patrols around Sicily. In the year from April 1942 he had managed to chalk-up a total of seventy-nine hours flying solo, largely on Spitfires. At the end of this period, Bennions' log book was annotated with the words 'above average', the flying assessment being elaborated with the comment: 'no general faults in flying to be watched' – a fact which was quite remarkable considering he only had the use of one eye.

With his vast experience as a Controller, Bennions received news of a new posting which would put him into a leading role in the Allies' struggle to regain control in the Mediterranean. He was posted to Algiers where he commanded the Ground Controlled Interception unit (GCI unit) which was to go ashore and operate on Corsica as a part of the invasion force.

Leading from the front, Bennions flew a number of calibration tests over Bo Rizzo, Sicily, during September in the run-up to the landings, making eight practice interceptions. The flights were arduous, lasting up to two hours and forty-five minutes and required maximum concentration, but Bennions rose to the task.

On 27 September, Bennions and his team flew on an American C47, taking off from Palermo on the ninety-minute flight to Tunis, where they took on more fuel for the longer second leg of the flight, which took them to Maison Blanche, Algiers.

It was vital that his unit be established on the island as soon as practicable and so Bennions found himself in one of the first waves of landing craft to hit the beaches at Ajaccio on 30 September 1943. As he descended the ramp, however, a glider bomb, launched from a *Dornier* Do 217, detonated, the blast throwing him onto the sands. Having received further shrapnel wounds, Bennions was evacuated back to England via Maison Blanche and Gibraltar. He duly recorded the flights in the 'Passenger' column of his log book, noting the aircraft types, the duration of each flight, altitude and courses.

Bennions' injuries had taken him out of the campaign, warranting a return to The Queen Victoria Hospital, East Grinstead, for treatment for splinter injuries. It was to be his last taste of action at the sharp end of the war.

The blast had destroyed his unit's radar and other secret equipment, while the rest of their gear was lost in the subsequent fire and sank with the remains of the landing craft. Such were the vagaries of the Services that Bennions might have faced a court-martial if there was any suggestion that he had been responsible for the losses. Consequently his CO wrote an explanatory letter exonerating him from any blame and this was submitted to the appropriate authorities and Bennions' personal kit and the unit's equipment duly written-off:

This is to clarify that I was on LST 79 to meet S/L Bennions who was in-charge of AMES 8003 arriving at Ajaccio on September 30th 1943 and that he was injured when the ship was set on fire by enemy aircraft and that all his kit was lost. It was quite impossible for his kit to have been recovered.

(Signed) P Laurence Brown
Wing Commander,
Northwest African Coastal Air Force.
15th November, 1943.

Following a period of convalescence, Bennions was posted to Fighter Command's Headquarters at Bentley Priory, where he worked in the Operations Department (OPS 3). For Bennions there was little opportunity to get behind the controls of an aircraft, let alone fly solo, but somehow he managed to travel to Northolt on 1 January 1944, from where he made a forty-minute flight in a Spitfire. But he would have to wait until July before he could get behind the controls again, making three, hour-long trips.

Bennions' outstanding abilities in his role was based on his practical experiences both as a fighter pilot and as a tactician, having on several occasions commanded No. 41 Squadron in combat. This led to him being selected to instruct the next generation of Fighter Controllers. With his course based at Newcastle-upon-Tyne, the posting meant that Bennions was once again able to live and work close to his family.

Bennions used the excuse that he needed to give practical demonstrations to his trainees to ensure he was able to keep his log book ticking-over: 'I persuaded the powers that be to give me an aircraft. I felt that if the pilots concerned were really "good boys" then they needed some reward, and I could take them flying!'

From August 1944 until late April 1945, Bennions' log book records numerous flights in Martinets and Oxfords. These were mainly made between Acklington and Catterick, Bennions, no doubt, taking the opportunity to see Avis and Connie.

Naturally, Bennions wanted to get back closer to the action and after several requests for a transfer he was offered a position as Controller of Night Fighter Operations at Chaterhall, which he accepted. Bennions was once again performing a role which fully suited his strengths. The role gave Bennions the opportunity to fly and his log book records a number of sector reconnaissance and communication flights between the end of May and late August 1945. Bennion made two hour-long flights on Hawker Hurricanes on 31 July and on 1 August, while he made two flights on a dual control Mosquito Mk III, the second of these was flown on 2 October with Flying Officer Moody as his instructor. This would be Bennions' last time at the controls of a fighter aircraft.

Meanwhile, Bennions' brother, Philip, who had earlier been turned down for military service owing to his being underage, had been called up. Following his basic training he was assigned to the RASC as a driver. Philip was later to teach jungle-fighting in Singapore before being transferred to Ceylon where he helped establish a new training centre. It was while in Ceylon that Philip met his first wife, the couple marrying in Colombo, before he was posted away to Trincomelee, where his eldest son was born.

Chapter 17

Post-War Years

Following the end of hostilities, George was offered a job in the Administration and Special Duties Branch of the RAF, but with little possibility of flying. Instead he opted for an early release and re-training as a teacher, a career which had always been in his mind to follow since childhood.

George was released from the RAF in 1946 with the rank of squadron leader, and, following a brief spell as welfare officer for a building contractor, he undertook a year-long emergency teacher training course, and became a schoolmaster.

George's daughter, Shirley Wilson recalled:

After his training and a short spell at Eston School, George was first at Peronne Lines School, which, when the new school was built, became Catterick Camp County Modern School (Secondary Modern), then later when the education system was restructured and the grammar school system became extinct, the school was re-named as Risedale School and catered for 'O' level exams but did not have a sixth form. Since Dad left, the school has become Risedale Community College.

For a very short while he was acting Head of Peronne School, but never actually head of the Secondary Modern school.

Built in 1952, Catterick Camp County Modern was one of the first 'County Moderns'. It had 1,000 pupils, roughly split evenly between the sexes. One pupil, Alan Clements, was a part of the first intake:

The school had fantastic facilities including a science lab any research team would have been proud of, a gym with showers – something completely unheard of at the time. There was also a fully equipped metalwork room, and of course a woodwork room, where Mr Bennions taught. As I recall there were about twenty woodwork benches, each with a cupboard at one end, which contained a full set of chisels, braces, mallets, set-squares and other tools.

Mr Bennions taught me woodwork from the ages of 11 to 15, when I left school. I think like many of his pupils, I have such fond memories of him. I can see him now, tall (at least he looked tall to us) steely grey/black hair and a moustache.

We all knew that he had been a fighter pilot, of course, and were a bit in awe of him. This was after all only seven years after the end of the war. I remember he was so calm and patient trying to teach us our mortice and tenon and dovetail joints etc. We were all hopeless!

When he wanted to explain something to us, he would whistle loudly through his teeth – a bit like a shepherd commanding his sheep dog – and shout 'Gather round this bench!', always the same, 'Gather round this bench!'

One thing that did stay with me all my life was the way he used to saw through a piece of timber and adjust his eye over it at an unusual angle in order to keep his cut 'square'. I've always had one eye stronger than the other and could never make a straight cut, but started to make the same adjustment, which I eventually mastered.

Of course, like many men at that time, he never talked about the war, but we knew that George – that was what we called him, but never to his face – had been a fighter pilot and was mentioned in Douglas Bader's book *Reach for the Sky* [first published in 1954].

Over the years whenever I have been doing a bit of DIY, I have often thought of him. On the wall, he used to have written in large letters: 'Keep Both Hands Behind the Cutting Edge!' This was about the only nod to Health and Safety there was in those days. Thinking about it; that could have been a metaphor for George's life up to that point, except he would probably have said: 'Keep both hands AT the cutting edge!'

I have forgotten many teachers from school, and remember others for the wrong reasons, but George Bennions left a deep impression. For his teaching yes, but for simply the way he carried himself, his example. You knew this was a man you could look up to.

George taught Woodwork and Metalwork, also specializing in Mathematics and, having always kept himself in good shape, took Physical Education lessons too. He taught for over twenty-eight years, rising to Head of Department.

Another pupil, Colin Crockett, explained to Shirley, Bennions' daughter:

I was a pupil at Catterick Camp County Modern School from 1953–55 and I remember an incident during a woodwork class. Your dad was explaining the way to mark out and subsequently remove the pieces of wood necessary to make a teapot stand. He also explained the possible consequences of using 'shortcuts' which could result in the 'legs' being chiselled off. We were warned that if this happened we would receive the cane for disobeying instructions. The cane that your dad used was the handle of a shinty stick, and I can tell you it hurt. One of these and you didn't want to get another one. [The method] To check the squareness of the finished product was to place it on a sheet of glass to see if it wobbled. When my teapot stand was taken to your father for assessment I received an A. I then owned up to your father that I had disobeyed his instructions and had "chopped" of one of the legs, sticking it back on with chewing gum, the gum looking like part of the woodgrain. Your father whistled up the attention of the class and told them what I had done, and what he said he would do if this happened. I awaited my punishment, as did the rest of the class, only to be told that as I had owned up I wouldn't be punished this time – I'm sure I saw a hint of amusement in your father's face as he warned the class that the next person to do this would receive the 'Cane'. Your father was indeed a man to be proud of and I feel privileged at having known him.

George was definitely 'old school'. He was known as a strict disciplinarian and 'a hard taskmaster'. He had 'little time for children who squandered their opportunities'. Shirley explained that:

Many ex-pupils of Catterick Camp County Modern School and Risedale School will testify to the punishment handed out by 'old man Bennions' but they are also quick to admit that it did them no harm and that they knew where they stood with him. There was definitely no 'messing about' in his workshop!

George finally left the education system when he felt that it was 'no longer considered fashionable to enforce any form of discipline', a sentiment many can echo.

In 1951 George and Avis had a son, who they named Anthony, after George's wartime friend Tony Lovell. Sadly, Anthony died in infancy, his loss deeply affecting the whole family. Shirley recalled:

George spent hours making a hardwood cross for the tiny grave. What a lot baby Tony has missed – what great expectations Ben might have had for him? They might have been impossible achievements for a post-war son of an air ace. Who knows?

That year George's mother fell ill and Philip returned to England and the family was once again reunited, Philip spending the next thirteen years working down the pits at the Florence Colliery. Four years after the death of his first wife in 1969, he married Pearl and the couple emigrated to Rhodesia where he worked in the mines.

Philip recalled that his brother came over on holiday to visit. George enjoyed the golf courses, although it was never a sport Philip played, his brother instead teaming-up with some of the ex-pats.

George, had a wicked sense of humour, and became known for leaving his glass eye on the table in their 'local' or pretending to have lost it and duping the unsuspecting. On one occasion he caught his brother out. Normally a quiet man, George surprised Philip when they were enjoying a dip in the pool:

> I remember that he suddenly shouted to everyone to get out of the pool. Once the bemused residents were all safely gathered at the poolside, he explained that he wanted them all to get back into the water to find his glass eye!

Having settled into life and his new role as a school master, George was very briefly recalled to the RAF during the Suez Crisis of 1956 but soon returned to Civvy Street and his teaching career. George continued to have links with the Service and three years later was made an honourary member of the Officers' Mess at Catterick, regularly attending Dinner Nights, including Ladies Nights, when Avis and later his daughters, accompanied him. Nearly a whole generation had passed and many old faces had left the scene. The new generation of officers were largely oblivious to George's wartime exploits and he remained quiet and unassuming.

George, like so many men who had left the Services, had had to largely turn his back on his former career. He was more fortunate than many, however, in that he had a wife and his children, who he adored. Teaching meant that, for the first time since they had married, Avis could relax a little, knowing that her husband wasn't going to be sent here or there at the apparent whim of the Air Ministry. His new job had fixed hours and terms. This allowed for planning, and the family was able to go on short breaks in England and, during the summer break, eventually venture further a field. Shirley remembered that:

> At the end of July 1959 he packed the car, a Zephyr Six, with a tent, sleeping bags, pressure cooker and much, much more for a six week trip to Italy. He drove all the way! We used the Dover to Calais ferry, camped in the Bois de Boulogne in Paris then travelled through Switzerland, then

into the north of Italy; arriving at Lake Garda for our 4 week stay by the lakeside. At the end of the holiday we packed up and Dad drove all the way back to Catterick. He dealt with breakdowns, the heat, very heavy storms and very short tempers! Believe it or not, he also repeated that holiday experience in the summer of 1961 and 1963.

In spite of the loss of one eye, George remained a keen sportsman and Shirley recalled that he played football for the village football team where he was often accused of 'dirty play', but his apology was: 'Sorry old boy, you were on my blind side!'

Their father encouraged Connie, Shirley and Georgina to play sports and, despite his reputation for heavy challenges, which in all fairness would quite genuinely have been down to his loss of judgment on distances, emphasized good sportsmanship and fair play:

He encouraged me in my sporting achievements. Here he insisted that it was more important to take part and encouraged my team participation as well as individually encouraging me to, in his words, 'do your best'.

Shirley also remembered that her father was a strong swimmer:

He was a keen swimmer and took an evening class teaching adults to swim. Ladies in the village still remind me of his great patience with them when they were very nervous of the deep water and thought that they were in danger of drowning!

He taught Georgina and I to swim when we were six and seven years old. He took us to Sandes Soldiers Home swimming baths at Catterick Garrison on a Saturday morning.

George enjoyed the lessons almost as much as the children and Shirley remembered that:

He came out refreshed and sang all the way home; only four miles. He had a repertoire of *'I'll take you home again Kathleen'*, *'Arrivederci Roma'* and a couple of patriotic hymns thrown in, which he sang with great gusto.

Having a father who was a teacher had its advantages and George was always there to give a helping-hand with homework, particularly Mathematics: 'He was a great help with any maths homework; taking time and patience to explain any process which was causing a problem.'

George loved poetry and, as his daughter Connie recalled: 'My father gave me my love for literature and Latin. He could recite lengthy passages from

Shakespeare even at the age of ninety. One of his favourite quotes was from *As You Like It.*'

George continued with many of his other hobbies too, including golf. He had begun playing a little after the war. Philip recalled:

George used to play in charity matches alongside Douglas Bader, Arthur Donaldson and members of the Guinea Pig club. He was elected captain of the Catterick Garrison Club and was later made an honoury life member....

Shirley remembered her father's passion for the game:

I remember at the age of about fourteen, on the back lawn, he handed me a book entitled *Play Golf with Player* and insisted that I compare his stance, grip and action with that of the photograph in the book and tell him when he was exactly the same as the great Player! He was attempting to perfect his swing!

Rather than become a golf widow Mum took up the game too. She played to a high standard and was at one time elected as Club Captain.

At RAF Halton, George had served his apprenticeship on Rolls Royce engines, consequently he was, as Shirley put it, a 'knight of the road'; always carrying a complete tool box in the boot of his car and took great delight in helping any unfortunate motorist who was stranded on the wayside.

A skilled craftsman in his own right, George used to make small pieces of furniture and even his own dinghy in which he used to go sailing with friends. He also worked in silver and other metals and had his own registered mark. Among the items George made was a solid silver tea service which is still in the family's procession.

A new phase in George's life began in 1958 when he met W P 'Bill' Meynell, former National Air Racing Champion. Bill had witnessed George's destruction of a Bf 110 near Barnard's Castle in the summer of 1940, the image of his heroics remaining the most powerful of the war. A shared love of all things aviation helped to forge their great friendship, and led to the pair teaming-up to pilot Bill's Tiger Moth G-ANEL, George's log book recording their first flight which took place at 13.05 hours on 15 August 1962, when they flew from Catterick to Coventry 'for Air Races at Bagington'. They made two practice flights the next day before coming second in the De Havilland Trophy Race at 17.45 hours the next day. Two days later they flew in the King's Cup Air Race, where they finished a creditable 14th.

Shirley explained that:

Over the next twelve years they performed aerobatics at air shows all across the country. They performed displays for RAF Regiment Catterick and at a whole host of air shows, including the Prestwick Air Show, at Turnhouse, Croft, Middleton St George, Edinburgh Air Show, Reeth, Pocklington and at Biggin Hill. In the process raising money for the RAF Benevolent Fund.

Dad thoroughly enjoyed his aerobatic practices and displays in the Tiger Moth with his great friend Bill Meynell. The Tiger Moth was hangared at RAF Catterick for many years and 'Ben' was presented to HRH Princess Margaret on 27 November 1979, during her visit to the Camp.

While he would never forget the thrill of flying the Supermarine Spitfire, which Mum always said had been his first love, he always found flying in an open cockpit biplane quite exhilarating. He used to say: 'You could feel the speed as the aircraft cut through the air.'

Shirley remembered that:

Their last public aerobatic display was at Biggin Hill where they took part in the Battle of Britain display on 13 September 1974. In total the pair flew 130 hours until their last recorded flight which was on 13 February 1977.

George eventually had to reluctantly give up flying. However, Shirley's son, David Wilson holds a pilot's licence, maintaining the family tradition in aviation.

On 2 November 1970, the wreckage of George's Spitfire was discovered at Henfield near Brighton and excavated by the Wealden Aviation Archaeology Group four years later, the proceedings being recorded by the press. George, still living in Mowbray Road, Catterick, was contacted by the group's Chairman, Mr Pat Nelson and was on-hand to witness the raising of his aircraft's Rolls-Royce Merlin engine. George noted that while many of the smaller fragments of his Spitfire had been smashed on impact and spread around as surface debris, the engine had plunged fifteen feet into the clay where it had been sealed and protected from the corrosive elements of air and moisture: 'I was amazed that some of the components were still oiled and working....'

The Spitfire (EB-J X4559) had been flown by Bennions over a period of four weeks, during which he had destroyed five enemy aircraft.

The aircraft recovery, and Bennions part in the proceedings, were covered by the national press, the *Sunday Express* of 15 September 1974 leading with:

Spitfire hero will dig up his 1940 plane
Sunday Express reporter

The last time pilot George Bennions saw his crippled Spitfire he was dangling on a parachute as the aircraft spun out of control high above Sussex.

That was 34 years ago next month, and Mr Bennions, now a 61-year-old teacher, had forgotten about it – until a telephone caller asked him: 'Would you like to see the wreckage of your old plane?'

The caller, an official of the Aircraft Archaeological Society, told Mr Bennions that part of the wreckage of his plane had been uncovered at a farm at Henfield, Sussex.

Wreckage
Now Mr Bennions, who lives at Catterick, Yorkshire, plans to join members of the society to dig up the rest of the wreckage and the remains of the German *Messerschmitt* he shot down in the same Battle of Britain dogfight.

Mr Bennions, a squadron leader who had already won a DFC, was then with 41 Squadron, based at Catterick, but that time was flying from Hornchuch, Essex.

The *Messerschmitt* 109 that he shot down on October 7 (sic), 1940, brought his tally to 12.

Then his plane was hit. Badly wounded, he parachuted to safety while his Spitfire plummeted to earth.

The landowner of the field where Bennions' Spitfire crashed later named a race horse *Bennions Spitfire*.

As a result of his treatment at The Queen Victoria Hospital, East Grinstead, in 1940, George had become a founder member of the Guinea Pig Club, which eventually numbered some 600 RAF pilots and air crew. The club came into being on 20 July 1941. To join its exclusive ranks, one had to be a member of aircrew who had been burned, frostbitten, or disfigured through air combat or crash injuries, and require plastic or maxillo – facial surgery. Bennions became an unofficial ambassador for the club, extolling the virtues of McIndoe and his team.

A keen writer and poet, in 1974, George was inspired to pen an additional verse to the famous poem *High Flight*, by John Gillespie McGee Jnr. George's verse read:

And now, through shades of Blue and Black and White,
I'll journey on to see the night of 'Outer Space',
And there is sanctity reposed, my mind encompassed,
No one knows what I may find.
Life's journey's end eternal bliss, or just
The everlasting kiss, of death.

George was always proud of the fact that he had been a founder member of the Guinea Pig Club and often wore the club tie. His daughter Connie recalled that they 'sent him a Guinea Pig Club umbrella. On wet days he walked round the village proudly bearing it.'

The club's reunion was held every September, when the Guinea Pigs gathered in East Grinstead, Sir Archibald McIndoe holding the place of honour up until his death in 1960. In 1979, the gathering was recorded by the cameras of Thames Television who were on-hand to record the events for a TV documentary.

Meanwhile, in June 1980 George received a letter from Hans Kettling, who had been taken prisoner when his Bf 110 M8 C- H had crash-landed at Barnard's Castle following combat with Ted Shipman and George Bennions. Kettling had initially been contacted by writer Christopher Goss, who had later written to all parties paving the way for further contact. In his letter the former *Luftwaffe* pilot explained what happened to him subsequent to their encounter:

After two weeks of interrogation at Cockfosters (and a nice healing of the burns on my hand) I was sent with several other officer PoWs to Grisedale Hall, where I met a bunch of air and navy men, also parachuters, who were the lucky ones to survive, some of them being able to tell hair-raising stories. Thanks to you and to your friends a steady supply of PoWs came in daily at that time. [At the] end of January 1941 we were shipped to Canada aboard the *Duchess of York*, where I was glad to meet *Unteroffizier* Volk, my former wireless operator and gunner, well restored, only a slight limp showing the effects of his wounds.

We left the ship at Halifax in midwinter, and I remember the newspapers boys shouting 'Tobruk fallen'. Going by railway for several days and nights, some of the PoWs manager to jump for freedom out of the windows, but lots of snow and extreme cold made them forget their intentions. All came back, sooner or later, except *Ob Lt* Franz, who was lucky and hard going enough to cross St Lawrence and over the ice and by boat, and who eventually reached the still neutral USA and later on Germany.

The following year I spent in different camps, from Lake Ontario to the Rocky Mountains. After some initial differences between guardians and

PoWs on the question whether to treat us as criminals or as soldiers, we went along very fine with the Canadian Veterans Guard, and after a while they even let us walk and roam in uninhabited parts of the country on parole, which they found 'as good as a Canadian Dollar'. Our favourite song at that time was '*Don't fence me in*'.

During his leisure time Kettling took up handicrafts and had already become quite skilled at carpentry and metalwork when he was finally repatriated in November 1946. Returning to his family in Germany, he found work with a Master Bookbinder, curiously sharing George's interests in working in wood and silver:

So in due course I became a master myself, enjoying my work and never regretting my choice. I am married and have a son 22. Retiring in May 1980, age 63, I hope to follow up some hobbies: working with silver, pewter and stone and turning wood.

Kettling went on to ask George if he would write back with details of his own story, adding that, now he was retired, he and his wife were planning a visit to England in the following year, suggesting that they might care to meet.

While Ted Shipman and Hans Kettling did meet and become friends, George felt that a meeting would somehow dishonour the memory of the pilots whom he had fought alongside and who had died in the cause of freedom. George politely declined, although he held no animosity towards the *Luftwaffe* air crews and later wrote:

You didn't think about who you were shooting down. You were out there to hit targets and that is what you did.

It was a game, but it was a professional game. We were there to win and we had to be professional about it.

At 25,000 feet there was no room to be afraid; you had to know you were the best.

My findings of the German Pilots can only be complimentary as, like myself, they were fully trained regulars who had joined the *Luftwaffe* prior to the War and, unlike our auxiliaries, had some considerable flying experience prior to hostilities.

George had, however, visited the site of the crash-landing at Broomielaw near Barnard's Castle on a number of occasions since the war, while Kettling and Shipman would later revisit the scene during one of their reunions.

There was a general renewal of interest in the events of 1940 during the fiftieth anniversary year, during which numerous books were published on the subject. There were official commemorations too and early in 1990, when preparations were already well advanced, George received a letter from the RAF surrounding the temporary recoding of the Battle of Britain Memorial Flight's Spitfire:

27th May, 1990.

Dear Sqd Ldr Bennions
…you will be please to know that the Memorial Flight's Spitfire Mk Vb AB910 now proudly carries the 'Guinea Pig' logo and the coding EB-J, representing the Spitfire you were flying on the day of your accident….

The same letter mentioned the fact that No. 41 Squadron was in the process of organizing a 75th Anniversary reunion at RAF Coltishall in 1991, to which Bennions was invited as a guest of honour.

This wasn't the only event that Bennions was invited to attend and Shirley recalled that her father: 'was thoroughly spoilt by the American Air Force personnel at Lakenheath, when he visited for long week-ends once a year for several years. It was a sad day for Catterick when the RAF handed over the station to the Army.'

In the late 1990s, during the expansion of Catterick village it was decided to name a street 'Bennions Way' in honour of George's service both as a fighter pilot and later as a teacher in the village. He was pictured proudly standing beside the new street name-plate.

Although an adopted Yorkshireman, now with a whole street named in his honour, George never forgot his roots, and in particular, his fondness for the Staffordshire Oatcake. When Philip and his wife Pearl used to travel north, the couple would often bring a fresh supply, and their visit during the 1998/9 Festive Season was no different. There was evidently a dilemma over supply and demand as revealed in an amusing letter Bennions wrote to his brother in which the Staffordshire delicacy was the sole subject of concern:

Thursday Feb 4 '99

Dear Philip and Pearl,
Just a little Thank You Note for a wonderful reunion and particularly for the OATCAKES, they are delicious.
    So much so that we need an umpire to decide the ownership of each individual cake, I wish you were here.
    I think, rightly or wrongly, that you intended that they should be divided 4 ways AVIS, CONNIE, BEN, FRANK.

Since you bought them for us I would welcome your interpretation. I have had 2, so far, and am simply dying to have another 2 – PLEASE ACT AS UMPIRE.

With Kindest Regards and Sincere THANKS
Your Loving Brother and In-Law
'George'

George lost Avis, his wife of sixty-five years, in 2000. The couple had been living with their daughter, Connie Slade, in the heart of Catterick Village for a number of years. With the loss of Avis, George's health fell into decline, but in 2002 he was guest of honour when residents of Bennions Way held a street party to mark Queen Elizabeth II's Jubilee. The *Northern Echo* of 13 June reported on how the event unfolded:

On Saturday, the 89-year-old veteran was given his own 'throne' and invited to judge the children's fancy dress competition, handing each a certificate to commemorate the occasion: 'I never expected anything like this,' he said. 'Having a street named after you is quite an honour, but I was thrilled to be invited to the residents' party and amazed so many of them knew so much about me. I was monarch of all I surveyed for a little while, and those involved organizing the party did a wonderful job.'

A sprightly eighty-nine year old, George was regularly to be seen striding around the village on his daily walk, more so after the DVLA required him to surrender his driving licence in the same year.

George was able to accept an invitation to attend the Battle of Britain Day celebrations at nearby RAF Catterick and RAF Leeming, which he attended in the company of his daughter Shirley Wilson.

Shirley recalled:

On these occasions were always very well hosted. Only some 18 months before he died, Dad was made a guest of honour at RAF Leeming's Battle of Britain Dinner night. We stood outside, at the front of the Officers' Mess, with other guests and serving officers watching the sky as the Battle of Britain Memorial Flight roared overhead. It was a very moving moment. For Dad the special highlight was seeing the beautiful Spitfire flying low over the Mess.

Reflecting on the events of 1940, Connie once asked her father why so many young brave pilots gave their lives so readily. He replied: 'If they hadn't the result would have been too horrendous to contemplate.'

Some years ago, the book shop Ottakers sponsored a competition for new writers. The winning entrants would have their stories published. Jim Davie, Ben's very good friend, decided to record the story of Pookie Overall's fateful flight on 6 November 1939, as his contribution. The book was launched at a number of locations, including nearby Northallerton.

Connie's memories of that fateful night were reinforced through conversations with her parents:

> My father had said that it was a very bad night, low cloud, poor visibility. He had seen Pookie Overall's plane go down and had thought it had landed on our house, No 2 Mowbray Road. He disobeyed orders and came home – typical Ben!

Shirley recalled that some years earlier, in 1993, George had received a letter from Flying Officer Overall's niece who was writing on her own behalf and for Overall's then aging mother. As was so often the case, Overall's family had been told little of the circumstances surrounding his death and they wanted some form of closure. It was difficult for George to rake-up the events of over half a century past but he sat down and wrote a detailed account of the events: two pages in all.

Rather than simply post a letter, George decided the reply needed to be more personal and so he set about recording a message based on his recollections. The result was: 'An account filled with the emotion of the horrific events and the loss of a friend and fellow aviator.'

The tape was posted to Canada where it was played by Overall's mother and brother and a few weeks later came an air mail letter from Canada in which Overall's family expressed their deep thanks for what Bennions had done for them: 'The emotion "Ben's" tape generated was electrifying – words seemed inadequate to express how they felt. They had made several copies of the tape for the family and next generation to cherish.'

Pookie Overall was buried in Catterick Cemetery, and each November since his death, George and his family visited the grave and laid flowers – a vigil his daughters maintain to this day.

In his late eighties, George was still exchanging letters with a number of historians and aviation enthusiasts. During correspondence with a local aviation enthusiast, Mr Ken Chester, George mentioned a Spitfire propeller blade signed by No. 41 Squadron pilots and used by them as a scoreboard: 'I was more than a little curious as to what had happened to the blade, and it seemed as though nobody knew where it might be, it certainly wasn't where it should have been, with No. 41 Squadron!'

On the back of George's enquiry, Chester made an appeal for information on the location of the blade, a feature appearing in the *Northern Echo* of 5

November 2003. In January the following year information was forwarded to George that the blade had been found and was at RAF Honington in Suffolk and it was duly returned to No. 41 Squadron's home base at RAF Coltishall.

With the onset of Alhziemer's and the sale of Connie's former home at The Birches in Swale Pasture Lane, George decided to remain close to his adopted roots in the village and moved into his own rooms with Shirley, where he remained until his death on 30 January 2004, at the age of ninety.

George Herman Bennions was buried in St Anne's Parish Church, in Catterick Village at 11 am on Saturday 7 February.

The pall-bearers were drawn from Tornado air crew from RAF Leeming, while representatives from the US Air Force paid their respects along with George's family and friends who filled the church.

Among the hymns were *O Valiant Hearts*, which includes the words 'Proudly you gathered, rank on rank, to war' – and *I Vow to Three My Country*.

Naturally it was a very difficult day for all of Bennions' family and close friends, but his daughter Shirley recalled:

It was a wonderful service and the RAF did him proud. The young officers were very smart and all in step and so many people from the village came to pay their respects.

If he was watching, I think he'll have been very pleased.

Proud to have lived, rather than to have died, for his country; proud to have been a Guinea Pig; proud to have met life face to face. Proud – and very thankful.

Squadron Leader George Herman Bennions, DFC, RAF Retd.

Directive No. 2 for the Conduct of the War

SUPREME COMMANDER OF THE ARMED FORCES MOST SECRET
Berlin 3 September 1939.

1. After the declaration of war by the English Government. The English Admiralty issued orders at 11.17 hours on 3rd September 1939, to open hostilities.

    France has announced that she will be in a state of war with Germany from 17.00 hours on 3rd September 1939.
2. The immediate aim of the German High Command remains the rapid and victorious conclusion of operations against Poland.

    The transfer of any considerable forces from the eastern front to the West will not be made without my approval.
3. The basic principles for the conduct of the war in the West laid down in Directive No. 1 remain unchanged.

    The declaration of war by England and France has the following consequences:

(a) In respect of England.

Navy.
Offensive action may now begin. In carrying out the war against merchant shipping, submarines also, for the time being, will observe prize regulations. Intensified measures leading to the declaration of danger zones will be prepared. I shall decide when these measures shall become effective.

The entrance to the Baltic will be mined without infringing neutral territorial waters.

In the North Sea the blockade measures envisaged for defensive purposes and for the attack on England will be carried out.

Air Force.
Attacks upon English naval forces at naval bases or on the high seas (including the English Channel), and on definitely identified troops transports, will only be made in the event of English air attacks on similar targets and where there are particularly good prospects of success. This applies also to action by the Fleet Air Arm.

I reserve to myself the decision about attacks on the English homeland.

(b) In respect of France.

Army.
The opening hostilities in the West will be left to the enemy. Commander-in-Chief Army will decide on the reinforcement of our forces in the West from such reserves as are still available.

Navy.
Offensive action against France will only be permitted if the enemy has first open hostilities. In that case the same instructions apply to France as have been laid down for England.

Air Force.
Offensive actions against France will only be undertaken after French attacks on German territory. The guiding principle must be not to provoke the initiation of aerial warfare by any action on the part of Germany.
In general the employment of the Air Force in the West is governed by the need to preserve its fighting strength after the defeat of Poland for decisive actions against the Western Powers.

4. Order X issued on 25 August 1939, is extended to all the Armed Forces with effect from 3 September 1939.

The conversion of the entire German economy to a war basis is hereby decreed.

Further measures for mobilization in civil life will be introduced by the High Command of the Armed Forces on the request of the highest government authorities.

(signed) Adolf Hitler.

Appendix 2

Directive No. 6 for the Conduct of the War

SUPREME COMMANDER OF THE ARMED FORCES MOST SECRET.
Berlin 9 October 1939.

1. It should become evident in the near future that England, and, under her influence, France, also, are not disposed to bring the war to and end, I have decided, without further loss of time, to go over to the offensive.
2. Any further delay will not only entail the end of Belgian and perhaps of Dutch neutrality, to the advantage of the allies; it will increasingly strengthen the military power of the enemy, reduce the confidence of neutral nations in Germany's final victory, and make it more difficult to bring Italy into the war on our side as a full ally.
3. I therefore issue the following orders for the further conduct of military operation:

   (a) An offensive will be planned on the northern flank of the western front, through Luxembourg, Belgium, and Holland. This offensive must be launched at the earliest possible moment and in greatest possible strength.
   (b) The purpose of this offensive will be to defeat as much as possible of the French Army and of the forces of the allies fighting on their side, and a the same time to win as much territory as possible in Holland, Belgium, and Northern France, to serve as a base for the successful prosecution of the air and sea war against England and as a wide protective area for the economically vital Ruhr.
   (c) The time of the attack will depend upon the readiness for action of the armoured and motorized units involved. These units are to be made ready with all speed. It will depend also upon the weather conditions obtaining and foreseeable at the time.

4. The Air Force will prevent attacks by the Anglo–French Air forces on our Army and will give all necessary direction support to its advance. It is also important to prevent the establishment of Anglo–French air bases and the landing of British forces in Belgium and Holland.
5. The Navy will do everything possible, while this offensive is in progress, to afford direct or indirect support to the operations of the Army and the Air Force.
6. Apart from these preparations for the beginning of the offensive in the West according to plan, the Army and Air Force must be ready at all times, in increasing strength, to meet the Anglo–French invasion of Belgium, immediately and as far forward as possible on Belgian soil, an to occupy the largest possible area of Holland in the direction of the West coast.

7. These preparations will be camouflaged in such a way that they appear merely to be precautionary measures made necessary by the threatening increase in the strength of the French and English forces on the frontier between France and Luxembourg and Belgium.
8. I request Commanders-in-Chief to submit to me their detailed plans based on this directive at the earliest moment and to keep me constantly informed of progress through the High Command of the Armed Forces.

(Signed) Adolf Hitler.

Appendix 3

Directive No. 13 for the Conduct of the War

SUPREME COMMANDER OF THE ARMED FORCES MOST SECRET
Berlin, 24 May 1940.

1. The next of our operations is to annihilate the French, English, and Belgian forces which are surrounded in Artois and Flanders, by a concentric attack by our northern flanks and by the swift seizure of the Channel coast in this area.
2. The task of the Air Force will be to break enemy resistance on the part of the surrounded forces, to prevent the escape of the English forces across the Channel, and to protect the southern flank of Army Group A.

The Enemy Air Force will be engaged whenever opportunity offers.

The Army will then prepare to destroy in the shortest possible time the remaining enemy forces in France. This operation will be undertaken in three phases:

Phase 1: A thrust between the sea and the Oise as far as the lower Seine below Paris, with the intention of supporting and securing with weak forces the later main operations on the right flank.

Should the position and reserves available permit, every effort will be made, even before the conclusion of hostilities in Artoi and Flanders, to occupy the area between the Somme and the Oise by a concentric attack in the direction of Montdidier, and thereby to prepare and facilitate the later thrust against the lower Seine.

Phase 2: An attack by the main body of the Army, including strong armoured forces, south–eastwards on either side of Reims, with the intention of defeating the main body of the French Army in the Paris–Metz–Belfort triangle and of bringing about the collapse of the Maginot Line.

Phase 3: In support of this main operation, a well–timed subsidiary attack on the Maginot Line with the aim of breaking through the Line with weaker forces at its most vulnerable point between St Avold and Sarreguemines in the direction of Nancy––Luneville.

Should the situation allow, an attack on the upper Rhine may be envisaged, with the limitation that not more than eight to ten division are to be committed.

3. Tasks of the Air Force.

(a) Apart from operations in France, the Air Force is authorized to attack the English homeland in the fullest manner, as soon as sufficient forces are available. This attack will be opened by an annihilating reprisal for English attacks on the Ruhr.

Commander-in-Chief Air Force will designate targets in accordance with the principles laid down in Directive No. 9 and further orders to be laid by the High Command of the Air Forces. The time and plan for this attack are to be reported to me.

The struggle against the English homeland will be continued after the commencement of land operations.

(b) With the opening of the main operation of the Army in the direction of Reims, it will be the task of the Air Force, apart from maintaining our air supremacy, to give direct support to the attack, to break up any enemy reinforcements which may appear, to hamper the regrouping of enemy forces, and in particular to protect the western flank of the attack.

The breakthrough of the Maginot line will also be support as far as necessary.

(c) Commander-in-Chief Air Force will also consider how far the air defence of the areas upon which the enemy is now concentrating his attacks can be strengthened by the employment of forces from less threatened areas.

In so far as the Navy is involved in any changes of his kind, Commander-in-Chief Navy is to participate.

4. Task of the Navy.

All restrictions on naval action in English and French waters are hereby cancelled and commanders are free to employ their forces to the fullest extent.

Commander-in-Chief Navy will submit a proposal for the delimitation of the areas in which the measures authorized for the coming siege may be carried out.

I reserve to myself the decision whether, and if so in what form, the blockade will be made public.

5. I request the Commanders-in-Chief to inform me, in person or in writing, of their intentions based on this directive.

(Signed) Adolf Hitler

Constitution of the Guinea Pig Club

The original constitution of the Guinea Pig Club as recorded in the minutes of the inaugural meeting taken by Pilot Officer Geoffrey Page.

The objects of the Club are to promote good fellowship among, and to maintain contact with, approved frequenters of Queen Victoria Cottage Hospital.

There are three classes of membership, all having equal rights:

1. The Guinea Pigs (patients)
2. The Scientists (doctors, surgeons and members of the medical staff).
3. The Royal Society for Prevention of Cruelty to Guinea Pigs (those friends and benefactors who by their interest in the hospital and patients make the life of the Guinea Pig a happy one).

The annual subscription for all members is 2/6d., due on 1st July each year. Women are not eligible for membership, but a 'ladies' evening may be held at the direction of the Committee.

The following members were proposed and seconded by members present.

President: Mr A H Minded, F.R.C.S.
Vice-President: Squadron Leader T Gleave
Secretary: FO W Towers Perkins
Treasurer: PO P C Weeks
Committee members: Messrs. Cotte, Edmonds, Faser, Gardiner, Hughes, Hunter, Eckoff, Morley, Overeyander, Livingstone, Page, Russell Davies and Wilton.
Other members present were: Messrs. Bodenham, Clarkson, Mappin and McLeod.
The following were proposed and seconded as members: Messrs. Banham, Bennions, Butcher, Dewar, Fleming, Harrison, Hart, Hillary, Kokal, Krasnordebski, Lock, Lord, Langdale, Mann, McPhail, Noble, Shephard, Smith-Barry and Truhlar.

Inspiration

Squadron Leader G H Bennions, DFC, RAF Retd.
Founder Member, Guinea Pig Club.

Inspiration by Archie, Tom and Jim,
Indulging in a literary whim,
I now attempt to eulogize
'The Guinea Pigs' so dear and wise.

What it is then, what makes them tick?
It's not a clock! It's not a trick!
It's simply that, with hearts of gold,
They have a story to unfold.

The story starts with sheer despair
Of men who've fallen from the air.
For, having fallen from their grace
They need to save 'their other face'.

How do this club so sanctified,
By members true both far and wide?
It's not a hall, it's not a den.
It's a compassion for their fellow men.

They stand or fall upon their pride
Once well sustained, then mortified.
The 'scrambled' from a ruined life
And overcame both fear and strife.

To show that 'men of guts and grit'
Do not 'fall down, stay down and quit'.
They proudly hold their heads on high
For inspiration from the sky.

The sky that once to them betold
Of glamour, glory, 'days of old'
And thus inspired. I do proclaim
To all the world their famous name
'The Guinea Pig Club'.

Archie – Sir Archibald McIndoe
Tom   – Group Captain Tom Gleave
Jim   – Jim Wright

Bennions' favourite quote from Shakespeare's *As You Like It*

'All the world's a stage,
And all the men and women merely players:
They have their exits and their entrances;
And one man in his time plays many parts,
His acts being seven ages. At first the infant,
Mewling and puking in the nurse's arms.
And then the whining school-boy, with his satchel
And shining morning face, creeping like snail
Unwillingly to school. And the lover,
Sighing like furnace, with a woeful ballad.
Made to his mistress' eyebrow. Then a soldier,
Full of strange oaths and bearded like the pard.
Jealous in honour, sudden and quick in quarrel,
Seeking the bubble reputation
Even in the cannon's mouth. And then the justice.
In fair round belly with good capon lined,
With eyes severe and beard of formal cut,
Full of wise saws and modern instances:
And so he plays his part. The sixth age shifts
Into the lean and slipper'd pantaloon,
With spectacles on nose and pouch on side,
His youthful hose, well saved, a world too wide
For his shrunk shank: and his big manly voice
Turning again toward childish treble, pipes
And whistles in his sound. Last scene of all,
That ends this strange eventful history,
Is second childishness and mere oblivion,
Sans teeth, sans eyes, sans taste, sans everything.'

Bibliography

Bishop, Edward, *Guinea Pig Club*, New English Library, 1963

Bishop, Patrick, *Fighter Boys: Saving Britain 1940*, Harper Perennial, 2004

Deere, Alan, *Nine Lives*, Hodder & Stoughton, 1985

Deighton, Len, *Fighter*, Jonathan Cape, 1977

Franks, Norman, *The Air Battle Of Dunkirk*, Grub Street Press, 2000

Gelb, Norman, *Scramble: A Narrative History Of The Battle Of Britain*, Michael Joseph, 1986

Mayhew, E R , *The Reconstruction of Warriors: Archibald McIndoe, The Royal Air Force And The Guinea Pig Club*, Pen & Sword, 2010

Ramsay, Winston, *Battle Of Britain Then And Now MkV*, After The Battle, 1980

Robinson, Anthony, *RAF Fighter Squadrons Of The Battle Of Britain*, Caxton Edition, 2000

Sarkar, Dilip, *Missing In Action: Resting In Peace?* Ramrod Publications, 1998

Shipman, John, *One Of The 'Few': The Memoirs of Wing Commander Ted 'Shippy' Shipman, AFC,* Pen & Sword, 2008

Shirer, William L , *This Is Berlin: A Narrative History; 1938–40*, Hutchinson, 1999

Shores, Christopher & Williams, Clive, *Aces High: A Tribute To The Notable Fighter Aces Of The British And Commonwealth Forces In WWII*, Grub Street Press, 1994

Smith, Richard C, *Hornchurch Scramble*, Grub Street Press, 2002

Trevor-Roper, H R, *Hitler's War Directives 1939–1945*, Pan, 1964

Wallens, R W 'Wally', DFC, *Flying Made My Arms Ache*, Self Publishing Association Ltd, Upton-upon-Seven, 1990

Williams, Peter & Harrison, Ted, *McIndoe's Army*, Pelham Books, 1979

Wood, Derek & Dempster, Derek, *The Narrow Margin*, Tri-Service Press Ltd., 1990

Wynn, Kenneth G, *Men Of The Battle Of Britain*, Gliddon Books, 1989

The London Gazette 1937–1945

The *Northern Echo*

The *Sunday Express*

Original Documents:

No. 41 Operational Record Book 27/424

No. 41 Squadron Combat Reports Air 50/18

Log Book belonging to Squadron Leader George Herman Bennions, DFC, RAF, Retd.

Unpublished Monograph
Browne, Giles, *Tony Lovell – A Very Proper Type* 1995–2010

Correspondence with:
Squadron Leader George Herman Bennions, DFC, RAF, Retd
Mr Philip Bennion
Hans Ulrich Kettling (via Mr Philip Bennion)
Squadron Leader J N Mackenzie, DFC, RAF, Retd.
Mrs Shirley Wilson

Index